QUE Bee

From Doubts to Distinction
Your ICSE 2026 Exams Partner

GIST OF THE TEXTBOOK
Crisp & Complete Theory - No need to go back to textbooks!

ALL TYPES OF LATEST PATTERN QUESTIONS
MCQs Including Statement Based, Arrange in Sequence Based Questions, Extract Based Questions, All in one place!

KEY WORDS HIGHLIGHTED
Important points neatly Underlined Never miss what matters

Coverage of Exam Questions
Coverage of all exam questions with solutions

COUNCIL-STYLE ANSWERS
Write responses like an examiner expects

SAMPLE & SPECIMEN PAPER
Practice in real-exam mode. Perfect your timing, strategy and confidence.

ARIHANT PRAKASHAN
(School Division Series)

ADMINISTRATIVE & PRODUCTION OFFICES

Regd. Office

'Ramchhaya' 4577/15, Agarwal Road, Darya Ganj, New Delhi -110002
Tele: 011- 47630600, 43518550; Fax: 011- 23280316

Head Office

Kalindi, TP Nagar, Meerut (UP) - 250002, Tel: 0121-7156203, 7156204

SALES & SUPPORT OFFICES

Agra, Ahmedabad, Bengaluru, Bareilly, Chennai, Delhi, Guwahati, Hyderabad, Jaipur, Jhansi, Kolkata, Lucknow, Nagpur & Pune.

PO No : TXT-XX-XXXXXXX-X-XX

Published By Arihant Publications (India) Ltd.

For further information about the books published by Arihant, log on to www.arihantbooks.com or e-mail at info@arihantbooks.com

Follow us on

PRICE ₹ 225.00

PRODUCTION TEAM

Publishing Manager
Keshav Mohan

Project Head
Manju

Cover Designer
Bilal Hashmi

Inner Designer
Ankit Tyagi

Page Layouting
Lalit Chaprana

Proof Reader
Harsh Agarwal

QUE Bee

ICSE
LITERATURE IN ENGLISH (PAPER 2)
Class 10

Major Elements in the Book

Drama (Julius Caesar)	Prose (Treasure Chest)	Poetry (Treasure Chest)
About the Author	Introduction	Introduction
About the Drama	About the Story	About the Poem
Themes of the Drama	Character Introduction	Exploring the Stanzas
Actwise Plot of Julius Caesar	Story at a Glance	Theme of the Poem
Major & Minor Characters	Theme	Message Conveyed by the Story
Summary of the whole Drama	Message Conveyed by the Story	Style, Tone & Mode
Actwise Scenewise Summary of	Style, Tone & Mode	Title
the Drama	Title, Figures of Speech	Literary Devices
Multiple Choice Questions (212)	Multiple Choice Questions (114)	Multiple Choice Questions (153)
Extract Based Questions (34)	Extract Based Questions (26)	Extract Based Questions (30)

Created by
Michael Anthony
MA, B.Ed,
PGT, St. Thomas' English Medium School, Meerut

Contributors
Parneet Kaur, Vaishali Jaiswal, Saba

From Learner to Leader

Step-Into the Spotlight

QUE Bee is more than just a book - it's a platform for young achievers like you to guide future toppers. If you've cracked the code to smart study or have insights that can make learning easier for others, this is your moment to shine!

What Can You Share?

- Your study techniques, time management tips, or motivation hacks
- Feedback or suggestions to make QUE Bee even better
- Real experiences that can guide other students through the exam maze

What's in It for You?

- Your name will be featured in our exclusive Student Panel in the next edition
- Win exciting & surprise rewards for impactful suggestions
- **Get published** - your photo, Ideas-or even interviews can be featured in the book
- **Become a student icon** - recognized and followed by peers across schools

Let your learning become someone else's ladder.
Be remembered. Be featured. Be the guide.

SCAN TO SHARE YOUR IDEA

Index

Latest
Course Structure

PAPER 2 - LITERATURE IN ENGLISH (Two hours) - 80 Marks

I. DRAMA: Julius Caesar: William Shakespeare (Acts III, IV & V)

II. TREASURE CHEST: A Collection of ICSE Short Stories & Poems (Evergreen Publications (India) Ltd. New Delhi)

PROSE (Short Stories)

1. With the Photographer – Stephen Leacock
2. The Elevator – William Sleator
3. The Girl Who Can – Ama Ata Aidoo
4. The Pedestrian – Ray Bradbury
5. The Last Lesson – Alphonse Daudet

POETRY

1. Haunted Houses – H.W. Longfellow
2. The Glove and the Lions – Leigh Hunt
3. When Great Trees fall – Maya Angelou
4. A Considerable Speck – Robert Frost
5. The Power of Music – Sukumar Ray

NOTE: *The ICSE (Class X) Examination paper will be set ONLY on the portion of the syllabus that is prescribed for Class X*

DRAMA : JULIUS CAESAR

Act 3 : Scene 1-3

Act 4 : Scene 1-3

Act 5 : Scene 1-5

JULIUS CAESAR

William Shakespeare

About the Author

An English playwright, actor and poet, **William Shakespeare** (1564-1616) is generally regarded as the greatest writer of the Elizabethan Era. His extensive work includes thirty-seven plays, one hundred and fifty-four sonnets and two long narrative poems.

Initially an actor, he started writing plays around 1589 with his early plays primarily being comedies and histories. He then wrote mainly tragedies until 1608 entering the last phase of his literary career with tragicomedies. His plays are marked with effective use of soliloquy, humour, clever rhetoric and double entendres (meaning). His works express the complete range of human experience with complex characters.

About the Drama

William Shakespeare's *Julius Caesar* was written in 1599 and is based on historical events surrounding the assassination of the Roman leader Gaius Julius Caesar in 44 BCE. The play, rich in political intrigue and moral complexity, explores themes of ambition, power, loyalty and the consequences of betrayal.

The story begins with Cassius convincing Brutus, a noble Roman, to join a conspiracy against Caesar, fearing his ambition might lead to tyranny. Despite personal loyalty, Brutus agrees believing it's for the greater good of Rome. Caesar ignores warnings and omens about his fate and is ultimately assassinated in the Senate by the conspirators.

Following Caesar's death, Mark Antony skilfully turns public opinion against the conspirators through a powerful funeral speech inciting a civil war. Brutus and Cassius face defeat on the battlefield leading to their suicides. Antony and Octavius, Caesar's heir, emerge victorious setting the stage for the rise of the Roman Empire.

The play delves into themes of power, betrayal, fate and the moral complexities of leadership and loyalty.
It examines the consequences of political machinations and personal ambition while raising enduring questions about loyalty, justice and the fine line between heroism and betrayal. Its vivid characters, poetic language and timeless themes make it the foundation of Shakespeare's dramatic legacy.

Themes of the Drama

- **Power and Corruption** The play examines the dangers of unchecked ambition and the corrupting influence of power. The fear that Caesar may become a tyrant drives the conspirators to assassinate him, showcasing how the pursuit and maintenance of power can lead to ethical compromises and destructive consequences.
- **Betrayal and Loyalty** Betrayal is a central theme with Brutus' betrayal of Caesar being the most significant. This theme underscores the tension between personal loyalty and public duty as Brutus justifies his actions as necessary for the republic's welfare despite his affection for Caesar.
- **Fate vs Free Will** Throughout the play, characters grapple with their ability to control their destinies. Caesar's dismissal of omens and prophecies highlights the tension between fate and human agency, suggesting that while fate may guide events, personal choices still play a crucial role.
- **Rhetoric and Manipulation** The power of language and rhetoric is vividly displayed in Mark Antony's funeral speech which manipulates the crowd's emotions and turns public opinion against the conspirators. This theme illustrates how persuasive speech can shape political outcomes and sway masses.
- **Public vs Private Self** Characters in the play often struggle with their public personas and private feelings. Brutus, in particular, embodies this conflict as he navigates his personal loyalty to Caesar and his perceived duty to Rome.

Act wise Plot of *Julius Caesar*

Act 1 : "The Seeds of Conspiracy"	This act sets the stage for the rising tension in Rome, with Caesar's growing power and the discontent among the conspirators.
Act 2 : "The Conspiracy Takes Shape"	Brutus wrestles with his conscience and ultimately joins the conspiracy as the plot to assassinate Caesar is finalised.
Act 3 : "The Fall of Caesar"	The pivotal act where Caesar is assassinated and the aftermath begins with the famous funeral orations.
Act 4 : "The Aftermath of Betrayal"	The power struggle continues as Brutus and Cassius face the consequences of their actions. The triad consolidates power.
Act 5 : "The Battle of Philippi"	The final act concludes with the battle, the deaths of key characters and the ultimate resolution of the conflict.

Major Characters

- **Julius Caesar** The leader of Rome whose assassination is the central event of the play
- **Brutus** A Roman senator and the main conspirator against Caesar, he is torn between loyalty to Caesar and his duty to Rome
- **Cassius** A senator who masterminds the plot to kill Caesar and a leader of the conspiracy
- **Mark Antony** A loyal friend of Caesar who seeks revenge for Caesar's assassination
- **Portia** Brutus' wife who is concerned about his secretive actions
- **Calpurnia** Caesar's wife who has ominous dreams about Caesar's death
- **Soothsayer** A mysterious figure who warns Caesar about the Ides of March
- **Octavius** Caesar's adopted son and heir who plays a role in the power struggle after Caesar's death

Minor Characters

- **Flavius** A tribune who opposes Caesar's rise to power
- **Marullus** A tribune who also opposes Caesar's ascent and is punished for removing decorations from Caesar's statues
- **Soothsayer** A mysterious figure who warns Caesar about the Ides of March
- **Artemidorus** A teacher of rhetoric who tries to warn Caesar of the conspiracy through a letter
- **Decius Brutus** A member of the conspiracy who persuades Caesar to go to the Senate on the day of his assassination
- **Metellus Cimber** A conspirator who asks for the repeal of his brother's banishment to create a reason for the assassination
- **Trebonius** A conspirator who leads Mark Antony away from Caesar at the Senate to help facilitate the assassination
- **Ligarius** A conspirator who joins Brutus and Cassius' cause despite initially being hesitant

- **Cicero** A respected Roman senator who is not involved in the conspiracy but is mentioned in passing
- **Cinna (the poet)** A poet who is mistaken for one of the conspirators and is killed by a mob
- **Varro and Claudius** Servants to Brutus
- **Strato** A servant to Brutus who assists in his final moments
- **Dardanius** Another servant of Brutus who is involved in his death
- **Aemilius Lepidus** He is a member of the second triumvirate and he basically does Antony's tasks.
- **Lucilius** He is a noble friend of Brutus (who pretends to be Brutus). He is captured by Antony's soldiers
- **Titinius** He is Brutus' servant who goes for a joy ride and ultimately commits suicide
- **Messala** He is a soldier of Brutus and Cassius and tells Brutus that his wife is dead

Summary of the Drama

The play begins with people celebrating Caesar's victory over Pompey. Flavius and Marullus, two tribunes, scold the citizens for changing their loyalty from Pompey to Caesar. Meanwhile, Cassius, a senator, is unhappy with Caesar's rise to power and begins plotting against him. He tries to persuade Brutus, Caesar's close friend, to join the conspiracy by playing on his love for Rome. Brutus is torn but agrees after thinking about Caesar's ambition.

Brutus decides to join the conspiracy believing that killing Caesar is the only way to save Rome from tyranny. Caesar's wife, Calpurnia, has a nightmare that Caesar will be killed and begs him not to go to the Senate. He initially agrees but is later persuaded by Decius who reinterprets the dream as a good omen. Caesar decides to go to the Senate. Brutus' wife, Portia, is anxious but is kept in the dark. Meanwhile, a man named Artemidorus tries to warn Caesar by giving him a letter but Caesar ignores it.

At the Senate, Caesar is assassinated by the conspirators. Brutus delivers the final blow claiming it was for Rome's good. After Caesar's death, Mark Antony, Caesar's loyal friend, pretends to accept the murder. However, he cleverly turns the people against the conspirators by showing them Caesar's will which leaves wealth to the people. The crowd becomes angry and starts hunting down the conspirators.

Antony, Octavius and Lepidus form a triad to rule Rome and punish Caesar's supporters. Brutus and Cassius, now in conflict, eventually reconcile. Brutus learns that his wife has died. Both sides prepare for battle with the stage set for a final confrontation.

The forces of Brutus and Cassius face off against those of Antony and Octavius in a final battle. Cassius believes his army is losing and asks his servant to kill him. However, Brutus' side continues fighting. Eventually, Brutus, realising defeat is near, asks his servant to hold his sword while he kills himself. Antony and Octavius emerge victorious. They mourn Brutus, calling him an honourable man, reflecting on the tragic events that unfolded.

ACT 3 : SCENE 1

Summary of Act 3 Scene 1

The scene begins with Caesar arriving at the Capitol, surrounded by a crowd that includes senators, supporters and the conspirators. Despite several warnings, including the Soothsayer's reminder to 'beware the Ides of March' and a letter from Artemidorus, Caesar dismisses the concerns and enters the Senate confidently.

Inside the Senate, Metellus Cimber approaches Caesar with a petition to pardon his banished brother. This request is a pretext to draw Caesar closer, and other conspirators, including Brutus and Cassius, join in the plea. Caesar, asserting his unwavering nature, refuses to change his decision, comparing himself to the North Star-constant and unyielding.

At this moment, the conspirators spring their trap. Casca strikes the first blow, followed by the others, with Brutus delivering the final stab. Caesar, shocked and heartbroken by Brutus' betrayal, famously says, 'Et tu, Brute?' before collapsing and dying. The conspirators proclaim they have liberated Rome from tyranny, attempting to justify their actions as a necessary act to save the Republic.

Following Caesar's death, chaos erupts. Mark Antony arrives, faking commitment to the conspirators while secretly mourning Caesar. He requests permission to speak at Caesar's funeral. Despite Cassius' reservations, Brutus grants Antony's request under the condition that Antony will not speak against the conspirators.

As the scene ends, Antony is left alone with Caesar's body, vowing revenge. He predicts that civil strife will engulf Rome, and Caesar's death will be avenged. This pivotal scene sets the stage for the power struggle and eventual downfall of the conspirators, with Antony preparing to turn public opinion against them through his funeral oration.

Vocab Vault

O'er read Read through
Sirrch, give place Fellow, get out of the way
Puissant Powerful
Low crooked courtesy Bending and stooping
Enfranchisement Restoration of the rights of citizenship
Disposing of new dignitaries Distribution of new honours and state appointments
Et tu, Brute? You too Brutus?
Doomsday Day of the judgement
Resolv'd Satisfied
Untrod state New and unknown circumstances
Apprehensive Intelligent
Corpse Dead body

Characters in the Scene

- **Julius Caesar** The ruler of Rome who is assassinated by the conspirators in this scene
- **Brutus** One of the main conspirators who believes killing Caesar is necessary for the good of Rome
- **Cassius** The mastermind behind the conspiracy who ensures the assassination plan is executed
- **Casca** The first conspirator to stab Caesar
- **Cinna** A conspirator who assists in the assassination
- **Decius Brutus** A conspirator who previously convinced Caesar to come to the Senate

- **Metellus Cimber** A conspirator who distracts Caesar by pleading for his brother's pardon
- **Trebonius** A conspirator who lures Antony away to prevent him from interfering in the assassination
- **Mark Antony** Caesar's loyal friend who flees after the assassination but later returns to shake hands with the conspirators while secretly planning revenge
- **Lepidus** A member of the Second Triumvirate, mentioned briefly but not actively involved in this scene
- **Servant of Antony** Delivers Antony's request to speak with the conspirators
- **Publius** A senator who is shocked by the assassination but is reassured by Brutus that no harm will come to him

EXAM ORIENTED QUESTIONS

TYPE - 1 Multiple Choice Questions

01 Mark

Q.1 Which character says the famous line, 'Et tu, Brute?'
(a) Mark Antony (b) Caesar
(c) Cassius (d) Brutus

Q.2 How does Caesar respond to the plea of Metellus Cimber to reverse his brother's exile?
(a) He agrees immediately
(b) He says he will consider it later
(c) He rejects it coldly
(d) He expresses sympathy but refuses

Q.3 What is the main reason Brutus decides to join the conspiracy against Caesar?
(a) He is jealous of Caesar's power
(b) He believes it is for the good of Rome
(c) He is forced by Cassius
(d) He wants to become king

Q.4 Who distracts Antony away from the Senate room?
(a) Brutus (b) Cassius
(c) Casca (d) Trebonius

Q.5 What is Caesar's attitude toward his own death in the final moments before he is assassinated?
(a) He pleads for mercy
(b) He accepts it without fear, believing in his destiny
(c) He begs for his life
(d) He runs away

Q.6 Where was Caesar put to death? **(ICSE Specimen 2025)**
(a) On a street in Rome
(b) On the battleground of Philippi
(c) At the foot of Pompey's statue
(d) In Brutus' orchard

Q.7 What do the conspirators shout after killing Caesar?
(a) 'Liberty, freedom, and tyranny is dead!'
(b) 'Hail, Caesar!'
(c) 'Revenge for Rome!'
(d) 'The Republic is saved!'

Q.8 What is the significance of Caesar's final words, 'Et tu, Brute?'
(a) They show his anger toward Brutus
(b) They express his disbelief that Brutus, whom he trusted, would betray him
(c) They show his sorrow over the loss of Rome
(d) They are a declaration of defiance

Q.9 Who is the last conspirator to stab Caesar?
(a) Cassius (b) Brutus
(c) Decius Brutus (d) Metellus Cimber

Q.10 Who asks permission to speak at Caesar's funeral? **(ICSE Specimen 2025)**
(a) Brutus (b) Antony
(c) Cassius (d) Octavius

Q.11 'Woe to the hand that shed this costly blood!
Over thy wounds now do I prophesy...'
These lines tell us that Antony is .... **(ICSE Specimen 2025)**
(a) enraged (b) sorrowful
(c) anxious (d) frustrated

Q.12 Why does Cassius oppose Mark Antony's request to speak at Caesar's funeral?
(a) He believes Antony will incite the crowd against them
(b) He does not trust Antony

(c) He fears Antony's eloquence
(d) All of the above

Q.13 Under what condition does Brutus allow Mark Antony to speak at the funeral?
(a) Antony must praise Brutus.
(b) Antony must not blame the conspirators.
(c) Antony must leave Rome afterward.
(d) Antony must promise loyalty to Brutus.

Q.14 What does Mark Antony do immediately after Caesar's assassination?
(a) He tries to escape from Rome
(b) He mourns Caesar's death
(c) He agrees to the conspirators' plan
(d) He seeks revenge on the conspirators

Q.15 What does Brutus claim in his speech after Caesar's death?
(a) That he killed Caesar because he was a tyrant
(b) That he was forced to kill Caesar
(c) That Caesar had planned to overthrow Rome
(d) That Caesar's death will bring peace to Rome

Q.16 What role does Artemidorus play in Act 3, Scene 1?
(a) He is part of the conspiracy
(b) He warns Caesar of the conspiracy with a letter
(c) He tries to intervene after Caesar's assassination
(d) He flees from Rome

Q.17 What does Brutus ask the conspirators to do after Caesar's assassination?
(a) Flee from Rome immediately
(b) Wash their hands in Caesar's blood to show their commitment
(c) Leave Caesar's body in the Senate
(d) Immediately announce themselves as rulers of Rome

Q.18 What strategy does Cassius suggest that the conspirators follow? **(ICSE Specimen 2025)**
(a) March towards Philippi
(b) Remain where they are
(c) Raise an army of foot soldiers
(d) Set fire to the surrounding villages

Q.19 Choose the option that lists the sequence of events in the correct order
1. Caesar arrives at the Senate.
2. The conspirators stab Caesar.
3. Antony is left alone with Caesar's body.
4. Antony shakes hands with the conspirators.

(a) 1, 2, 3, 4 (b) 1, 4, 3, 2
(c) 1, 2, 4, 3 (d) 4, 3, 2, 1

Q.20 'O world, thou were the forest to this hart, and this indeed, O world, the heart of thee.' **(Competency Based Que.)**
Which of the following uses the same literary device as given above?
(a) The bees buzzed around the flower-filled garden.
(b) Her eyes are buttons.
(c) She caught the scent of mothballs in the abandoned home.
(d) Broken pencils are pointless.

Q.21 What does Antony predict will happen after Caesar's death?
(a) Peace will reign in Rome
(b) Civil war will engulf Rome
(c) Rome will become a democracy
(d) The conspirators will be celebrated as heroes

Q.22 How does Antony show respect to Caesar after his death?
(a) He swears vengeance over Caesar's body.
(b) He calls him the most noble Roman.
(c) He covers Caesar's body with his cloak.
(d) He requests a proper burial.

Q.23 What action does Antony plan after being left alone with Caesar's body?
(a) He plans to leave Rome.
(b) He plans to gather his supporters for war.
(c) He plans to turn the people against the conspirators.
(d) He plans to burn Caesar's body in secret.

Q.24 Why does Artemidorous urge Caesar to go through his letter first?
(a) It is concerning Rome
(b) It is concerned with the conspiracy against Caesar
(c) It is concerned with a matter of national importance
(d) It is he who came first to Caesar

Q.25 What does Cassius say he would do if their purpose is revealed?
(a) Make another plan
(b) Kill Casca
(c) Kill the one who it
(d) Kill himself

Q.26 According to Caesar, what will be the effect of Metellus Cimber's stooping and cringing an ordinary men?
(a) Incite others to stoops low
(b) Inflame the pride of ordinary men
(c) Invoke the ordinary men to rebel
(d) None of the above

Q.27 How do the conspirators make requests to Caesar regarding Publius Cimber?

(a) Appealing to his divine night
(b) Appealing to his supreme self
(c) Feigned servility
(d) None of the above

Q.28 How do the people of Rome run after Caesar's murderers?

(a) As if an earthquake had occurred
(b) As if doomsday had came
(c) As if a boam had blasted
(d) As if a large building had collapsed

Q.29 What appears as the main cause of Brutus failure in this scene of the play?

(a) Lack of experience (b) Lack of brutality
(c) Error of Judgement (d) None of these

Q.30 Select the option that shows the correct relationship between statements (1) and (2).

Statement 1 Caesar refuses to pardon Metellus Cimber's banished brother.

Statement 2 Caesar believes that changing his decision would make him appear weak and inconsistent.

(a) Statement 1 is true and Statement 2 is false
(b) Statement 2 is true and Statement 1 is false.
(c) Statement 2 is the cause for Statement 1.
(d) Both statements are false.

Q.31 Select the option that shows the correct relationship between statements (1) and (2).

Statement 1 Mark Antony shakes hands with the conspirators after Caesar's assassination.

Statement 2 Antony wants to show his approval of Caesar's murder and join the conspiracy.

(a) Statement 1 is true and Statement 2 is false
(b) Statement 2 is true and Statement 1 is false.
(c) Statement 2 is the cause for Statement 1.
(d) Both statements are false.

Answers

1. (b)	2. (c)	3. (b)	4. (d)	5. (b)	6. (c)	7. (a)	8. (b)	9. (b)	10. (b)
11. (a)	12. (d)	13. (b)	14. (b)	15. (a)	16. (b)	17. (b)	18. (b)	19. (c)	20. (b)
21. (b)	22. (a)	23. (c)	24. (b)	25. (d)	26. (c)	27. (c)	28. (b)	29. (c)	30. (c)
31. (a)									

Explanations

20. The given quote uses a metaphor by comparing Caesar (the 'hart' or deer) to a hunted animal in a forest (the world) emphasising his vulnerability and tragic fate.
Similarly, option (b) also uses metaphor and draws comparison between 'eyes' and 'buttons' without using as or like.

30. In Act 3, Scene 1, Metellus Cimber kneels before Caesar, begging for the repeal of his banished brother's sentence. However, Caesar refuses to grant the pardon.
He justifies his refusal by claiming that he is 'constant as the Northern Star', meaning he does not change his mind once he has made a decision. Caesar believes that reversing his ruling would make him appear weak and inconsistent.
Hence, statement 2 is the cause for statement 1.

31. After Caesar's assassination in Act 3, Scene 1, Mark Antony shakes hands with the conspirators to appear friendly and avoid immediate danger. Antony does not approve of Caesar's murder or want to join the conspiracy. Instead, he is secretly plotting revenge while pretending to make peace.
Hence, statement 1 is true and statement 2 is false.

TYPE - 2 Extract Based Questions 16 Marks

Extract 1

Caesar Are we all ready? What is now amiss.

That Caesar and his Senate must redress?

Metellus Most high, most mighty and most puissant Caesar, Metellus Cimber throws before thy seat.

A humble heart, --- [He kneels] **(ICSE Specimen 2025)**

(i) Where are the speakers?
What does 'puissant' mean?
Explain: Metellus Cimber throws before thy seat a humble heart'. **(3)**

Ans. The speakers are at the Capitol, Senate.

'Puissant' means powerful/mighty.

The given line means Metellus Cimber begs the mighty Caesar most humbly to listen to his plea.

(ii) At the beginning of the scene, Caesar says, 'The Ides of March are come'.
Why do you think Caesar said this'?
What does the Soothsayer say in response? **(3)**

Ans. Caesar said this because he had been warned earlier by the Soothsayer to be aware of the Ides of March.

He said the words to remind the Soothsayer that nothing had happened to him even though the day has arrived.

In response, the Soothsayer tells Caesar that though it had come, it had not yet gone.

(iii) What specific duties do the conspirators allot to Trebonius and Casca?
Why does Cassius become nervous when Popilius Lena speaks to him as they enter? **(3)**

Ans. Trebonius has the duty of taking Antony out of the way and ensuring that he wouldn't be near when Caesar is attacked. Casca has been asked to attack Caesar first.

Popilius Lena speaks to Cassius as they enter the Senate House and addresses him directly wishing him success in his enterprise that day. This makes Cassius the conspiracy against Caesar has been discovered.

(iv) What does Artemidorus want of Caesar?
How does Caesar respond to his plea? **(3)**

Ans. Artemidorus pleads that Caesar read the scroll that he had been just given as it concerns him very closely.

Caesar responds by saying that whatever concerned him personally would be dealt with last.

(v) Shortly after this exchange, Caesar is stabbed to death by the conspirators. Whom do you sympathise with — Julius Caesar or the conspirators? Give reasons for your choice. **(4)**

Ans. I sympathise with Julius Caesar because he was betrayed by those he trusted, particularly Brutus whom he considered a close friend. The betrayal by someone so dear adds a layer of personal tragedy to Caesar's death.

Despite any flaws Caesar might have had, such as ambition or arrogance, he genuinely believed he was acting in Rome's best interest. His assassination was brutal and deceitful, taking place under the guise of friendship and loyalty.

Extract 2

Caesar 'I could be well moved, if I were as you;
If I could pray to move, prayers would move me:
But I am constant as the northern star,
Of whose true-fixed and resting quality
There is no fellow in the firmament.
The skies are painted with unnumber'd sparks,
They are all fire and every one doth shine;
But there's but one in all doth hold his place:
So in the world; 'tis furnish'd well with men,
And men are flesh and blood, and apprehensive;
Yet in the number I do know but one
That unassailable holds on his rank,
Unshaked of motion: and that I am he,
Let me a little show it, even in this,
That I was constant Cimber should be banish'd,
And constant do remain to keep him so.'

(i) What does Caesar mean when he compares himself to the 'northern star'?
What is the 'northern star' known for? **(3)**

Ans. Caesar uses the metaphor of the 'northern star' to convey his resolute nature. The northern star is a celestial body known for its fixed position in the sky symbolising constancy and reliability.

By comparing himself to the northern star, Caesar is asserting that he is firm and resolute in his decisions.

He is stating that he doesn't yield to any external pressures or influences, just as the northern star is constant.

(ii) How does Caesar justify his decision to keep Metellus Cimber's brother banished? (3)

Ans. Caesar justifies his decision by emphasising his constancy and firmness. He states that he is 'unshaked of motion', meaning he is steadfast and will not be swayed by emotional appeals or petitions.

He reinforces this by declaring that he was constant in his decision to banish Metellus Cimber's brother. He remains constant in upholding that decision.

(iii) What does the phrase 'men are flesh and blood, and apprehensive' imply about Caesar's view of others? (3)

Ans. The given phrase suggests that Caesar views other men as being vulnerable, emotional and easily swayed by fears and uncertainties. By contrast, he sees himself as superior, immune to such human weaknesses.

This reflects Caesar's perception of himself as a unique and exceptional figure, distinct from the common man in his ability to remain resolute and unaffected by emotional appeals.

(iv) How does Caesar's speech reflect his attitude towards power and leadership? (3)

Ans. Caesar's speech reflects an attitude of self-assuredness and absolute confidence in his authority. He believes that a leader must be steadfast and unyielding, maintaining decisions once made, regardless of external pressures.

This reveals his belief in the importance of strong, decisive leadership/However, it also hints at potential arrogance as he sees himself as the singular, unquestionable figure in a world of fallible men.

(v) What is the significance of Caesar's use of celestial imagery in this speech? (4)

Ans. The celestial imagery serves to elevate Caesar's status, likening him to a star-an-eternal and unchanging force in the universe. By comparing himself to the northern star and other heavenly bodies, Caesar implies that his role and decisions are divinely ordained and irreversible.

This use of grand imagery underscores his self-perceived greatness and the inevitability of his authority, reinforcing his belief in his unique and irreplaceable position in the world.

Extract 3

Caesar "Et tu, Brute? Then fall, Caesar!" [Dies.]

Cinna "Liberty! Freedom! Tyranny is dead!
Run hence, proclaim, cry it about the streets."

Cassius "Some to the common pulpits, and cry out
'Liberty, freedom, and enfranchisement!"

Brutus "People and senators, be not affrighted;
Fly not; stand still: ambition's debt is paid."

(i) What is the significance of Caesar's last words, 'Et tu, Brute? Then fall, Caesar!'? (3)

Ans. Caesar's last words 'Et tu, Brute?' express his shock and betrayal upon seeing his close friend Brutus among the conspirators. The phrase signifies the ultimate betrayal as Caesar trusted Brutus completely.

The addition of 'Then fall, Caesar!' suggests that with Brutus' participation, Caesar feels utterly defeated and resigns himself to his fate, symbolising the end of his reign and life.

(ii) How does Cinna's exclamation, 'Liberty! Freedom! Tyranny is dead!' reflect the conspirators' justification for Caesar's assassination? (3)

Ans. Cinna's exclamation reflects the conspirators' belief that Caesar's death is a necessary act to restore liberty and freedom to Rome. They view Caesar as a tyrant whose ambition threatened the Republic's democratic values. By proclaiming 'Tyranny is dead', Cinna suggests that Caesar's death marks the end of autocratic rule and the beginning of freedom for the Roman people.

(iii) What does Cassius mean by urging others to 'cry out 'Liberty, freedom, and enfranchisement!'' in the common pulpits? (3)

Ans. Cassius is instructing the conspirators to publicly announce the death of Caesar as a victory for the ideals of liberty, freedom and enfranchisement.

He wants to ensure that the people perceive Caesar's assassination as an act of liberation from tyranny. By doing so, he aims to gather public support and justify their actions as being in the best interest of Rome.

(iv) How does Brutus attempt to calm the crowd with his statement, 'People and senators, be not affrighted; Fly not; stand still: ambition's debt is paid'? (3)

Ans. Brutus addresses the crowd to reassure them and prevent panic. By telling them 'be not affrighted' and 'Fly not; stand still', he urges them to remain calm and composed.

He justifies Caesar's assassination by stating that 'ambition's debt is paid', implying that Caesar's excessive ambition has been dealt with, and the Republic is now free from the threat of dictatorship.

(v) How do these lines collectively convey the theme of betrayal and the conspirators' justification of their actions? (4)

Ans. The lines highlight the deep personal betrayal felt by Caesar, especially from Brutus, and the justification the conspirators use to rationalise their actions. Caesar's shock and resignation upon recognising Brutus among his killers underscore the personal nature of the betrayal.

Meanwhile, the conspirators' proclamations about liberty and freedom suggest that they believe their actions are necessary for the greater good of Rome. The juxtaposition of personal betrayal with political justification reflects the complex motivations and moral ambiguity surrounding the assassination of Caesar.

Extract 4

Antony 'O mighty Caesar! Dost thou lie so low?
Are all thy conquests, glories, triumphs, spoils,
Shrunk to this little measure? Fare thee well.
I know not, gentlemen, what you intend,
Who else must be let blood, who else is rank:
If I myself, there is no hour so fit
As Caesar's death hour; nor no instrument
Of half that worth as those your swords, made rich
With the most noble blood of all this world.
I do beseech ye, if you bear me hard,
Now, whilst your purpled hands do reek and smoke,
Fulfill your pleasure. Live a thousand years,
I shall not find myself so apt to die:
No place will please me so, no mean of death,
As here by Caesar, and by you cut off,
The choice and master spirits of this age.'

(i) How does Antony's opening question 'O mighty Caesar! Dost thou lie so low?' reflect his emotional response to Caesar's death? (3)

Ans. Antony's question reflects his shock and sorrow at the sight of Caesar's lifeless body. The phrase 'lie so low' contrasts Caesar's former greatness with his current state, emphasising the tragic fall from power and glory.

Antony's tone is one of mourning and disbelief. It highlights the profound loss he feels for the once-mighty leader.

(ii) What does Antony imply by asking, 'Are all thy conquests, glories, triumphs, spoils, Shrunk to this little measure?' (3)

Ans. Antony is lamenting the futility of Caesar's achievements in the face of death. He implies that all of Caesar's victories and accomplishments have now been reduced to insignificance by his death that he lies in the dust at pompey's feet.

This question underscores the theme of the fleeting nature of power and glory.

(iii) Why does Antony refer to the conspirators' swords as being 'made rich with the most noble blood of all this world'? (3)

Ans. Antony uses this phrase to emphasise the enormity of the conspirators' act by pointing out that they have stained their swords with Caesar's blood. It suggests both a condemnation of their deed and an acknowledgment of Caesar's greatness.

This indicates that they have killed not just a man but someone of immense importance and virtue. Their swords have became valuable with the blood of Caesar.

(iv) What does Antony mean when he says, 'If I myself, there is no hour so fit As Caesar's death hour'? (3)

Ans. Antony is suggesting that if the conspirators intend to kill him as well, then this would be the perfect time.

He expresses a willingness to die alongside Caesar, seeing no more appropriate or honourable moment for his own death than the one that claimed Caesar.
This demonstrates his loyalty to Caesar.

(v) How does Antony's speech serve as both a subtle challenge to the conspirators and a declaration of loyalty to Caesar? (4)

Ans. Antony's speech is a complex mix of grief, loyalty and subtle provocation. While outwardly expressing his sorrow and willingness to die, Antony also subtly challenges the conspirators. He does so by reminding them of Caesar's greatness and the gravity of their crime.

His declaration that no other means of death would please him as much as dying by Caesar's side also serves as a testament to his unwavering loyalty.

This duality in his speech sets the stage for Antony's later actions as it conveys both his personal loss and the potential for future retribution.

Extract 5

Antony 'O pardon me, thou bleeding piece of earth,
That I am meek and gentle with these butchers!
Thou art the ruins of the noblest man
That ever lived in the tide of times.
Woe to the hand that shed this costly blood!
Over thy wounds now do I prophesy,-
Which, like dumb mouths, do ope their ruby lips,
To beg the voice and utterance of my tongue,-
A curse shall light upon the limbs of men;
Domestic fury and fierce civil strife
Shall cumber all the parts of Italy;

(i) What does Antony mean by addressing Caesar's body as 'thou bleeding piece of earth'?

How does this imagery contribute to the overall tone of the speech? (3)

Ans. Antony uses vivid imagery to depict Caesar's corpse as lifeless and reduced to (mere earth) symbolising both his death and his connection to Rome.

This imagery emphasises the gravity of Caesar's fall from a powerful ruler to a lifeless body and sets a sombre, mournful tone. It also highlights the disrespectful nature of the murder, suggesting that the conspirators have desecrated something sacred.

(ii) How does Antony's use of the word 'butchers' to describe the conspirators reflect his attitude towards them and their actions? (3)

Ans. Antony's use of 'butchers' conveys his deep disdain and condemnation for the conspirators. The term dehumanises them reducing their act to a brutal and senseless slaughter rather than a justified political assassination.

It reflects Antony's belief that their actions were brutal and dishonourable. This further emphasises his anger and the moral outrage he feels toward those who killed Caesar.

(iii) Analyse the significance of Antony's prophecy about 'domestic fury and fierce civil strife' in Italy. How does this foreshadow the events to come? (3)

Ans. Antony's prophecy serves as a powerful foreshadowing of the chaos and civil war that will overwhelm Rome following Caesar's assassination. By predicting 'domestic fury and fierce civil strife', Antony foresees the violent outcomes of the conspirators' actions.

This suggests that Caesar's death will destabilise the Republic and lead to widespread conflict. This prophecy underscores the theme of political turmoil and the consequences of power struggles.

(iv) What is the significance of Antony personifying Caesar's wounds as 'dumb mouths' that 'ope their ruby lips'?

How does this metaphor enhance the speech's impact? (3)

Ans. Antony's personification of Caesar's wounds as 'dumb mouths' that 'ope their ruby lips' creates a haunting image of the wounds demanding justice and speaking through Antony's tongue.

This metaphor suggests that the wounds are silently crying out for retribution and that Antony feels compelled to be their voice.

It enhances the speech's emotional impact by emphasising the grievousness of the murder and Antony's role as an avenger, giving a voice to the injustice done to Caesar.

(v) There are two functions that Antony's speech serves. Identify them and elaborate. (4)

Ans. Antony's speech functions on two levels: as a lamentation for the loss of Caesar and as a veiled call to action against the conspirators. His mournful tone and expressions of grief underscore his sorrow and respect for Caesar.

However, his references to 'domestic fury', 'civil strife' and the curse that will fall upon the conspirators hint at a desire for vengeance and retribution.

Antony subtly incites the audience by portraying the conspirators as butchers and predicting the turmoil their actions will cause, thereby sowing the seeds for rebellion and revenge.

Extract 6

Antony Post back with speed, and tell him what hath chanc'd
Here is a mourning Rome, a dangerous Rome,
No Rome of safety for Octavius yet;
Hie hence and tell him so. Yet, stay awhile;
Thou shalt not back till I have borne this corpse
Into the marketplace; there shall I try,
In my oration, how the people take
The cruel issue of these bloody men;
According to which, thou shalt discourse
To young Octavius of the state of things.
Lend we your hand. **(Competency Based Que.)**

(i) **What instructions does Antony give the servant?** **(3)**

Ans. Antony instructs the servant to inform Octavius about the recent events in Rome particularly the killing of Caesar, emphasising that the city is dangerous and not safe for him yet. He insists that the servant wait until after his speech to the crowd, to observe their reaction to his oration and then relay the situation to Octavius.

This highlights Antony's strategic approach in ensuring that Octavius is aware of the political climate and his own assessment of the people's mood following Caesar's assassination.

(ii) **Why does Antony say 'Rome is dangerous'? Whom is it not safe for? Why?** **(3)**

Ans. Antony describes Rome as 'dangerous' because of the political instability and the threat posed by the conspirators. It is particularly unsafe for Octavius, Caesar's here, as the conspirators might target him next to establish their power.

Antony's description of Rome as 'mourning' reflects the grief over Caesar's death and foreshadows the civil unrest that might follow.

(iii) **Mention any three predictions that Antony makes when he left alone with Julius Caesar's dead body.** **(3)**

Ans. Antony predicts that a curse will fall upon the Limbs of conspirators, that civil strife will plague Italy and that Caesar's death will lead to widespread chaos and revenge.

These predictions reveal Antony's deep grief and anger over Caesar's death as well as his determination to avenge him by inciting public unrest and turning the people against the conspirators.

(iv) **What was Brutus' and Cassius' opinion of Antony? whose assessment about Antony was correct? Justify your answer.** **(3)**

Ans. Brutus views Antony as harmless and believes he can be trusted allowing him to speak at Caesar's funeral. Cassius, on the other hand, is more cautious and distrustful, fearing Antony's potential influence over the people. Cassius' assessment proves to be more accurate as Antony uses his funeral speech to sway public opinion against the conspirators leading to their eventual downfall.

(v) **What aspects of Antony's character are revealed during Act III and Act IV?** **(4)**

Ans. In Act III and Act IV, Antony's character is revealed as both politically astute and deeply loyal to Caesar. His manipulative use of rhetoric in his funeral speech demonstrates his skill in influencing the masses.

His willingness to confront the conspirators and his strategic planning for Octavius' arrival show his political sense. Additionally, his profound grief and determination to avenge Caesar highlight his loyalty and personal commitment to justice.

ACT 3 : SCENE 2

Summary of Act 3 Scene 2

In this scene, the citizens of Rome gather in the Forum, eager to understand the reasons behind Caesar's assassination. Brutus addresses the crowd first, presenting a rational and composed justification for Caesar's murder. He argues that Caesar's ambition posed a threat to the Republic and the freedom of Rome. Brutus insists that his love for Rome outweighed his loyalty to Caesar. Furthermore, he claims that Caesar's death was necessary to prevent him from becoming a tyrant. His speech is calm and logical. It appeals to the citizens' sense of duty and patriotism. The crowd initially supports Brutus believing that he acted for the greater good of Rome, they became blind followers of Brutus.

However, the mood shifts dramatically when Mark Antony steps forward to speak. Antony, despite appearing to respect the conspirators, strategically incites doubt and stirs the emotions of the crowd. He begins by repeatedly referring to Brutus and the conspirators as 'honourable men' but the irony in his tone becomes increasingly apparent. Antony then reads Caesar's will revealing Caesar's generosity to the people. Caesar has left his wealth and lands for them. He also displays Caesar's body pointing out the brutal wounds inflicted by the conspirators. The sight of Caesar's corpse, coupled with Antony's passionate speech, arouses anger and sorrow among the citizens. Antony's masterful manipulation of words turns the crowd against the conspirators. The citizens, now enraged and feeling betrayed, riot and rush to avenge Caesar's death. The scene ends with the mob setting fire to the conspirators' homes and preparing for civil war. This pivotal scene showcases Antony's rhetorical skill and marks the beginning of the downfall of the other conspirators as Rome descends into chaos.

Characters in the Scene

- **Brutus** One of the conspirators, who addresses the Roman crowd, justifying Caesar's assassination by claiming it was for the good of Rome
- **Mark Antony** Caesar's loyal friend, who delivers his famous funeral speech, turning the people against the conspirators
- **Plebeians** (Roman Citizens) The common people of Rome who initially support Brutus but are later swayed by Antony's powerful rhetoric

Vocab Vault

Censure Strong disapproval or criticism
Base Low, dishonourable or immoral
Lamented Mourned or grieved for, especially when someone has died
Exterminated Belittled
Bequeathing Will
Dint Impression
Ruffle Rouse
Drachmas Silver coins
Pricked Stirred or provoked
Fates In Roman mythology, the three goddesses who controlled human destiny

EXAM ORIENTED QUESTIONS

TYPE - 1 Multiple Choice Questions

01 Mark

Q.1 What does Brutus urge the Roman citizens to do in his speech?
(a) Leave the city
(b) Listen carefully to his explanation
(c) Seek revenge on Antony
(d) Support the conspirators

Q.2 What reason does Brutus give for Caesar's assassination?
(a) Caesar was a tyrant
(b) Caesar was ambitious
(c) Caesar wanted to destroy Rome
(d) Caesar planned to kill the Senate

Q.3 How do the citizens initially react to Brutus' speech?
(a) With outrage
(b) With understanding and support
(c) With confusion
(d) By leaving the scene

Q.4 What does Brutus offer to do if the people disagree with his actions?
(a) Leave Rome forever
(b) Go into exile
(c) Kill himself with the same dagger
(d) Hand over power to Antony

Q.5 How does Antony address the citizens when he begins his speech?
(a) 'Friends, Romans, countrymen'
(b) 'Citizens of Rome'
(c) 'Dear comrades'
(d) 'Loyal subjects'

Q.6 'Ambition should be made of <u>sterner stuff</u>.'
What literary device is used in Antony's argument when he mentions Caesar's refusals of the crown?
(a) Irony (b) Hyperbole (c) Alliteration (d) Simile

Q.7 Mark Antony stirs the emotions of the crowd in his .... **(Competency Based Que.)**
(a) farewell speech (b) eulogy (Funeral Speech)
(c) prologue (d) epilogue

Q.8 What is Antony's main purpose in his speech?
(a) To honour Brutus
(b) To calm the citizens
(c) To incite anger and turn them against the conspirators
(d) To declare himself the new leader of Rome

Q.9 How does Antony refer to Brutus and the conspirators in his speech?
(a) As noble men (b) As honourable men
(c) As traitors (d) As saviours of Rome

Q.10 What does Antony use to persuade the crowd about Caesar's kindness?
(a) Caesar's will (b) Caesar's speeches
(c) Caesar's letters (d) Caesar's victories

Q.11 What does Antony claim Caesar left to the people in his will?
(a) His wealth
(b) His gardens and orchards
(c) A public park
(d) His title

Q.12 How does Antony subtly discredit Brutus' claim about Caesar's ambition?
(a) By citing Caesar's refusals of the crown
(b) By showing Caesar's generosity
(c) By questioning Brutus' motives
(d) By praising Caesar's military campaigns

Q.13 What effect does Antony's speech have on the crowd?
(a) They leave to mourn Caesar quietly
(b) They grow angry and riot
(c) They continue to support Brutus
(d) They call for Antony's death

Q.14 What is Antony's final statement about Caesar's wounds?
(a) They are a symbol of Rome's downfall
(b) They are silent witnesses to his murder
(c) They beg for justice
(d) They should be forgotten

Q.15 What does the crowd decide to do after Antony's speech?
(a) Destroy the homes of the conspirators
(b) Bury Caesar with honour
(c) Exile Antony from Rome
(d) Demand a new leader

Q.16 How does Antony show Caesar's body to the crowd?
(a) He uncovers it dramatically
(b) He describes its wounds
(c) He lets the crowd view it closely
(d) He refuses to show it

Q.17 Why does Antony claim to weep for Caesar?
(a) He feels guilty for not protecting him
(b) He has lost a friend
(c) He is manipulating the crowd
(d) He fears for his own life

Q.18 What is the crowd's reaction to Antony's reading of Caesar's will?
(a) They are indifferent
(b) They are enraged and ready to revolt
(c) They feel grateful to Antony
(d) They demand the conspirators' immediate execution

Q.19 What does Antony call the conspirators towards the end of his speech?
(a) Tyrants (b) Betrayers
(c) Butchers (d) Liberators

Q.20 What does Antony predict for Rome after Caesar's death?
(a) Peace and prosperity
(b) Civil strife and chaos
(c) A new golden age
(d) Military conquest

Q.21 How does Antony's speech contrast with Brutus' speech in this scene?
(a) Antony uses logic while Brutus appeals to emotions.
(b) Antony praises Brutus while Brutus criticizes Caesar.
(c) Antony appeals to the emotions of the crowd while Brutus uses logic.
(d) Antony uses brief statements while Brutus uses rhetorical questions.

Q.22 What is the attitude of the mob in this scene? **(Competency Based Que.)**
(a) Clever (b) Intelligent
(c) Sensitive (d) Irrational

Q.23 Who has been referred to by Mark Antony as 'Caesar's angle'?
(a) Calpurnia (b) Octavius
(c) Brutus (d) None of these

Q.24 How does Antony describe Caesar's wounds?
(a) Meek creatures
(b) Unfortunate mouths
(c) Poor dumb mouths
(d) Closed mouths

Q.25 According to Antony, what would the people of Rome do after reading Caesar's will?
(a) They will kiss Caesar's wound reverently
(b) They will avenge his murder
(c) They will start destruction in Rome
(d) They will crown his best friend as king

Q.26 Select the option that shows the correct relationship between statements (1) and (2).
Statement 1 Antony calls the conspirators "honourable men" in his speech.
Statement 2 Antony genuinely believes that the conspirators acted with honour.
(a) Statement 1 is true and Statement 2 is false
(b) Statement 2 is true and Statement 1 is false.
(c) Statement 2 is the cause for Statement 1.
(d) Both statements are false.

Q.27 Arrange the following statements in the correct order as per Act 3, Scene 2.
(i) Antony reads Caesar's will.
(ii) Brutus assures the crowd he acted for the good of Rome.
(iii) The citizens initially agree with Brutus.
(iv) Antony's speech incites the citizens to revolt.
(a) (ii), (iii), (i), (iv) (b) (i), (ii), (iv), (iii)
(c) (iii), (ii), (iv), (i) (d) (ii), (iv), (iii), (i)

Q.28 Select the option that shows the correct relationship between statements (1) and (2). **(Competency Based Que.)**
Statement 1 They will kiss dead Caesar's wounds with reverence.
Statement 2 The people of Rome have just heard Antony read out Caesar's will to them.
(a) Statement 1 is true, and Statement 2 is false.
(b) Statement 2 is the cause of Statement 1.
(c) Statement 1 and Statement 2 are independent of each other.
(d) Statement 2 is true, and Statement 1 is false.

Answers

1. (b)	2. (b)	3. (b)	4. (c)	5. (a)	6. (c)	7. (b)	8. (c)	9. (b)	10. (a)
11. (b)	12. (a)	13. (b)	14. (c)	15. (a)	16. (a)	17. (b)	18. (b)	19. (c)	20. (b)
21. (c)	22. (d)	23. (c)	24. (c)	25. (a)	26. (a)	27. (a)	28. (b)		

Explanations

26. In Act 3, Scene 2, during his funeral speech, Antony repeatedly calls the conspirators 'honourable men' (e.g., 'Brutus is an honourable man').

    Antony does not genuinely believe the conspirators acted with honour. Instead, he uses irony to make the crowd question their actions, ultimately turning the people against them.

    Hence, statement 1 is true and statement 2 is false.

28. Antony reads out Caesar's will, which leaves money and land for the citizens, further inflaming their anger against the conspirators.

    Since the reading of Caesar's will moves the crowd to deep sorrow and reverence, Statement 2 is the cause of Statement 1.

TYPE - 2 Extract Based Questions 16 Marks

Extract 1

Romans, countrymen, and lovers, hear me for my
cause, and be silent that you may hear. Believe
me for mine honor, and have respect to mine
honor that you may believe. Censure me in your
wisdom,
and awake your senses that you may the better
judge. If there be any in this assembly, any dear
friend of Caesar's, to him I say that Brutus' love
to Caesar was no less than his. If then that
friend
demand why Brutus rose against Caesar, this is
my
answer: not that I loved Caesar less,
but that I loved
Rome more. Had you rather Caesar were living,
and die all slaves, than that Caesar were dead,
to live all freemen?
As Caesar loved me, I weep for him.
As he was fortunate, I rejoice at it. As he was
valiant, I honor him. But, as he was ambitious,
I slew him.

(i) **What appeal does Brutus make to the crowd at the beginning of his speech?**

How does he ask them to judge him? (3)

Ans. Brutus appeals to the crowd by asking them to hear him out for his cause and be silent so they can listen.

He asks them to believe him for his honour and to respect his honour so that they may trust his words. He requests that they use their wisdom and senses to better judge his actions.

(ii) **How does Brutus justify his participation in Caesar's assassination? (3)**

Ans. Brutus justifies his participation in Caesar's assassination by stating that his love for Caesar was equal to his love for Rome. He explains that he did not kill Caesar because he loved him less but because he loved Rome more. He suggests that allowing Caesar to live would have led to the people becoming slaves whereas Caesar's death ensures their freedom.

(iii) **What contrasting emotions does Brutus express about Caesar?**

How do they reflect his internal conflict? (3)

Ans. Brutus expresses contrasting emotions by saying he weeps for Caesar's love, rejoices at his fortune, honours his bravery but kills him for his ambition.

These contrasting emotions reflect Brutus' internal conflict between his personal affection for Caesar and his perceived duty to Rome.

(iv) **How does Brutus use rhetorical questions in his speech?**

What is their purpose? (3)

Ans. Brutus uses rhetorical questions such as "Had you rather Caesar were living, and die all slaves, than that Caesar were dead, to live all freemen?" to challenge the crowd and make them reflect on their choices.

The purpose of these questions is to justify Caesar's assassination by framing it as a choice between personal freedom and slavery under Caesar's rule.

(v) **What does Brutus mean by the statement, "not that I loved Caesar less, but that I loved Rome more"?**

How does this define his character? (4)

Ans. By this statement, Brutus means that his decision to kill Caesar was not due to a lack of affection for him; rather, due to a greater loyalty to Rome.

This defines Brutus' character as someone who prioritises the greater good and the welfare of the state over personal relationships and emotions.

Extract 2

"Friends, Romans, countrymen, lend me your ears;
I come to bury Caesar, not to praise him.
The evil that men do lives after them;
The good is oft interred with their bones;
So let it be with Caesar. The noble Brutus
Hath told you Caesar was ambitious:
If it were so, it was a grievous fault,
And grievously hath Caesar answer'd it.
Here, under leave of Brutus and the rest-
For Brutus is an honourable man;
So are they all, all honourable men-
Come I to speak in Caesar's funeral.
He was my friend, faithful and just to me:
But Brutus says he was ambitious;
And Brutus is an honourable man."

(i) **How does Antony's opening line, "Friends, Romans, countrymen, lend me your ears", set the tone for his speech? (3)**

Ans. Antony's opening line is an appeal for attention and establishes a connection with the audience. By addressing them as "Friends, Romans, countrymen", he emphasises unity and respect setting a pacifying and engaging tone for his speech.

(ii) **What rhetorical strategy does Antony use when he says, "I come to bury Caesar, not to praise him"?**

What effect does this have on the audience? (3)

Ans. Antony uses irony and subtle contradiction in the given statement. While he claims not to praise Caesar, his speech gradually highlights Caesar's virtues.

This strategy engages the audience and makes them question the truth of Brutus' accusations against Caesar.

(iii) **Analyse Antony's repeated use of the phrase "Brutus is an honourable man".**

How does this repetition serve his overall argument? (3)

Ans. The repetition of "Brutus is an honourable man" is a form of verbal irony. While Antony outwardly appears to agree with Brutus' honour, the repeated phrase casts doubt on Brutus' credibility.

It subtly undermines Brutus' claims by juxtaposing them with evidence of Caesar's virtues.

(iv) **What is the significance of Antony's statement, "The evil that men do lives after them; The good is oft interred with their bones", in the context of Caesar's assassination? (3)**

Ans. This statement suggests that people's negative deeds are remembered more than their good actions after death. In the context of Caesar's assassination, Antony implies that Caesar's positive contributions are being overlooked and buried along with him while his alleged ambition (a supposed fault) is being used to justify his murder.

(v) **How does Antony's reference to Caesar as 'faithful and just to me' contrast with Brutus' accusation of ambition?**

What impact does this have on the audience? (4)

Ans. Antony's reference to Caesar as 'faithful and just to me' contrasts sharply with Brutus' accusation of ambition by portraying Caesar as loyal and honourable. He emphasises Caesar's virtues and his commitment to Rome challenging Brutus' justification for the assassination.

This creates doubt in the audience's mind about Brutus' motives shifting their sympathy toward Caesar. The contrast heightens the emotional appeal, leading the crowd to question the righteousness of Caesar's death. Ultimately, this stirs their anger against the conspirators and inciting them to seek revenge.

Extract 3

"But here's a parchment with the seal of Caesar;
I found it in his closet, 'tis his will:
Let but the commons hear this testament-
Which, pardon me, I do not mean to read-
And they would go and kiss dead Caesar's wounds
And dip their napkins in his sacred blood,
Yea, beg a hair of him for memory,
And, dying, mention it within their wills,
Bequeathing it as a rich legacy
Unto their issue."

(i) What do you think Antony's tone conveys in his statement about Caesar's will?

How does it reflect his intentions toward the crowd? **(3)**

Ans. Antony's tone is dramatic and filled with a sense of withheld emotion. By mentioning the will but not reading it immediately, he creates a sense of suspense and mystery leading the crowd to anticipate something significant.

His tone is calculated and it reflects his intention to manipulate the crowd's emotions. He aims to make them eager to learn more; and, in doing so, he subtly guides their emotions toward anger and desire for revenge for Caesar's death.

(ii) Why does Antony mention that he does not intend to read Caesar's will aloud?

How does this add to the suspense of the scene? **(3)**

Ans. Antony's refusal to immediately read Caesar's will builds suspense by keeping the audience in anticipation of what the will contains. By hinting that the will holds something important, Antony fuels the crowd's curiosity making them more likely to side with him.

The withholding of the information increases the emotional stakes which in turn makes the crowd more eager to hear what he has to say.

(iii) What is the significance of the imagery of the commons kissing Caesar's wounds and dipping napkins in his blood?

How does this imagery serve Antony's purpose in rallying the crowd? **(3)**

Ans. The imagery of the commons kissing Caesar's wounds and dipping napkins in his blood serves to deify Caesar and turn him into a martyr.

By invoking this powerful imagery, Antony stirs up feelings of sympathy and reverence for Caesar. This emotional appeal not only paints Caesar as a victim but also arouses anger toward his assassins. It is meant to inspire them to avenge his death and take action against the conspirators.

(iv) How does the reference to Caesar's will act as a strategic move in Antony's speech?

What effect do you think it will have on the public's emotions? **(3)**

Ans. The reference to Caesar's will is a strategic move because it promises the crowd something of great value heightening their interest and emotional investment. Antony suggests that Caesar's will contains a generous bequest which increases the public's desire to hear it.

This tactic effectively shifts the crowd's emotions from grief to hope and excitement, making them more susceptible to Antony's subsequent appeal for vengeance. It plays into the desire for justice and retribution, and the anticipation of the will's contents acts as a tool to inflame their feelings.

(v) In what ways does Antony manipulate the public's sentiment toward Caesar in this speech?

Do you think he genuinely cares for Caesar or is he using his death for personal gain? **(4)**

Ans. Antony manipulates the public's sentiment by emphasising Caesar's good qualities, his martyrdom and the injustice of his death. He skilfully stirs emotions casting the conspirators as villains and Caesar as a victim.

Antony's feelings toward Caesar appear genuine as he expresses deep grief and loyalty. However, his actions also suggest he is using Caesar's death for personal gain. Antony skilfully manipulates the crowd's emotions to turn them against the conspirators and shift power in his favour.

While his sorrow seems real, his ultimate goal is to strengthen his own political power making his mourning a strategic tool in his pursuit of authority. Thus, his care for Caesar is intertwined with his ambition.

Extract 4

Antony You all do know this mantle.
I remember
The first time ever Caesar put it on;
Twas on a summer's evening, in his tent,
That day he overcame the Nervii.

(Competency Based Que.)

(i) Who were the 'Nervii'?

Why does Antony mention the names of Cassius, Casca and Brutus as he shows the mob the mantle? **(3)**

Ans. The 'Nervii' were a Gallic tribe. Caesar had won against them.

Antony mentioned the names of Cassius, Casca and Brutus as he showed the mob the mantle to stir the emotions of the crowd. Through it, Antony indirectly reminds the crowd that it was Brutus (a well-loved figure) who stabbed Caesar.

This highlights the personal and emotional impact of the assassination and manipulates the crowd's feelings of anger and betrayal.

(ii) **State three arguments put forward by Antony earlier to prove that Caesar was not ambitious.** **(3)**

Ans. Three arguments put forward by Antony earlier to prove that Caesar wasn't ambitious are

(a) **Caesar's Refusal of the Crown** Antony points out that when Caesar was offered the crown three times, he rejected it each time, suggesting that Caesar was not ambitious.

(b) **Caesar's Generosity to the People** Antony mentions that Caesar wept for the poor, showing his compassion. He also mentions that Caesar left money to the people in his will, further disproving any claim of ambition.

(c) **Caesar's Refusal to Accept Praise** Antony reminds the crowd that Caesar, after his military victories, did not act arrogantly or demand excessive recognition. Instead, he showed humility and a sense of duty to Rome.

(iii) **Why does Antony refer to Brutus as well-beloved?**

Why was the stabbing of Caesar by Brutus referred to as the 'most unkindest cut of all'? **(3)**

Ans. Antony refers to Brutus as 'well-beloved' because Brutus was viewed as an honourable and respected figure in Rome. He was also Caesar's friend and trusted confidant which made his betrayal even more painful and shocking.

The stabbing of Caesar by Brutus is referred to as the 'most unkindest cut' because it was the ultimate betrayal. Caesar trusted Brutus making the act of stabbing him feel the most painful of all the blows. It emphasises the personal nature of Brutus' betrayal.

(iv) **Mention three ways Brutus' speech differs from Antony's.** **(3)**

Ans. Brutus' speech is logical, calm and appeals to reason, presenting the assassination as a noble act done for the greater good of Rome. Antony's speech, on the other hand, is emotional, impassioned and aimed at stirring up the crowd's emotions.

Brutus relies on his own reputation and honour, showing himself as a trusted and respected figure to justify his actions. On the other hand, Antony uses emotions to stir the crowd, making them feel anger and sadness to turn them against the conspirators.

Brutus' speech is aimed at justifying the assassination of Caesar and persuading the crowd that it was for Rome's benefit. Antony, however, seeks to turn the crowd against the conspirators stirring them to seek revenge for Caesar's death.

(v) **What characteristic of the mob is highlighted in this scene?**

State any two characteristic traits of mark Antony revealed in this scene.

Justify your answer by giving a suitable reason. **(4)**

Ans. The mob's fickleness and susceptibility to emotional manipulation are highlighted in this scene. They quickly turn from supporting Brutus and the conspirators to calling for vengeance after Antony's emotional appeal and the revelation of Caesar's will.

Two Characteristic Traits of Mark Antony revealed in Act 3 Scene 2 are

(a) Cunning and strategic (b) Emotional and persuasive

His use of Caesar's will and the imagery of Caesar's blood being kissed manipulates the mob's emotions to suit his political agenda. He portrays Brutus' betrayal as the 'most unkindest cut'. This highlights Antony's ability to manipulate public sentiment and sway the crowd's opinion.

Extract 5

I am no orator, as Brutus is,
But, as you know me all, a plain blunt man
That love my friend, and that they know full well
That gave me public leave to speak of him.
For I have neither wit, nor words, nor worth,
Action, nor utterance, nor the power of speech
To stir men's blood.

(i) **What does Antony mean by saying he is 'no orator, as Brutus is'?**

How does this reflect his humility or strategy in the speech? **(3)**

Ans. Antony is acknowledging that he is not as skilled in speechmaking as Brutus. However, this statement is strategic because it makes Antony appear humble and self-criticising.

By downplaying his abilities, he gains the crowd's sympathy and prepares them to be more receptive to his speech which is, in fact, deeply emotional and persuasive.

(ii) **Why does Antony describe himself as a 'plain blunt man'?**

How does this affect the audience's perception of him? **(3)**

Ans. Antony describes himself as a 'plain blunt man' to convey sincerity and honesty presenting himself as someone who is straightforward.

This contrast to Brutus' more formal, reasoned approach helps the crowd see him as more relatable and trustworthy. It builds a connection with the audience making them more likely to listen to his emotional appeal.

(iii) **What does Antony's statement "I love my friend, and that they know full well" reveal about his relationship with Caesar?** **(3)**

Ans. Antony's statement emphasises his deep affection and loyalty toward Caesar making it clear that his grief is personal. By reminding the crowd that they know how much he loved Caesar, Antony strengthens the emotional impact of his speech. It also establishes that his mourning is genuine making his forthcoming emotional appeal more powerful.

(iv) **Why does Antony say he 'has neither wit, nor words, nor worth'?**

How does this affect the credibility of his speech? **(3)**

Ans. Antony's claim of lacking wit, words and worth is a strategy meant to disarm the audience. By claiming to be without the qualities of an effective speaker, he sets up the expectation that his words will not be sophisticated or manipulative. This irony enhances his credibility-when he does deliver a compelling and emotional speech, the crowd is more likely to trust him because he didn't appear to be trying to manipulate them.

(v) **How does Antony's self-deprecation about his lack of 'action, utterance, or power of speech' contribute to the effectiveness of his speech?** **(4)**

Ans. Antony's self-deprecation is a deliberate tactic to lower expectations and make his speech appear more genuine. By stating that he lacks the ability to 'stir men's blood' with his words, Antony sets up the contrast for when he actually does stir the crowd's emotions. His humility allows the crowd to focus on the sincerity of his message; and, when he appeals to their emotions, it becomes more impactful because he didn't try to manipulate them with elaborate speechcraft.

ACT 3 : SCENE 3

Summary of Act 3 Scene 3

In this scene, chaos ensues as the enraged citizens of Rome take to the streets following Caesar's assassination. The mob, incited by Mark Antony's speech, seeks vengeance against the conspirators. They encounter Cinna, the poet. However, they think that he is Cinna, the conspirator.

Despite his desperate attempts to explain his innocence and clarify his identity, the furious crowd, driven by blind rage, ignores his pleas. They accuse him simply for sharing a name with one of the conspirators. The scene ends with the mob violently attacking and killing him.

This brief yet powerful scene illustrates the dangerous consequences of political manipulation and mob mentality highlighting the complete breakdown of order in Rome. It serves as a stark reminder of how reason can be easily overcome by emotion and sets the stage for the further turmoil and violence that will follow.

Characters in the Scene

- **Cinna the Poet** An innocent poet who is mistaken for Cinna the conspirator and is brutally attacked by the angry mob
- **Plebeians** (Roman Citizens) The enraged crowd, influenced by Antony's funeral speech, who turn violent and seek revenge on the conspirators

Vocab Vault

Plebeians The common people of Rome, as opposed to the elite or aristocracy (the patricians)

Triumvirate A political group consisting of three individuals who share power

Throng A large, densely packed crowd

Consolation Comfort or solace given to someone who is distressed or grieving

Reverence Deep respect, often shown through actions

REVISION NOTES

EXAM ORIENTED QUESTIONS

TYPE - 1 Multiple Choice Questions

01 Mark

Q.1 What does the mob initially demand from Cinna the poet?
(a) To recite a poem
(b) To identify himself
(c) To lead them to the conspirators
(d) To confess to Caesar's murder

Q.2 What is the primary reason the mob is so furious in Act 3, Scene 3?
(a) They are grieving Caesar's death
(b) They are manipulated by Antony's speech
(c) They have been ordered to riot by Brutus
(d) They are seeking revenge for Caesar's murder

Q.3 What is the significance of the mob attacking Cinna the poet?
(a) It reflects the growing chaos in Rome after Caesar's death
(b) It shows the mob's loyalty to Caesar
(c) It highlights the importance of poets in Roman politics
(d) It foreshadows Brutus' downfall

Q.4 How does the mob react to Cinna the poet's plea for his life?
(a) They listen to him and spare him
(b) They laugh at him and kill him anyway
(c) They arrest him for questioning
(d) They offer him a chance to explain himself

Q.5 What does the mob's treatment of Cinna the poet demonstrate about the political climate in Rome?
(a) The political situation is stable and controlled
(b) The citizens of Rome are acting with reason and justice
(c) The mob is easily swayed and chaotic in their decisions
(d) The plebeians are highly loyal to the conspirators

Q.6 How does the mob's behaviour in Act 3, Scene 3 contrast with the earlier scenes in the play?
(a) The mob was previously peaceful but now they are violent and irrational
(b) The mob has always been hostile to Caesar's supporters
(c) The mob remains calm and reflective in this scene
(d) The mob is more focused on the death of the conspirators

Q.7 What purpose does this scene serve?
(a) It highlights the effect of Antony's speech
(b) It signifies the love of the comman man for Caesar
(c) It highlights Antony's speech
(d) All of the above

Q.8 According to a citizen, Cinna's reply that he was a bachelor, tantamount to saying
(a) only bachelors are trustworthy
(b) those who marry are fools
(c) those who are bachelors are fools
(d) None of the above

Q.9 Select the option that shows the correct relationship between statements (1) and (2).
Statement 1 Cinna the poet's death is symbolic of the chaos in Rome after Caesar's assassination.
Statement 2 His death is caused by a mistaken identity, showing the irrational and violent behaviour of the mob.
(a) Statement 1 is true and Statement 2 is false
(b) Statement 2 is true and Statement 1 is false.
(c) Statement 2 is the cause for Statement 1.
(d) Both statements are false.

Answers

1. (b) 2. (d) 3. (a) 4. (b) 5. (c) 6. (a) 7. (a) 8. (b) 9. (c)

TYPE - 2 Extract Based Questions

16 Marks

Extract 1

Third Plebeian Your name, sir, truly.

Cinna Truly, my name is Cinna.

First Plebeian Tear him to pieces! He's a conspirator.

Fourth Plebeian Tear him for his bad verses, tear him for his bad verses!

Fourth Plebeian it is no matter. His name's Cinna. Pluck but his name out of his heart, and turn him going.

Third Plebeian Tear him, tear him! Come, brands, ho, firebrands! To Brutus', to Cassius', burn all! Some to Decius' house, and some to Casca's, some to Ligarius'. Away, go!

(i) Why does the First Plebeian immediately accuse Cinna of being a conspirator?

What does this reveal about the mob's state of mind? (3)

Ans. The First Plebeian accuses Cinna of being a conspirator simply because his name is 'Cinna' which is the same as one of the conspirators.

This shows how easily the mob can be manipulated and how quickly they jump to conclusions without considering the truth. The mob's state of mind is one of chaos and anger, fuelled by emotional reactions rather than rational thought.

(ii) How does Cinna's attempt to clarify his identity as a poet contribute to the tragicomic nature of the scene? (3)

Ans. Cinna's attempt to distinguish himself as 'Cinna the poet' highlights the absurdity of the mob's actions.

The fact that the crowd, in its blind rage, refuses to listen to his defense and instead decides to tear him apart for 'bad verses' adds an element of dark humour to the tragedy.

This moment reflects the danger of mob mentality and the ease with which innocent people can be swept up in violent actions.

(iii) What does the Fourth Plebeian's insistence on tearing Cinna apart for his 'bad verses' reveal about the mob's irrational behaviour? (3)

Ans. The Fourth Plebeian's focus on 'bad verses' instead of the actual reason for the mob's anger (the conspiracy) emphasises how irrational and unreasonable the crowd is.

They are so consumed by rage that they no longer care about facts or justice. Instead, they lash out indiscriminately, targeting anyone with the name 'Cinna', even if the person is innocent and unrelated to the conspiracy.

(iv) How does the scene reflect the consequences of Antony's speech to the plebeians? (3)

Ans. This scene directly reflects the consequences of Antony's speech where he stoked the crowd's emotions and turned them against the conspirators.

The mob's violent reaction to the name 'Cinna' shows how easily they can be manipulated and how quickly their anger has been directed toward anyone associated with Caesar's assassination. The scene exemplifies the chaos and bloodlust Antony's speech has incited.

(v) What is the significance of the plebeians' decision to attack Cinna, even after he claims to be a poet and not a conspirator? (4)

Ans. The plebeians' decision to attack Cinna despite his explanation reflects the crowd's complete loss of reason and their overwhelming desire for vengeance.

It symbolises the dangers of mob mentality where personal identity and truth are disregarded in favour of collective anger.

This scene demonstrates how the mob, once stirred, can become irrational and destructive. As a result, they make decisions based on impulse and confusion rather than understanding.

Act 4 : Scene 1

Summary of Act 4 Scene 1

In this scene, Antony, Octavius and Lepidus meet to discuss their plans after Caesar's assassination. They form a Triumvirate and start making a list of their enemies who must be killed. Even Lepidus' own brother and Antony's nephew are included in the list, showing how ruthless they have become.

After Lepidus leaves to carry out their orders, Antony and Octavius talk about him. Antony sees Lepidus as weak and unworthy comparing him to an animal that is only useful when controlled. However, Octavius defends Lepidus. Antony still insists that they should use him and then get rid of him when he is no longer needed.

This scene shows how Antony has become just as power-hungry as the conspirators he opposed. He no longer speaks about justice for Caesar but is instead focused on gaining and keeping power. Meanwhile, Octavius, though young, shows strength and hints that he might challenge Antony's authority later.

The scene sets up conflict between the new rulers and Brutus and Cassius leading to the civil war that will decide Rome's future.

Characters in the Scene

- **Mark Antony** Now a powerful leader of Rome, he is ruthless and manipulative. He plans to eliminate enemies and dismisses Lepidus as weak and unimportant.
- **Octavius Caesar** Julius Caesar's adopted son and heir. He is young but confident, standing up to Antony and showing early signs of leadership.
- **Lepidus** He is obedient and willing to follow orders, but Antony sees him as weak and plans to remove him once he is no longer useful.

Vocab Vault

Proscription A public list of people condemned to death or exile

Tried Tested or proven

Orts and limitations Leftovers and restrictions

Bay'd Cornered or trapped (like a hunted animal)

EXAM ORIENTED QUESTIONS

TYPE - 1 Multiple Choice Questions

01 Mark

Q.1 Who are the members of the Second Triad in Act 4, Scene 1?
(a) Antony, Octavius and Brutus
(b) Antony, Cassius and Lepidus
(c) Antony, Octavius and Lepidus
(d) Antony, Octavius and Decius

Q.2 What is the main purpose of the meeting between Antony, Octavius and Lepidus?
(a) To plan a celebration for Caesar
(b) To divide Caesar's wealth
(c) To create a list of their enemies
(d) To discuss peace with Brutus and Cassius

Q.3 What does Antony suggest about Lepidus after he leaves the meeting?
(a) Lepidus is a loyal and valuable ally
(b) Lepidus is untrustworthy and must be eliminated
(c) Lepidus is a tool to be used and discarded
(d) Lepidus should lead the army against Brutus and Cassius

Q.4 When Antony says, 'This is a slight unmeritable man, /Meet to be sent on errands', he refers to ....
(ICSE Specimen Paper 2025)
(a) Lepidus (b) Octavius (c) Pindarus (d) Lucilius

Q.5 Towards whose inclusion in the execution list does Antony express no personal objection?
(a) His nephew (b) Octavius' uncle
(c) Lepidus' son (d) Cassius' cousin

Q.6 Which of the following sentences does Mark Antony not use to describe Lepidus in Act 4, Scene 1?
(Competency Based Que.)
(a) He needs to be taught and trained.
(b) High-spirited fellow with ideas of his own.
(c) He follows trends and fashion.
(d) He is a piece of property.

Q.7 What opinion does Octavius hold about Lepidus?
(Competency Based Que.)
(a) He is industrious.
(b) He is responsible.
(c) He is a good statesman.
(d) He is a tried and valiant soldier.

Q.8 What metaphor does Antony use to describe Lepidus?
(a) A loyal dog (b) A burdened mule
(c) A mighty lion (d) A broken shield

Q.9 What does the discussion between Antony and Octavius reveal about their relationship?
(a) They are completely united in their plans
(b) They have underlying tensions and differing opinions
(c) Octavius blindly follows Antony's lead
(d) They plan to betray each other

Q.10 Select the option that shows the correct relationship between statements (1) and (2).
Statement 1 The triumvirate discusses dividing power among themselves.
Statement 2 They want to ensure there is no single ruler to prevent the rise of another Caesar.
(a) Statement 1 is true and Statement 2 is false
(b) Statement 2 is true and Statement 1 is false.
(c) Statement 2 is the cause for Statement 1.
(d) Both statements are false.

Q.11 "Your brother too must die." Whose brother is referred to?
(a) Antony's (b) Brutus' (c) Octavius' (d) Lepidus'

Q.12 Which of the following adjective is not used by Mark Antony for Lepidus?
(a) 'Stone of provender' (b) 'Unmeritable man'
(c) 'Barren-spirited fellow' (d) 'A property'

Q.13 Mark Antony's dismissal of Lepidus reflect which of the following traits of his personality?
(a) Shrewd manipulator (b) Power-hungry
(c) Betrayer of friendship (d) All of these

Q.14 Arrange the following events from Act 4, Scene 1 in the correct sequence.
1. Antony, Octavius and Lepidus create a list of enemies to be executed.
2. Lepidus is sent to fetch Caesar's will.
3. Antony and Octavius discuss Lepidus' worth and role in the triumvirate.
4. Antony suggests that they alter Caesar's will to reduce the bequests to the people.

(a) 1, 2, 3, 4 (b) 1, 3, 2, 4 (c) 1, 4, 2, 3 (d) 2, 1, 3, 4

Answers

1. (c) 2. (c) 3. (c) 4. (a) 5. (a) 6. (b) 7. (d) 8. (b) 9. (b) 10. (a)
11. (d) 12. (a) 13. (d) 14. (b)

TYPE - 2 Extract Based Questions

16 Marks

Extract 1

Antony "These many, then, shall die; their names are pricked."

Octavius "Your brother too must die; consent you, Lepidus?"

Lepidus "I do consent."

Antony "Prick him down, Octavius."

(i) What is the significance of Antony saying, "These many, then, shall die; their names are pricked"? (3)

Ans. Antony's statement signifies the cold and ruthless nature of the new leadership. The act of 'pricking' names on the list shows the methodical and detached way in which they decide who will be executed. This further highlights the brutal political climate and their determination to eliminate opposition.

(ii) Why does Octavius mention Antony's nephew and ask Lepidus for consent to his death? (3)

Ans. Octavius mentions Antony's nephew to demonstrate the impersonal and merciless nature of their decisions. By seeking Lepidus' consent, he ensures unity and agreement within the triumvirate, even when it involves difficult personal sacrifices. This emphasises the political expediency over familial ties.

(iii) How does Lepidus' response, 'I do consent', reflect his character and position within the triumvirate? (3)

Ans. Lepidus' quick consent reflects his submissive and passive role within the triumvirate. It shows his willingness to comply with Antony and Octavius' decisions, highlighting his weaker position and lack of influence compared to the other two leaders.

(iv) What does Antony's command, 'Prick him down, Octavius', reveal about his leadership style? (3)

Ans. Antony's command reveals his ruthlessness. It shows that he is willing to take swift and harsh actions without hesitation, prioritising political strategy and control over personal relationships or moral considerations.

(v) What theme is emphasised by the exchange of dialogue in these lines? (4)

Ans. The theme emphasised by this exchange of dialogue is ruthlessness and the corrupting nature of power. The casual and impersonal manner in which Antony, Octavius and Lepidus decide on executions illustrates how their thirst for control has led them to prioritise political power over moral considerations. By quickly listing individuals to be killed, including even Lepidus' own brother, they show a complete disregard for personal connections and the sanctity of life.

This exchange highlights the moral decay that often accompanies the pursuit of absolute power as well as the manipulation and use of others as tools in political gain.

Extract 2

And having brought our treasure where we will,
Then take we down his load and turn him off
(Like to the empty ass) to shake his ears
And graze in commons.

Octavius You may do your will,
But he's a tried and valiant soldier.

(i) What is the significance of Antony comparing Lepidus to 'the empty ass' in these lines? (3)

Ans. Antony's comparison of Lepidus to an 'empty ass' highlights his low opinion of Lepidus. The image of an 'empty ass' suggests that Lepidus is a mere beast of burden carrying their orders without any real influence or worth. Antony sees him as a tool to be used and discarded, rather than a valuable ally.

(ii) What does Octavius mean when he refers to Lepidus as 'a tried and valiant soldier'? (3)

Ans. Octavius' statement reflects his more favourable view of Lepidus. By calling him a 'tried and valiant soldier', Octavius acknowledges Lepidus' past military service and bravery. It suggests that Octavius values Lepidus' loyalty and military contributions, even if Antony sees him as expendable in political matters.

(iii) How do Antony and Octavius' differing opinions on Lepidus highlight their relationship in this scene? (3)

Ans. The contrasting opinions of Antony and Octavius about Lepidus reveal the tension and differing perspectives within the triumvirate. Antony's dismissive attitude toward Lepidus shows his more cynical, power-driven approach. Meanwhile, Octavius' defense of Lepidus indicates his more pragmatic and perhaps more generous approach to alliances highlighting their political dynamics.

(iv) What is implied by Antony's suggestion to 'take we down his load and turn him off'? (3)

Ans. Antony's suggestion to 'take we down his load and turn him off' implies that they will use Lepidus for a while but once he has served his purpose, they will discard him. This reflects Antony's belief that Lepidus is only useful as a tool to help them achieve their goals and that he is not worthy of long-term trust or power.

(v) What theme is highlighted by the way Antony and Octavius view Lepidus in this exchange? (4)

Ans. The theme of power and manipulation is highlighted in this exchange. It shows how political leaders like Antony and Octavius use others to further their own ambitions. They view their allies and subordinates as expendable commodities. The discussion underscores the corrupting influence of power and the lack of loyalty in their leadership.

ACT 4 : SCENE 2

Summary of Act 4 Scene 2

In this scene, Brutus and his army arrive at a military camp near Sardis. Brutus meets with Lucilius who informs him that Cassius is approaching with his forces. However, Lucilius hints that Cassius has not been as friendly or respectful as before indicating a strain in their relationship.

Shortly after, Cassius arrives with his forces and it is clear that there is a rift between him and Brutus. Cassius feels slighted and accuses Brutus of wronging him. Brutus, aware of the tension, suggests they discuss their issues privately in his tent to avoid airing their grievances in front of the troops.

This scene highlights the internal conflict and strain in the leadership of the conspirators. It foreshadows potential challenges in their unity as they prepare for battle against Antony and Octavius. The personal tensions between Brutus and Cassius reflect the weakening alliance and growing mistrust within their ranks.

Characters in the Scene

- **Brutus** One of the main conspirators against Caesar. He is worried about Cassius' behaviour and senses tension in their friendship.
- **Lucilius** A loyal officer and friend to Brutus. He brings news about Cassius' change in attitude and warns Brutus that Cassius is no longer as friendly as before.
- **Pindarus** Cassius' loyal servant. He arrives with Cassius and serves as his messenger.
- **Cassius** Another key conspirator against Caesar. He enters angrily, ready to confront Brutus over some grievances.
- **Soldiers (Attendants)** They accompany Cassius and Brutus as they prepare for war.

Vocab Vault

Ill officers Bad or dishonest officers
Jades Lazy or worn-out horses
Sink in the trial Fail in the test or challenge
Speak the word along Pass the order down the line
Wrangle Argue or fight bitterly

EXAM ORIENTED QUESTIONS

TYPE - 1 Multiple Choice Questions

01 Mark

Q.1 Who informs Brutus about the change in Cassius' demeanour?

(a) Lucilius (b) Titinius (c) Messala (d) Pindarus

Q.2 What does Lucilius say about Cassius' behaviour toward Brutus?

(a) Cassius has been warm and friendly.
(b) Cassius has been cold and distant.
(c) Cassius has remained indifferent.
(d) Cassius has shown great respect.

Q.3 Brutus and Cassius did not argue in front of their men because **(Competency Based Que.)**

(a) they did not want an audience.
(b) they did not want to demoralise their troops.
(c) they wanted witnesses to collaborate in their discussion.
(d) they wanted to discuss in a calm environment.

Q.4 How does Brutus plan to handle the disagreement with Cassius?

(a) By ignoring it and focusing on the battle
(b) By confronting Cassius publicly
(c) By discussing it privately in his tent
(d) By writing a letter to Cassius

Q.5 What is the significance of the tension between Brutus and Cassius in this scene?

(a) It shows their strong alliance.
(b) It highlights the unity of the conspirators.
(c) It foreshadows internal conflict and weakening trust.
(d) It reveals Cassius' complete loyalty to Brutus.

Q.6 What does the arrival of Cassius signify in this scene?

(a) A moment of unity and celebration
(b) The beginning of military preparations
(c) Rising tensions and potential discord between leaders
(d) Cassius' submission to Brutus' leadership

Q.7 Who is referred to as Pindarus' master?

(a) Brutus (b) Cassius
(c) Antony (d) Octavius

Q.8 According to Brutus, what does a friend begin to do when his love begins to decline and diminish?

(a) He tries to part ways
(b) He uses forced formalities
(c) He uses corrupt means
(d) He does not bother for anything

Q.9 With whom has Brutus compared an insincere man?

(a) Worthless horse (b) Worthless runner
(c) Worthless friend (d) None of these

Q.10 According to Cassius, what hides the wrong done by Brutus?

(a) Dignified appearance
(b) His fear
(c) His outer personality
(d) None of the above

Q.11 Select the option that shows the correct relationship between statements (1) and (2).

Statement 1 Brutus feels hopeful about their upcoming battle against Antony and Octavius.

Statement 2 The conspirators' internal conflicts do not affect their military strategy.

(a) Statement 1 is true and Statement 2 is false
(b) Statement 2 is true and Statement 1 is false.
(c) Statement 2 is the cause for Statement 1.
(d) Both statements are false.

Answers

1. (a) 2. (b) 3. (b) 4. (c) 5. (c) 6. (c) 7. (b) 8. (b) 9. (a) 10. (a) 11. (a)

TYPE - 2 Extract Based Questions

16 Marks

Extract 1

Thou hast described
A hot friend cooling. Ever note, Lucilius,
When love begins to sicken and decay
It useth an enforcèd ceremony.
There are no tricks in plain and simple faith;
But hollow men, like horses hot at hand,
Make gallant show and promise of their mettle

(i) What does Brutus mean when he says, 'Thou hast described a hot friend cooling'? **(3)**

Ans. Through the given line, Brutus is acknowledging that Lucilius has accurately described the situation between him and Cassius where their once close friendship has cooled.

The phrase 'hot friend cooling' refers to the waning intensity of their bond as their relationship becomes strained and distant.

(ii) Why does Brutus suggest that 'when love begins to sicken and decay, it useth an enforcèd ceremony'? **(3)**

Ans. Brutus is commenting on outward formalities that often accompanies the diminishing of genuine love and friendship. He is indirectly pointing out at the behaviours of Cassius, who did not welcome Lucilius with warmth and love.

(iii) What is the meaning of the phrase 'There are no tricks in plain and simple faith'? **(3)**

Ans. Through the given phrase, Brutus is emphasising the value of honesty and sincerity in relationships. He believes that true faith and loyalty are straightforward and free of deceit or manipulation. In contrast, when someone pretends to be faithful, it is often insincere and deceptive, marked by tricks and falsehoods.

(iv) What does Brutus imply about 'hollow men, like horses hot at hand, make gallant show and promise of their mettle'? **(3)**

Ans. In the given phrase, Brutus is critiquing those who make grand displays of loyalty and strength but lack true substance or integrity. The metaphor of 'hollow men' suggests individuals who appear strong and committed on the surface but are actually empty and weak.

Horses in the stable pretend to be very energetic and fast but when put to trial in actual race they bow down their head like deciteful jades.

Similarly, 'horses hot at hand' may look ready and promising but lack the true strength to follow through.

(v) How do these lines reflect Brutus' perspective on friendship and loyalty in the context of his relationship with Cassius? **(4)**

Ans. These lines reveal Brutus' disillusionment with the shifting dynamics of his friendship with Cassius.

He perceives the cooling of their relationship as a natural decline of true loyalty, with both sides now engaging in pretenses ('enforcèd ceremony') rather than genuine connection.

The metaphor of 'hollow men' suggests that Brutus feels Cassius may show outward love but when is tried he betrays.

Extract 2

Cassius Brutus, this sober form of yours hides wrongs,
And when you do them-
Brutus Cassius, be content.
Speak your griefs softly. I do know you well.
Before the eyes of both our armies here
Let us not wrangle. Bid them move away.
Then in my tent, Cassius, enlarge your griefs,
And I will give you audience.

(i) What does Cassius mean when he says, 'Brutus, this sober form of yours hides wrongs'? **(3)**

Ans. In the given phrase, Cassius is accusing Brutus of hiding his true feelings and grievances behind a calm and composed exterior. He implies that Brutus' outward appearance of soberness conceals his anger or dissatisfaction, particularly regarding Cassius' actions or decisions.

(ii) Why does Brutus ask Cassius to 'speak your griefs softly'? **(3)**

Ans. Brutus is urging Cassius to express his frustrations in a calm and controlled manner rather than in an angry or confrontational way. He wants to avoid causing a scene or disrupting the unity of their forces, especially in front of their soldiers and prefers that they discuss their issues privately.

(iii) What is Brutus emphasising in 'Before the eyes of both our armies here, let us not wrangle'? **(3)**

Ans. Brutus is emphasising the importance of maintaining unity and discipline in front of their armies. He wants to avoid public disputes as they could weaken the morale of their troops and cause division within their forces.

He is trying to preserve their authority and control in front of the soldiers.

(iv) **Why does Brutus invite Cassius to his tent to 'enlarge your griefs'?** **(3)**

Ans. Brutus invites Cassius to his tent to offer him a private space to vent his frustrations and explain his grievances in detail. By inviting him to his tent, Brutus hopes to resolve the conflict between them in a more intimate and controlled setting. In this way, they can speak freely without the risk of undermining their authority. Moreover he did not want their army's to witness their conflicts.

(v) **How do these lines illustrate the strained relationship between Brutus and Cassius?** **(4)**

Ans. These lines show that there is tension between Brutus and Cassius as Cassius is frustrated and feels wronged by Brutus. Meanwhile, Brutus is trying to maintain composure and resolve the conflict diplomatically.

The need for privacy and the tone of their conversation reflect underlying issues in their relationship where personal grievances are affecting their professional alliance.

ACT 4 : SCENE 3

Summary of Act 4 Scene 3

The scene takes place in the military camp near Alexandria where Brutus and Cassius are having a private conversation discussing their disagreements and the state of the war. The scene begins with Brutus and Cassius being at odds over various matters and tension builds up. Brutus accuses Cassius of bribery and Cassius defends himself. He says that he has always acted honourably in the cause of Rome. Cassius is offended by Brutus' accusations and is hurt by what he perceives as a betrayal of their friendship.

As the quarrel intensifies, both men express frustration with one another. Brutus accuses Cassius of being greedy and corrupt while Cassius counters that Brutus has been too harsh on him. This dispute is complicated further when Brutus reveals the personal grief he has been suffering. He mentions the recent suicide of Portia and how it has affected him emotionally. He also expresses his disillusionment with the war and his growing anxiety about their political situation.

Eventually, after a heated exchange, the two men reconcile, with Cassius apologising and Brutus forgiving him. Their reconciliation shows their deep friendship and shared commitment to the cause of liberty despite their disagreements. They agree to move forward and unite their forces for the upcoming battle against the forces of Mark Antony and Octavius.

The scene is a crucial moment in the play as it highlights the tension between Brutus and Cassius who have been the central leaders of the conspiracy against Caesar. Their personal and ideological differences threaten to divide the army.

Furthermore, Brutus encounters Caesar's ghost in his tent. When Brutus asks why it has come, the spirit warns him that they will meet again at Philippi. The ghost is a symbol of Brutus, guilt. It predicts that Brutus will die at Philippi. This further adds to the supernatural element in the play.

However, in the end, their shared goal of defeating Antony and Octavius brings them back together. The scene emphasises the complexity of their relationship blending political ambition, personal grief and loyalty. It also foreshadows the eventual tragic fate of the characters as the instability within the ranks suggests that the forces of Rome are unravelling.

Vocab Vault

Hedge me in Hinder or disrupt my action

Mirth Cheerfulness or joy

Waspish Bad tempered

Conn'd by rote Learned by memorisation without true understanding; recited mechanically

Yoked Bound or enslaved

Flint A hard stone, often used metaphorically to represent toughness or harshness

Chides Scolds or reprimands

Jigging fools People who behave foolishly or frivolously, often engaging in silly or superficial amusements

O'erswell Overflows

Legions Large groups of soldiers, typically used to describe Roman military units

Ventures Risky or daring undertakings

Characters in the Scene

- **Brutus** One of the main conspirators. He argues with Cassius over money and corruption but later reconciles with him. He also sees Caesar's ghost, which foreshadows his fate.
- **Cassius** Another key conspirator. He is angry at Brutus for accusing him of corruption but after a heated argument, they make peace and prepare for battle.
- **Lucilius** A loyal officer of Brutus. He helps deliver messages and observes that Cassius is not as friendly as before.
- **Titinius** Another soldier loyal to Cassius. He stays with Cassius and helps in the war preparations.
- **Messala** A messenger who brings news of Antony and Octavius' growing power and the execution of senators, including Cicero.
- **Poet** A random poet who enters Brutus' tent and tries to stop Brutus and Cassius from fighting. His interruption is ignored.
- **Caesar's Ghost** A supernatural figure that appears to Brutus at night, calling itself his 'evil spirit' and warning that they will meet again at Philippi, foreshadowing Brutus' downfall.

EXAM ORIENTED QUESTIONS

TYPE - 1 Multiple Choice Questions

01 Mark

Q.1 What is the main reason for the quarrel between Brutus and Cassius in this scene?
(a) Disagreement over battle strategy
(b) Personal grievances and accusations
(c) Their failure to defeat Octavius
(d) Their different views on Caesar's assassination

Q.2 What does Brutus accuse Cassius of in this scene?
(a) Being too lenient with their soldiers
(b) Being greedy and corrupt
(c) Failing to take charge of the army
(d) Disrespecting Caesar

Q.3 How does Cassius react to Brutus' accusations?
(a) He apologises immediately
(b) He defends himself arguing he has always acted honourably
(c) He ignores Brutus and walks away
(d) He challenges Brutus to a duel

Q.4 What personal tragedy does Brutus reveal to Cassius?
(a) The death of his father
(b) The death of Portia, his wife
(c) The death of his brother
(d) His banishment from Rome

Q.5 What is Cassius' response to Brutus' grief over Portia's death?
(a) He offers his condolences
(b) He criticises Brutus for letting emotions interfere with leadership
(c) He suggests Brutus forget about his grief and focus on battle
(d) He says that all leaders suffer personal losses

Q.6 How does Brutus carry anger within his nature?
(a) As a flint carries fire
(b) As a ball of fire
(c) As a wick of a lamp
(d) As a drop of water

Q.7 Who would overlook a friend's fault, according to Brutus?
(a) A gossip monger (b) A wicked friend
(c) An arrogant man (d) A flatter's eye

Q.8 Messala brings the news of killing of which of the following senators by Antony and Octavius?
(a) Lucius (b) Titinus (c) Cicero (d) Cassius

Q.9 What does the ghost of Caesar stands for?
(a) Spirit of Caesar, restless for revenge
(b) Spirit of Caesar, restless for saving Roman Republic
(c) Spirit of Caesar, restless on being betrayed by Brutus
(d) None of the above

Q.10 How does Portia die?
(a) By jumping from Mount Olympus
(b) By drowning in the sea
(c) By swallowing poison
(d) By swallowing burning coals

Q.11 What does Brutus say is the cause of Portia's death?
(a) Illness
(b) Suicide/Brutus is absence
(c) The strain of the war
(d) She was killed by Octavius' forces

Q.12 How does Brutus feel about the war in Act 4, Scene 3?
(a) He is confident they will win
(b) He is disillusioned and increasingly anxious
(c) He wants to retreat from battle
(d) He is excited about the prospect of victory

Q.13 What does Cassius accuse Brutus of in response to his accusations?
(a) Being too idealistic
(b) Being a coward
(c) Being too harsh on him
(d) Not taking care of the army properly

Q.14 How does Brutus react to Cassius' apology?
(a) He refuses to forgive him
(b) He accepts the apology and they reconcile
(c) He walks away in silence
(d) He demands Cassius be removed from the army

Q.15 What does Cassius offer Brutus to regain his favour?
(a) To step down from leadership
(b) A lavish gift
(c) A written apology
(d) An apology and an offer to make amends

Q.16 What is the significance of the reconciliation between Brutus and Cassius?
(a) It strengthens their resolve to defeat Octavius and Antony
(b) It marks the beginning of their eventual betrayal of each other
(c) It indicates Brutus' willingness to take control
(d) It highlights their mutual fear of Octavius

Q.17 Which of the following characters is mentioned by Cassius as being loyal to Brutus?
(a) Octavius (b) Antony
(c) Lucilius (d) Messala

Q.18 'O Cassius, you are yoked with a lamb.' [Act 4] Which of the following uses the same literary device as given above? **(Competency Based Que.)**
(a) The man fought as bravely as a lion.
(b) His voice is velvet.
(c) The sky was dotted with fluffy, white clouds.
(d) The juicy apple tasted sweet.

Q.19 What does Brutus plan to do after reconciling with Cassius?
(a) Retreat from the battle
(b) Attack Octavius immediately
(c) Continue with their military preparations for the second battle
(d) Focus on strengthening the Roman economy

Q.20 Who is tasked with managing the army's logistics in Act 4, Scene 3?
(a) Brutus and Cassius themselves
(b) Labeo and Flavius
(c) Octavius and Antony
(d) Lucilius and Messala

Q.21 What does Brutus say about his actions against Caesar in this scene?
(a) He regrets killing Caesar
(b) He justifies them as being for the good of Rome
(c) He plans to fight Octavius and Antony for revenge
(d) He says he was forced into it by Cassius

Q.22 What event does Brutus recall as affecting him deeply?
(a) The betrayal by his friends
(b) Portia's death
(c) The assassination of Caesar
(d) The loss of Rome's support

Q.23 How does Cassius view Brutus' leadership after their argument?
(a) He believes Brutus is too weak to lead
(b) He is angry and wants to take over leadership
(c) He recognises Brutus' nobility and offers his support
(d) He is indifferent to Brutus' leadership

Q.24 What does Brutus believe will be the outcome of their next battle?
(a) Victory for their cause
(b) Defeat and retreat
(c) Another stalemate
(d) The death of one of the generals

Q.25 What does Brutus do to relieve the tension between him and Cassius?
(a) He offers Cassius a greater role in leadership
(b) He apologises for his harsh words
(c) He calls for peace talks with Octavius
(d) He withdraws from the army

Q.26 How does Brutus feel about his current military position?
(a) He feels hopeful and prepared for victory
(b) He is concerned and fearful about the war
(c) He plans to surrender to Octavius
(d) He is indifferent to the outcome

Q.27 What does Brutus mean when he says, 'The sufferance of the time is now' (referring to their situation)?
(a) The time has come to fight for freedom
(b) They must endure the hardships of war
(c) They have no other choice but to keep fighting
(d) Their suffering is a result of their own actions

Q.28 What does Brutus instruct his soldiers to do after the reconciliation with Cassius?
(a) Prepare for battle
(b) Retreat to a safer location
(c) Rest and gather strength
(d) Search for supplies

Q.29 What does Cassius fear Brutus will do as a result of their argument?
(a) Betray him
(b) Abandon the army
(c) Lead them to defeat
(d) Join forces with Octavius

Q.30 How does Brutus handle the news of Portia's death?
(a) He is openly distraught
(b) He is stoic and keeps his emotions hidden
(c) He demands a funeral immediately
(d) He leaves the army to mourn her

Q.31 What role does Lucilius play in this scene?
(a) A mediator between Brutus and Cassius
(b) A trusted officer in Brutus' army
(c) A messenger for Octavius
(d) A bystander who offers advice

Q.32 How does Brutus justify his decision to continue fighting despite the loss of Portia?
(a) He believes the cause is greater than personal loss
(b) He is motivated by revenge for Caesar's death
(c) He hopes to secure peace for Rome
(d) He has no other option

Q.33 What is Brutus' attitude towards death and destiny in this scene?
(a) He accepts it as part of the natural order
(b) He seeks to avoid it at all costs
(c) He fears it and is overwhelmed by anxiety
(d) He believes that fate will lead him to victory

Q.34 What is the tone of Act 4, Scene 3?
I. Optimistic II. Tense III. Conflicted
IV. Peaceful V. Celebratory
(a) I and II
(b) II and III
(c) III and IV
(d) IV and V

Q.35 Which literary device is most evident in Brutus' speech when he says, 'There is a tide in the affairs of men/Which, taken at the flood, leads on to fortune'?
(a) Metaphor
(b) Allusion
(c) Personification
(d) Simile

Q.36 Select the option that shows the correct relationship between statements (1) and (2).
Statement 1 Brutus' attitude toward the death of Caesar is emotional, revealing his inner turmoil.
Statement 2 Brutus' actions in the civil war reveal a constant conflict between personal loyalty and political duty.
(a) Statement 1 is true and Statement 2 is false
(b) Statement 2 is true and Statement 1 is false.
(c) Statement 2 is the cause for Statement 1.
(d) Both statements are false.

Q.37 Select the option that shows the correct relationship between statements (1) and (2).
Statement 1 Brutus' refusal to listen to Cassius' counsel during the argument shows his growing belief in his own judgement.
Statement 2 The conflict between Brutus and Cassius in Act 4, Scene 3 is resolved peacefully and they work together harmoniously for the rest of the play.
(a) Statement 1 is true and Statement 2 is false
(b) Statement 2 is true and Statement 1 is false.
(c) Statement 2 is the cause for Statement 1.
(d) Both statements are false.

Q.38 Arrange the following actions in the correct sequence as they occur in Act 4, Scene 3.
1. **Brutus and Cassius decide on their strategy for the upcoming battle.**
2. **Brutus accuses Cassius of being corrupt and taking bribes.**
3. **Brutus contemplates his wife Portia's death.**
4. **Brutus and Cassius reconcile and swear to fight together against their enemies.**

(a) 2, 3, 1, 4
(b) 1, 2, 4, 3
(c) 3, 2, 1, 4
(d) 4, 3, 1, 2

Answers

1. (b)	2. (b)	3. (b)	4. (b)	5. (a)	6. (a)	7. (d)	8. (c)	9. (a)	10. (d)
11. (b)	12. (b)	13. (c)	14. (b)	15. (d)	16. (a)	17. (c)	18. (b)	19. (c)	20. (b)
21. (b)	22. (b)	23. (c)	24. (a)	25. (b)	26. (b)	27. (b)	28. (a)	29. (a)	30. (b)
31. (b)	32. (a)	33. (a)	34. (b)	35. (a)	36. (c)	37. (a)	38. (a)		

Explanations

36. A metaphor is a figure of speech that compares two things without the use of 'as' or 'like'. In the given line, 'tide in the affairs of men' represents opportunities that must be seized at the right moment. Additionally, 'Taken at the flood' suggests that just like a high tide can carry a ship forward, taking advantage of the right moment leads to success.

37. Brutus struggles emotionally with the consequences of Caesar's assassination. Even though he justifies the killing as necessary for Rome, he feels guilt and sorrow. Throughout the play, Brutus is torn between his love for Caesar and his sense of duty to Rome. He joins the conspiracy not out of hatred but because he believes it is best for the republic.

    Hence, statement 2 is the cause for statement 1.

38. Brutus disregards Cassius' advice and insists on marching to Philippi instead of waiting for Antony and Octavius to come to them. This shows Brutus' growing confidence in his own judgement, even though Cassius warns him against it. While Brutus and Cassius resolve their argument peacefully, their unity remains fragile. Their poor strategic choices lead to their defeat at Philippi.

    Hence, statement 1 is true and statement 2 is false.

TYPE - 2 Extract Based Questions

16 Marks

Extract 1

Brutus You wrong'd yourself to write in such a case.

Cassius In such a time as this it is not meet
That every nice offence should bear his comment. **(Competency Based Que.)**

(i) Where are Brutus and Cassius?

Why does Brutus make the above statement? **(3)**

Ans. Brutus and Cassius are in Brutus' tent within the army camp. Brutus makes this statement because he feels that Cassius has wronged him by writing a letter in support of Lucius Pella who was accused of taking bribes from the Sardians.

(ii) Immediately after this extract, what does Brutus accuse Cassius of?

Why does he do so?

How does Cassius react to it? **(3)**

Ans. Brutus accuses Cassius of being greedy and accepting bribes eitching palm. He does so because he is angered by the idea of compromising their moral integrity in the war against Caesar's corruption. Cassius reacts defensively denying the accusation and feeling insulted by Brutus' harsh words.

(iii) Later, in what context does Brutus remind Cassius of the Ides of March?

How does Brutus express his distaste for accepting bribes? **(3)**

Ans. Brutus reminds Cassius of the Ides of March to recall their joint commitment to rid Rome of corruption and ambition *i.e.,* Julius Caesar. Brutus expresses his distaste for accepting bribes by arguing that they must remain morally upright and not stoop to the level of the corrupt individuals they opposed.

(iv) What reason does Brutus give for not being afraid of Cassius' threats later in the scene?

What does he accuse Cassius of, then?

What was Cassius' reply? **(3)**

Ans. Brutus states that he is not afraid of Cassius' threats because he believes in his own integrity and righteousness. He accuses Cassius of withholding money needed to pay Brutus' soldiers. Cassius responds by offering his dagger saying that if Brutus no longer trusts him, he can kill him and take his heart which is more valuable than pluto's mine.

(v) Give one character trait to each of Cassius and Brutus, as revealed in this scene.

Justify with the help of instances from the scene. **(4)**

Ans. Brutus: Principled Brutus is portrayed as a man of integrity who values honour above personal relationships. He confronts Cassius for supporting Lucius Pella, accused of taking bribes and condemns corruption saying, 'Shall we now contaminate our fingers with base bribes?'

This reflects his unwavering commitment to justice and morality.

Cassius: Emotional Cassius displays his emotional and sensitive nature. When Brutus accuses him, Cassius feels deeply hurt and dramatically offers his dagger saying, 'Strike, as thou didst at Caesar.' This reveals his vulnerability and how personally he takes criticism, especially from a close ally.

Extract 2

Brutus I did send to you
For certain sums of gold, which you denied me;
For I can raise no money by vile means;
By heaven, I had rather coin my heart,
and drop my blood for drachmas, than to wring
From the hard hands of peasants their vile trash
By any indirection. **(ICSE Specimen 2025)**

(i) To whom are these words addressed?
Why is Brutus angry with this person? (3)

Ans. Brutus is addressing the above words to Cassius.

Brutus is expressing his anger and disappointment after learning that Cassius was accepting bribes in exchange of power. He also expresses his frustration when Cassius refused to send him money when he needed it.

(ii) How does this person feel when he hears these words?
What does he say to defend himself? (3)

Ans. Cassius felt angry and hurt after hearing Brutus' accusations.

He defends himself by clarifying that he didn't intend to refuse help. Instead, the messengers had made a mistake and caused a miscommunication between them.

(iii) Why did Brutus need 'certain sums of gold'?
Why was he unable to raise these sums of money? (3)

Ans. Brutus needed the money to help pay the soldiers of his battalion.

He was unable to gather such a sum as he didn't have any funds of his own and refused to raise money using vile means. He argues that he would rather turn his own heart into gold and his blood drops into silver coins than rob poor and innocent villagers of their hard-earned money.

(iv) Earlier in this scene, Brutus refers to Lucius Pella.
What had been accused of?
Who had supported him and how? (3)

Ans. Lucius Pella was accused of taking away money from the Sardians. Brutus humiliated Pella by condemning his actions and disgraced him.

Cassius had written to Brutus defending Pella and requesting him to absolve Pella of these accusations. He says so because he knew the man well.

(v) Mention any two aspects of Brutus' character that are revealed in the above extract.
What do you understand about the relationship between Brutus and the person he addresses? (4)

Ans. The above extract showcases Brutus' high morals.

He holds honesty and loyalty on the highest pedestal and expects others to do the same. In the extract, Brutus condemns Cassius for accepting bribes.

He expresses his disappointment in Cassius for committing such a shameful act.

However, this scene also showcases the double standards. As he criticises Cassius' act of accepting bribes, he also argues with Cassius for not aiding him financially to pay his battalion. By doing this, he establishes that he can never extort money from the poor.

The relationship between Cassius and Brutus is shown to be strained in the above dialogue. They quarrel and find faults in each other without accepting their own mistakes. It showcases evident differences in their personalities and value system that leads to clashes between them.

Extract 3

Sheathe your dagger.
Be angry when you will, it shall have scope.
Do what you will, dishonor shall be human.
O Cassius, you are yokèd with a lamb
That carries anger as the flint bears fire,
Who, much enforcèd, shows a hasty spark
And straight is cold again.

(i) What does Brutus mean by 'dishonour shall be humour' in the context of this passage? (3)

Ans. Brutus is telling Cassius that his dishonourable behaviour, such as accepting bribes or wrongdoing, will be treated lightly as if it were merely a whimsical or humorous act. This reflects Brutus' ability to tolerate Cassius' faults despite his anger emphasising Brutus' restrained and forgiving nature.

(ii) How does Brutus describe his own temperament in this passage?
What metaphor does he use? (3)

Ans. Brutus describes himself as calm and patient, likening himself to a lamb, which symbolises gentleness.

He further compares his anger to a flint stating that when struck, it produces a brief spark but quickly returns to coldness. This shows that his anger is short-lived and controlled.

(iii) What does Brutus' comparison of his anger to flint suggest about his character? **(3)**

Ans. The comparison shows that Brutus is a person of restraint and self-control. While he is capable of anger, it is momentary and does not linger or consume him. This reflects his rational and composed demeanour even during conflicts.

(iv) What is the significance of Brutus telling Cassius to 'sheathe your dagger'? **(3)**

Ans. Brutus' command for Cassius to sheathe his dagger symbolises his refusal to escalate the conflict. It demonstrates his leadership and calm approach to resolving disputes emphasising his focus on unity and reason over emotional outbursts.

(v) What does this exchange reveal about the relationship between Brutus and Cassius? **(4)**

Ans. The exchange highlights the tension and contrasting personalities between the two. Brutus is calm, rational and forgiving. Meanwhile, Cassius is emotional and prone to dramatic expressions of his feelings.

Despite their differences, Brutus' willingness to diffuse the situation and maintain their alliance underscores the strength of their bond and shared purpose.

Extract 4

Brutus Speak no more of her. Give me a bowl of wine.
In this I bury all unkindness, Cassius [Drinks]
Cassius My heart is thirsty for that noble pledge.
Fill, Lucius, till the wine O'erswell the crup,
I cannot drink too much of Brutus' love.

(Competency Based Que.)

(i) Who is referred to as 'her' in the first line of the extract?
What had she done?
Why did she take that step? **(3)**

Ans. The person referred to as 'her' is Portia, Brutus' wife. She committed suicide by swallowing hot coals. Portia took this step because of her distress over Brutus' absence, the growing power of Octavius and Antony and her fear for Brutus' safety.

(ii) How was Brutus related to the above lady?
Why did he wish not to discuss the matter related to her?
What does this tell us about his nature? **(3)**

Ans. Brutus was Portia's husband. He avoided discussing her death as he wanted to focus on the pressing military matters at hand and maintain composure. This shows Brutus' stoic nature and his ability to suppress personal grief for the greater good.

(iii) Who comes to meet Brutus and Cassius immediately after the quoted lines?
What news do they bring? **(3)**

Ans. A messenger arrives to inform Brutus and Cassius about the advancement of Octavius and Antony's army. They bring news that the enemy forces are approaching and preparation for battle is necessary.

(iv) Explain the term 'Triumvirate' in this context.
Name the members of the Second Triumvirate. **(3)**

Ans. The term 'Triumvirate' refers to the political alliance formed by three leaders.

In the context of Julius Caesar, the Second Triumvirate consisted of Octavius Caesar, Mark Antony and Lepidus who shared power after Caesar's assassination.

(v) Brutus and Cassius had different ideas about how best to defeat the enemy.
What were their strategies? Whose strategy was adopted? **(4)**

Ans. Brutus wanted to march to Philippi to confront Antony and Octavius believing it would be advantageous to face them before their army grew stronger. Cassius, on the other hand, preferred to wait and let the enemy exhaust themselves by travelling. Brutus' strategy was ultimately adopted.

Extract 5

Under your pardon. You must note besides
That we have tried the utmost of our friends,
Our legions are brim full, our cause is ripe.
The enemy increaseth every day;
We, at the height, are ready to decline.
There is a tide in the affairs of men
Which, taken at the flood, leads on to fortune;
Omitted, all the voyage of their life
Is bound in shallows and in miseries.
On such a full sea are we now afloat,
And we must take the current when it serves
Or lose our ventures.

(i) What does Brutus mean by 'We, at the height, are ready to decline'?
How does it reflect his understanding of the situation? **(3)**

Ans. Through the given line, Brutus acknowledges that their cause has reached its peak and is poised to weaken if they delay taking action. Literally it means they are at Mount Sardis and can only came down.

It reflects his strategic insight that opportunities are fleeting and the momentum they currently hold will diminish as time passes and the enemy grows stronger.

(ii) Analyse the significance of the metaphor 'the tide in the affairs of men' in the context of Brutus' leadership decisions. **(3)**

Ans. The metaphor underscores Brutus' belief in seizing opportunities at their peak for success. As a leader, this reflects his understanding that hesitation can lead to failure.

The 'tide' symbolises the perfect moment for action. Brutus emphasises that missing it will result in stagnation and misery highlighting his urgency and decisiveness.

(iii) How does Brutus' speech reveal his philosophical outlook on fate and free will? **(3)**

Ans. Brutus' speech suggests a belief in a balance between fate and free will. While he acknowledges that circumstances create opportunities (fate), he emphasises the importance of taking action at the right moment (free will).

This duality reflects his rational yet idealistic worldview.

(iv) What is the rhetorical purpose of the line 'On such a full sea are we now afloat'?

How does it persuade others? **(3)**

Ans. The given line uses a vivid metaphor to compare their current situation to a ship on a high tide, poised for a successful journey.

It conveys a sense of urgency and inevitability persuading his comrades to recognise that they must act decisively to achieve success or risk losing everything.

(v) Mention any two aspects of Brutus' character that are revealed in the above extract.

What do you understand about the relationship between Brutus and the person he addresses? **(4)**

Ans. Two aspects of Brutus' character revealed in the given extract are

(a) **Practical and Strategic Thinker** Brutus demonstrates a clear understanding of timing and strategy.

(b) **Philosophical and Idealistic Nature** Brutus' use of the metaphor about 'the tide in the affairs of men' reflects his belief in fate and the importance of decisive action.

Brutus is addressing Cassius in this extract and their relationship is one of mutual respect but also occasional conflict. Brutus' tone here is firm yet rational indicating his leadership and ability to persuade Cassius. The relationship is strained at times but moments like these reveal Brutus' dominance in decision-making.

Extract 6

Ha, who comes here?-
I think it is the weakness of mine eyes
That shapes this monstrous apparition.
It comes upon me.-Art thou any thing?
Art thou some god, some angel, or some devil,
That mak'st my blood cold and my hair to stare?
Speak to me what thou art.

(i) How does Brutus' reaction to the apparition reflect his psychological state? **(3)**

Ans. Brutus' reaction, marked by fear and uncertainty, reveals his inner turmoil and guilt. The apparition symbolises his anxiety about his decisions, particularly the assassination of Caesar.

His questioning of whether it is a god, angel or devil demonstrates his confusion and vulnerability indicating that his rational composure is faltering.

(ii) Why does Brutus refer to the apparition as a 'monstrous apparition'?

What does this choice of words suggest? **(3)**

Ans. The phrase 'monstrous apparition' reflects Brutus' perception of the ghost as something unnatural and terrifying.

This choice of words suggests that Brutus sees the ghost as a manifestation of his guilt or a supernatural warning emphasising his fear and unease about the consequences of his actions.

(iii) In what ways does this interaction with the apparition serve as a turning point in Brutus' character arc? **(3)**

Ans. The apparition confronts Brutus with his guilt and foreshadows his downfall marking a shift from confident leadership to self-doubt and fear. It forces Brutus to face the moral weight of his decisions.

It further highlights the internal conflict that has been building throughout the play and setting the stage for his tragic end.

(iv) How does the imagery in Brutus' words ('mak'st my blood cold and my hair to stare') enhance the dramatic tension of the scene? **(3)**

Ans. The imagery vividly conveys Brutus' physical and emotional reaction to the apparition heightening the scene's eerie and ominous atmosphere. The description of his blood running cold and his hair standing on end reflects his deep fear reinforcing the supernatural and foreboding tone.

(v) **Brutus' reaction to seeing the apparition reveals his internal conflict and sense of guilt over the assassination. Elaborate.**

Do you sympathise with Brutus? Give reasons for your choice. **(4)**

Ans. Brutus' reaction to seeing the apparition reveals the depth of his internal conflict and guilt. The apparition symbolises his unresolved remorse and the moral weight of his actions. Despite justifying Caesar's assassination as necessary for Rome, the ghost confronts him with the personal cost of his betrayal, emphasising his psychological torment.

This moment humanises Brutus showing him as a man grappling with the consequences of his choices.

One might sympathise with Brutus because his actions stemmed from a genuine, though flawed sense of duty. His suffering evokes pity as he bears the burden of his moral struggle alone.

Extract 7

Brutus Why, I will see thee at Philippi, then.

Now I have taken heart, thou vanishest.

Ill spirit, I would hold more talk with thee.-

Boy, Lucius!-Varro, Claudius, sirs, awake!

Claudius!

Lucius The strings, my lord, are false.

Brutus He thinks he still is at his instrument.

Lucius, awake!

Lucius My lord?

Brutus Didst thou dream, Lucius, that thou so criedst out?

Lucius My lord, I do not know that I did cry.

(i) **What does Brutus' determination to 'see thee at Philippi' reveal about his character at this moment in the play?** **(3)**

Ans. Brutus' declaration reflects his stoic resolve and acceptance of fate. Despite being unsettled by the ghost, he regains composure and decides to confront the forewarning head-on.

This highlights his bravery as well as his commitment to fulfilling his perceived destiny, regardless of the personal cost.

(ii) **How does the ghost's vanishing contribute to the dramatic tension of the scene?**

What does it symbolise for Brutus? **(3)**

Ans. The ghost's vanishing intensifies the dramatic tension by leaving Brutus in a state of unresolved fear and uncertainty.

It symbolises the fleeting but inescapable nature of guilt and foreshadowing. The ghost serves as a reminder of Brutus' moral conflict and the impending consequences of his actions.

(iii) **What is the significance of Lucius' response, 'The strings, my lord, are false'?**

How does it contrast with Brutus' experience? **(3)**

Ans. Lucius' response reflects his innocence and detachment from the intense psychological turmoil Brutus is experiencing.

The mention of 'false strings' metaphorically contrasts with Brutus' inner discord and emotional strain. It emphasises the gap between the ordinary world and Brutus' haunted state of mind.

(iv) **Why does Brutus question Lucius about his dream?**

What does this suggest about Brutus' mental state? **(3)**

Ans. Brutus questions Lucius in an attempt to validate his own experience with the ghost.

This suggests Brutus' growing uncertainty and paranoia. His need for external confirmation reflects his inner turmoil and fear that the supernatural encounter may be a product of his own guilty conscience.

(v) **How does Shakespeare use the interaction between Brutus and Lucius to highlight Brutus' isolation and responsibility as a tragic hero?** **(4)**

Ans. The interaction underscores Brutus' loneliness, as he faces the ghost and its implications alone while Lucius remains unaware of the gravity of the situation.

This isolation highlights the burden of leadership and moral responsibility that defines Brutus as a tragic hero emphasising his internal conflict and eventual downfall.

ACT 5 : SCENE 1

Summary of Act 5 Scene 1

This scene takes place on the plains of Philippi where the forces of Brutus and Cassius face off against those of Antony and Octavius. Before the conflict begins, both sides engage in a war of words trying to intimidate and discredit one another.

The scene begins with Brutus and Cassius discussing their strategy and their fears acknowledging that they may not win the battle. Antony and Octavius arrive and the two armies prepare for combat. The tension between the opposing forces is palpable and the leaders of both sides exchange insults and threats. Antony condemns Brutus and Cassius for assassinating Caesar. He calls them 'villains' and compares them with 'apes', 'hounds' and 'bondmen'. In response, Cassius screams 'flatterers' angrily and reminds Antony that he once benefitted from Caesar's kindness. Cassius expresses concern about the battle but Brutus reassures him that they are fighting for the right cause. The two armies then engage in a fierce battle. During the battle, various individuals have their moments of glory and tragedy. Ultimately, the outcome of the battle will determine the fate of the conspirators and the future of Rome.

This scene sets the stage for the final resolution of the conflict where the forces of the triumvirs (Antony, Octavius and Lepidus) will confront the last remains of the republican forces led by Brutus and Cassius. The fate of the main characters is sealed as the scene transitions into the final act of the play.

Characters in the Scene

- **Octavius Caesar** Julius Caesar's adopted son and heir. He is confident and assertive, standing up to Antony and taking command of the right side of the battlefield.
- **Mark Antony** A skilled orator and military leader, Antony is focused on avenging Caesar's death and defeating Brutus and Cassius.
- **Brutus** One of the main conspirators against Caesar, Brutus remains calm and honourable, refusing to engage in petty insults and staying focused on the battle ahead.
- **Cassius** Brutus ally and fellow conspirator, Cassius is pessimistic in this scene. He expresses fear of bad omens and believes that defeat is inevitable.
- **Messala** A soldier and messenger in Brutus' army, Messala helps deliver information and plays a role in the battle.
- **Lucilius** Another officer in Brutus' army, Lucilius remains loyal to Brutus throughout the battle.
- **Lepidus** (mentioned, but not present) He is part of the triumvirate with Antony and Octavius but is not involved in this scene.

Vocab Vault

Exigent Critical time
Parley Talk or discussion
Hybla A district in Sicily known for its honey bees
Peevish Easily annoyed by things that are not important
Presage Be a sign or warning of
Canopy A cover that hangs or spreads above something

EXAM ORIENTED QUESTIONS

TYPE - 1 Multiple Choice Questions

01 Mark

Q.1 Where does the battle between Brutus and Cassius' forces and Antony and Octavius' forces take place?
(a) Rome (b) The Senate (c) Philippi (d) The Capitol

Q.2 Which two leaders meet on the battlefield at the beginning of Act 5, Scene 1?
(a) Brutus and Cassius (b) Brutus and Octavius
(c) Cassius and Antony (d) Antony and Octavius

Q.3 Who expresses concern about the outcome of the battle before it begins?
(a) Brutus (b) Cassius (c) Octavius (d) Antony

Q.4 How does Brutus respond to Cassius' concerns about the battle?
(a) He agrees with Cassius' doubts
(b) He reassures Cassius believing in their cause
(c) He becomes angry with Cassius
(d) He ignores Cassius' concerns

Q.5 What is the general mood between the two armies before the battle?
(a) Cheerful and hopeful (b) Tense and hostile
(c) Neutral and indifferent (d) Indifferent but civil

Q.6 What feeling does Cassius' words convey when he refers to Octavius as 'a peevish schoolboy' and to Antony as 'a masker and a reveller'?
(Competency Based Que.)
(a) Fear (b) Disdain (c) Worry (d) Regret

Q.7 Cassius' reference to ravens, crows and kites taking the place of two mighty eagles that accompanied their armies from Sardis tells us that he is ....
(Competency Based Que.)
(a) filled with superstitious dread
(b) an expert bird watcher
(c) happier in the company of birds
(d) not a believer in superstition

Q.8 Who offers Brutus and Cassius the chance to make peace and avoid the battle?
(a) Octavius (b) Lepidus
(c) Antony (d) Their soldiers

Q.9 What is the primary cause of the hostility between Brutus and Antony?
(a) Antony's ambition
(b) The assassination of Caesar
(c) Personal differences
(d) Disagreement on military strategy

Q.10 What does Brutus ask his army to do before the battle begins?
(a) To wait for further orders
(b) To fight bravely for their cause
(c) To withdraw from the battle
(d) To give up arms

Q.11 What happens after Brutus and Cassius exchange harsh words with Antony and Octavius?
(a) They agree to a ceasefire
(b) They prepare for battle
(c) They retreat to their camps
(d) They make peace

Q.12 What does Octavius claim about Brutus during the confrontation?
(a) That Brutus is a traitor to Caesar
(b) That Brutus is an honourable man
(c) That Brutus is afraid of war
(d) That Brutus should have never joined the conspiracy

Q.13 Cassius and Brutus make up their minds to die rather than be taken as prisoners. **(Competency Based Que.)**

What trait of character is revealed in their behaviour?
(a) Pride (b) Sadism
(c) Resignation (d) Pessimism

Q.14 What role does the weather play in Act 5, Scene 1?
(a) It symbolises the fate of the battle
(b) It reflects the tension between the two armies
(c) It is not mentioned
(d) It helps in strategising for the battle

Q.15 What is the tone of the interaction between Brutus and Cassius before the battle?
(a) Fearful
(b) Cooperative and hopeful
(c) Angry and accusing
(d) Friendly and casual

Q.16 Which of the following is not an example of irony?
(Competency Based Que.)
(a) Cassius calls Caesar a God while describing how weak he was.
(b) Antony refers to Brutus as an honourable man while disproving his claims.
(c) One of the plebeians suggested crowning Brutus king.
(d) Antony compares the conspirators' killing of Caesar to apes and hounds.

Q.17 Which hopes of Octavius are 'answered'?

(a) The conflict between Brutus and Cassius.
(b) The armies of the conspirators' advance towards Philippi
(c) The surrender by the armies of the conspirators
(d) None of the above

Q.18 What reason does Antony give for the enemy's advance towards Philippi?

(a) To hide their fear and show their unity
(b) To hide their conflicts and show their unity
(c) To show their patriotism and friendship
(d) None of the above

Q.19 When does Octavius say his sword will go back into its sheath?

(a) When Caesar's ghost will disappear
(b) When another Caesar will appeal
(c) When thirty-three wounds of Caesar have be avenged
(d) When he becomes Caesar

Q.20 Who has been described by Cassius as 'A pevish schoolboy'?

(a) Marcus Brutus (b) Mark Antony
(c) Octavius Caesar (d) Lucius

Q.21 With whom has Cassius compared himself in this scene

(a) Brutus (b) Pompey (c) Caesar (d) Lucius

Q.22 Cassius has changed his mind about the doctrine of Epicurus regarding which of the following?

(a) Superstitious
(b) Ghosts
(c) Republicanism
(d) Omens and Premonitions

Q.23 Who according to Cassius has formed a 'canopy most fatal' over their heads?

(a) Two huge eagles (b) Enemy soldier
(c) Sparrows (d) Crows and Kites

Q.24 How does Brutus define Cato's act of committing suicide?

(a) Mean and short-sighted
(b) Low and cowardly
(c) Sensible and timely
(d) None of the above

Q.25 Cassius compares Antony's sweet words with which of the following.

(a) Honey made by Sybla bees
(b) Honey made by Hybla bees
(c) Honey made by Queen bee
(d) Honey made by Olypus bee

Q.26 Select the option that shows the correct relationship between statements (1) and (2).

Statement 1 The exchange of insults between the leaders intensifies the tension before the battle.

Statement 2 Both sides are determined to prove their superiority and justify their actions.

(a) Statement 1 is true and Statement 2 is false
(b) Statement 2 is true and Statement 1 is false.
(c) Statement 2 is the cause for Statement 1.
(d) Both statements are false.

Q.27 Arrange the following events from Act 5, Scene 1 in the correct order.

1. Antony and Octavius arrive and confront Brutus and Cassius.
2. Cassius expresses concerns about the loyalty of his troops.
3. Brutus and Cassius exchange harsh words with Antony and Octavius.
4. Brutus reassures Cassius that their cause is just.
5. The armies prepare for battle.

(a) 2, 4, 1, 3, 5 (b) 1, 2, 3, 4, 5
(c) 4, 2, 1, 3, 5 (d) 2, 1, 4, 3, 5

Answers

1. (c)	2. (a)	3. (b)	4. (b)	5. (b)	6. (b)	7. (a)	8. (c)	9. (b)	10. (b)
11. (b)	12. (b)	13. (a)	14. (b)	15. (c)	16. (d)	17. (b)	18. (a)	19. (c)	20. (c)
21. (b)	22. (d)	23. (d)	24. (b)	25. (b)	26. (c)	27. (a)			

Explanations

16. Irony occurs when there is contrast between expectation and reality or when words convey a meaning apposite to their literal interpretation.
In option (d), metaphor has been used to make a comparison.

26. Before the battle of Philippi, Antony, Octavius, Brutus and Cassius exchange harsh words, adding to conflict. The leaders on both sides strongly believe in their cause. They are determined to prove their superiority.
Hence, statement 2 is the cause for statement.

TYPE - 2 Extract Based Questions

16 Marks

Extract 1

Brutus Words before blows; is it so, countrymen?

Octavius Not that we love words better, as you do.

Brutus Good words are better than bad strokes, Octavius.

Antony In your bad strokes, Brutus, you give good words.
Witness the hole you made in Caesar's heart,
Crying 'Long live, hail, Caesar!'

Cassius Antony, The posture of your blows are yet unknown,
But, for your words, they rob the Hybla bees
And leave them honeyless.

(i) What does Brutus mean when he says, 'Good words are better than bad strokes, Octavius'? (3)

Ans. Brutus implies that diplomacy and peaceful dialogue are preferable to violence and conflict. He criticises Octavius for favouring action over thoughtful words suggesting that resorting to violence without trying to resolve matters verbally is reckless.

(ii) How does Antony use irony in his response to Brutus mentioning Caesar's heart? (3)

Ans. Antony uses irony by highlighting the contradiction in Brutus' actions. He accuses Brutus of giving 'good words' while committing a grievous act-murdering Caesar. Antony sarcastically notes that Brutus spoke respectfully of Caesar even as he betrayed him by stabbing him.

(iii) What is the significance of Cassius' comment about Antony's words robbing the Hybla bees of their honey? (3)

Ans. Cassius uses this metaphor to criticise Antony's verbal skill, suggesting that his words are sweet and persuasive but ultimately harmful, as they leave others (like the bees) deprived. This comment reflects Cassius' mistrust of Antony's rhetoric viewing it as manipulative and deceitful.

(iv) How does the dialogue between Brutus, Octavius, Antony and Cassius reflect the tension between the two factions? (3)

Ans. The dialogue underscores the hostility and mistrust between the factions. Brutus and Cassius emphasise the value of honourable intentions and dialogue.

Meanwhile, Antony and Octavius focus on the perceived hypocrisy and treachery of the conspirators. The exchange reveals the deep animosity and sets the stage for the impending conflict.

(v) Octavius' response to Brutus reveal a lot about his character and attitude toward the confrontation. Elaborate. (4)

Ans. Octavius' response shows his direct and confrontational nature. He dismisses the value of words indicating a preference for decisive action.

This reflects his confidence and determination to fight, contrasting with Brutus' more reflective and diplomatic approach. It also highlights Octavius' growing assertiveness as a leader.

Extract 2

This is my birthday, as this very day
Was Cassius born. Give me thy hand, Messala.
Be thou my witness that against my will
(As Pompey was) am I compelled to set
Upon one battle all our liberties.
You know that I held Epicurus strong
And his opinion. Now I change my mind
And partly credit things that do presage.

(i) What significance does Cassius attach to his birthday in this scene?

How does it reflect his state of mind? (3)

Ans. Cassius mentioning his birthday highlights a personal and reflective moment suggesting a sense of fatalism or destiny.

He is aware of the irony that the day of his birth may also mark his death which underscores his inner turmoil and premonition about the battle.

This reflection reveals his growing doubts and resignation to the events unfolding.

(ii) How does Cassius' reference to Pompey's compulsion to fight a single battle parallel his own situation? (3)

Ans. Cassius draws a parallel between his current predicament and Pompey's past suggesting that both were forced into decisive battles that they were reluctant to engage in.

This comparison emphasises Cassius' sense of being trapped by circumstances, compelled to stake everything on a single battle for freedom, despite his reservations.

(iii) **How does Cassius' shift from Epicurean beliefs to partly believing in omens signify a change in his character? (3)**

Ans. Cassius' shift from adhering to Epicurean philosophy, which dismisses superstition, to acknowledging omens signifies a profound change in his character.

It shows that the pressures of war and impending conflict have eroded his rationalist beliefs making him more susceptible to fear and superstition.

This change illustrates his growing uncertainty and vulnerability.

(iv) **What role does Messala play in this dialogue?**

Why does Cassius ask him to be a witness? (3)

Ans. Messala serves as a confidant and a witness to Cassius' inner thoughts and decisions. Cassius' request for Messala to be a witness reflects his desire to document his reluctance and sense of compulsion in fighting this battle.

It underscores Cassius' need for validation and acknowledgment of his honourable intentions despite the dire circumstances.

(v) **How do Cassius' reflections on fate and free will contribute to the themes of the play? (4)**

Ans. Cassius' reflections on fate and free will contribute to the play's exploration of human agency versus destiny.

His acknowledgment of foreshadowing omens and his feeling of compulsion suggest a tension between his belief in controlling one's fate and the inescapable forces of destiny.

This internal conflict highlights the broader theme of whether characters in the play are masters of their fate or pawns of predetermined outcomes.

Extract 3

Even by the rule of that philosophy
By which I did blame Cato for the death
Which he did give himself (I know not how,
But I do find it cowardly and vile,
For fear of what might fall, so to prevent
The time of life), arming myself with patience
To stay the providence of some high powers
That govern us below.

(i) **How does Brutus' reflection on Cato's suicide reveal a conflict in his own philosophy? (3)**

Ans. Brutus' reflection reveals a conflict between his Stoic beliefs and his personal feelings about suicide.

While he initially blames Cato for what he views as a cowardly act, his current situation forces him to reconsider the morality of suicide.

This inner conflict highlights Brutus' struggle to reconcile his philosophical ideals with the harsh realities he faces.

(ii) **What does Brutus mean by 'arming myself with patience'?**

How does this phrase reflect his approach to dealing with adversity? (3)

Ans. The phrase 'Arming myself with patience' indicates Brutus' resolve to endure hardship and uncertainty with composure.

This reflects his Stoic philosophy which emphasises self-control and acceptance of fate. By embracing patience, Brutus aims to face whatever the future holds without surrendering to fear or impulsiveness.

(iii) **How does Brutus' attitude toward providence contrast with his earlier actions in the play? (3)**

Ans. Brutus' mention of 'providence of some high powers' marks a shift from his earlier reliance on rationality and personal agency. Initially, he believed in the power of human action to shape events as seen in his role in Caesar's assassination. Now, he expresses a more fatalistic view, recognising the limits of human control and acknowledging a higher power's influence on earthly affairs.

(iv) **What philosophical critique is Brutus making about suicide? How does this critique align with Stoic principles? (3)**

Ans. Brutus critiques suicide as an act of cowardice and a pre-emptive avoidance of potential suffering. This critique aligns with Stoic principles which value endurance and resilience in the face of adversity. Stoicism teaches that one should accept the natural course of life and death, rather than attempting to escape it out of fear.

(v) **In what ways does Brutus' contemplation of fate and governance by higher powers reflect the broader themes of the play? (4)**

Ans. Brutus' contemplation reflects the play's broader themes of fate, free will and the limits of human agency. His acknowledgment of higher powers governing earthly events underscores the tension between the characters' attempts to control their destinies and the overarching influence of fate.

This theme resonates throughout the play as characters grapple with their roles in shaping or surrendering to historical forces beyond their control.

ACT 5 : SCENE 2

Summary of Act 5 Scene 2

In this brief scene, Brutus orders Messala to take a message to the troops. The message instructs them to move forward with a surprise attack on Octavius' forces. Brutus notices a weakness in Octavius' position and believes that now is the opportune moment to strike. He hopes to exploit this perceived vulnerability and gain an advantage in the battle.

The scene underscores Brutus' strategic thinking and his desire to take decisive action to secure victory for his army.

Characters in the Scene

- **Brutus** The leader of the remaining conspirators, Brutus gives orders to attack Octavius' forces. He remains confident in their strategy.
- **Messala** A loyal officer under Brutus. In this scene, Brutus sends Messala with instructions to charge against Octavius' troops, hoping to take advantage of a perceived weakness.

EXAM ORIENTED QUESTIONS

TYPE - 1 Multiple Choice Questions — 01 Mark

Q.1 What does Brutus observe about Octavius' army in this scene?
(a) They are retreating.
(b) They show signs of weakness.
(c) They are overpowering Cassius' forces.
(d) They have formed an alliance with Antony's forces.

Q.2 Who does Brutus send to deliver orders to his troops?
(a) Lucilius
(b) Messala
(c) Titinius
(d) Pindarus

Q.3 What action does Brutus order his troops to take?
(a) Retreat to a safer position
(b) Prepare for a defensive stand
(c) Launch an attack on Octavius' forces
(d) Join forces with Cassius' troops

Q.4 What is the main theme reflected in this scene?
(a) Betrayal among allies
(b) The unpredictability of war
(c) The power of rhetoric
(d) The inevitability of fate

Q.5 What does Brutus believe is the opportune moment in this scene?
(a) To negotiate peace with Octavius and Antony
(b) To exploit a perceived weakness in Octavius' forces
(c) To retreat and regroup with Cassius
(d) To send messengers to Antony's camp

Q.6 Why is this scene significant to the play's overall conflict?
(a) It shows Brutus' hesitation to fight.
(b) It highlights a critical turning point in the battle.
(c) It marks Brutus' reconciliation with Cassius.
(d) It demonstrates the superiority of Octavius' strategy.

Q.7 Which characteristic trait of Brutus is seen in this scene?
(a) Impulsive (b) Calm (c) Rational (d) Patriotic

Q.8 What message does Brutus give to Messala for Cassius?
(a) Wait for him at Sardis
(b) Attack the enemy
(c) Send money to him
(d) All of the above

Q.9 Which error does Brutus make in this scene?
(a) He misinterprets his army's message
(b) He misinterprets his army's strength
(c) He order an attack on Octavius army too early
(d) None of the above

Q.10 What is referred to by the term 'Legians' in this scene?
(a) Areas (b) Troops
(c) Boundaries (d) Battlefields

Q.11 Select the option that shows the correct relationship between statements (1) and (2).
Statement 1 Brutus orders his troops to attack Octavius' forces immediately believing that they show signs of weakness.
Statement 2 Brutus thinks that an immediate offensive will turn the tide of the battle in his favour.
(a) Statement 1 is true and Statement 2 is false
(b) Statement 2 is true and Statement 1 is false.
(c) Statement 2 is the cause for Statement 1.
(d) Both statements are false.

Answers

1. (b) 2. (b) 3. (c) 4. (b) 5. (b) 6. (b) 7. (a) 8. (b) 9. (c) 10. (b) 11. (c)

TYPE - 2 Extract Based Questions 16 Marks

Extract 1

Let them set on at once, for I perceive
But cold demeanour in Octavius' wing,
And sudden push gives them the overthrow.
Ride, ride, Messala! Let them all come down.

(i) What does Brutus perceive about Octavius' wing in the battle?

How does he plan to use this observation to his advantage? (3)

Ans. Brutus perceives 'cold demeanour' in Octavius' wing suggesting that the enemy forces are unprepared or demoralised. Seeing this weakness, Brutus decides that a sudden push would be enough to overthrow them. This indicates his strategic intent to take advantage of the momentary vulnerability in Octavius' forces.

(ii) How does the urgency in Brutus' command to Messala reflect his state of mind during the battle? (3)

Ans. Brutus' command to 'Ride, ride, Messala!' reflects his urgency and desire to act quickly. The battle is at a critical point and Brutus believes that swift action can turn the tide in their favour. His focus on making an immediate push shows his determination to capitalise on any opportunity for victory.

(iii) What does Brutus mean by 'cold demeanour'? Why does he interpret this as a sign of potential victory? (3)

Ans. 'Cold demeanour' refers to the lack of enthusiasm, energy or confidence in Octavius' forces. Brutus interprets this as a sign of vulnerability and weakness believing that the enemy's apparent lack of preparation and morale will make them easier to defeat. He sees this as an opportunity to launch a decisive attack.

(iv) In what way does Brutus' decision to 'let them set on at once' demonstrate his leadership qualities during the battle? (3)

Ans. Brutus' decision to attack immediately reflects his decisive nature and ability to make quick decisions in the heat of battle. His willingness to act without hesitation, based on his observation of the enemy's weakness, shows his confidence in seizing opportunities and leading his forces with conviction.

(v) How does the line 'Let them all come down' suggest Brutus' outlook on the battle and his resolve for the outcome? (4)

Ans. The line 'Let them all come down' suggests that Brutus is ready for a full confrontation willing to face the enemy head-on. It conveys his confidence in overcoming the enemy and his belief that a direct, aggressive approach will lead to victory. This line demonstrates his resolve and commitment to fighting until the end.

ACT 5 : SCENE 3

Summary of Act 5 Scene 3

In this scene, the battle intensifies as both sides suffer losses. Cassius, stationed on a hill, observes the fight from a distance. Pindarus, his servant, brings news that Titinius has been surrounded by enemy troops. Cassius, feeling despondent and believing that the battle is lost, decides to take his own life. He asks Pindarus to assist him in his suicide by using the same sword that killed Caesar.

Pindarus reluctantly complies and Cassius dies. Shortly afterward, Titinius returns revealing that he was not captured but instead greeted by friendly troops who were celebrating a victory. When Titinius finds Cassius dead, he is overcome with grief. In his despair, he takes Cassius's sword and kills himself.

Brutus arrives with Messala and learns of Cassius's death. Though saddened, Brutus remains resolute to continue fighting. He declares that Cassius's spirit will inspire their troops to keep battling.

This scene emphasises themes of miscommunication, loyalty and the tragic consequences of misinterpretation.
It marks the downfall of Cassius and the deepening tragedy of the conspirators' defeat.

Characters in the Scene

- **Cassius** One of the main conspirators. In this scene, Cassius faces despair and tragically commits suicide, mistakenly believing his forces have been defeated.
- **Titinius** A loyal soldier and friend to Cassius. He is sent to check on nearby troops but returns too late, only to find Cassius dead. Overwhelmed by grief, Titinius takes his own life beside Cassius.
- **Pindarus** Cassius' loyal servant. At Cassius' command, Pindarus reluctantly assists in his master's suicide and then flees the battlefield.
- **Messala** A messenger and officer in Brutus' army. He delivers news to Cassius and later discovers the bodies of Cassius and Titinius, reporting back to Brutus.
- **Brutus** (briefly mentioned) Although he doesn't appear directly in this scene, his actions influence the events. His success in battle is misinterpreted, leading to the tragic misunderstandings.
- **Cato the Younger** (mentioned) An ally of Brutus, leading troops in the battle.
- **Lucilius** (mentioned) An officer under Brutus, still fighting for their cause.
- **Caesar's Spirit** A spirit who is active in this scene or Cassius commits suicide with the sword he uses to kill Caesar.

Vocab Vault

Fell to spoil To damage, harm or impair something

Sirrah Fellow

Parthia Part of Asia minor

The Sun of Rome is set The death of Cassius and the figurative end of his influence and legacy in the Roman cause

Envenomed Poisoned

EXAM ORIENTED QUESTIONS

TYPE - 1 Multiple Choice Questions

01 Mark

Q.1 What is Cassius' reaction when he believes Titinius has been captured by the enemy?

(a) He orders his troops to retreat.
(b) He decides to take his own life.
(c) He tries to send reinforcements.
(d) He runs toward the battlefield.

Q.2 Who does Cassius ask to help him commit suicide?

(a) Brutus (b) Messala
(c) Pindarus (d) Titinius

Q.3 When Cassius says, 'My life is run his compass', he means that .... **(ICSE Speciment 2025)**

(a) it is the day on which Brutus was born
(b) his life had come full circle
(c) his life could be measured with a compass
(d) his life could be compared to a race

Q.4 Why does Cassius feel the need to die?

(a) He is overcome with guilt.
(b) He believes the battle is lost.
(c) He fears Octavius' forces.
(d) He wants to join Caesar in death.

Q.5 What is Titinius' reaction when he finds Cassius dead?

(a) He curses the enemy. (b) He rejoices in victory.
(c) He kills himself. (d) He runs away in fear.

Q.6 What does Titinius initially think when he sees the soldiers around him?

(a) They are his enemies.
(b) They are celebrating his capture.
(c) They are his friends who have come to rescue him.
(d) They are reinforcements for Cassius.

Q.7 How does Brutus respond to the news of Cassius' death?

(a) He immediately orders a retreat.
(b) He vows to avenge Cassius' death.
(c) He expresses deep sorrow but resolves to continue the fight.
(d) He blames himself for Cassius' death.

Q.8 What does Titinius do with Cassius' sword after finding him dead?

(a) He uses it to kill Brutus.
(b) He throws it away in despair.
(c) He uses it to take his own life.
(d) He hands it over to Messala.

Q.9 What tragic misunderstanding leads to Cassius' death?

(a) Cassius believes Titinius has been captured by the enemy but Titinius is actually surrounded by friendly forces.
(b) Cassius thinks Brutus has been defeated.
(c) Cassius mistakes the enemy's movements for his own troops.
(d) Cassius believes Pindarus is betraying him.

Q.10 What motivates Brutus to continue fighting after Cassius' death?

(a) His loyalty to Caesar.
(b) His desire to avenge Cassius.
(c) His belief that victory is still possible.
(d) His fear of being captured by the enemy.

Q.11 To whom does Brutus refer when he says, 'Are yet two romans living such as these? **(Competency Based Que.)**
'The last of all the Romans fare thee well!'?

(a) Antony and Octavius (b) Cassius and Titinius
(c) Pindarus and Lucius (d) Strato and Lucillius

Q.12 Cassius tells Pindarus to observe Titinius from a hill because of which deformity of his (Cassius)?

(a) Weak eyesight (b) Weak legs
(c) Weak heart (d) None of these

Q.13 Who says the following sentences. "Caesar thou art revenged"?

(a) Octavius (b) Cassius (c) Brutus (d) Pindarus

Q.14 Select the option that shows the correct relationship between statements (1) and (2).

Statement 1 Brutus is deeply affected by the death of Cassius but remains determined to continue the fight.

Statement 2 Brutus believes that Cassius' death must be avenged in the ongoing battle.

(a) Statement 1 is true, and Statement 2 is false
(b) Statement 2 is true, and Statement 1 is false.
(c) Statement 2 is the cause for Statement 1.
(d) Both statements are false.

Q.15 Arrange the following events from Act 5, Scene 3 in the correct sequence.

1. Titinius is sent by Cassius to check on the situation and the enemy's movements.
2. Pindarus reports to Cassius that Titinius has been captured by the enemy.
3. Cassius decides to take his own life and asks Pindarus to help him.
4. Titinius returns and reveals that he was not captured but surrounded by friendly troops.
5. Titinius, upon finding Cassius dead, kills himself with Cassius' sword.

(a) 1, 2, 3, 4, 5 (b) 1, 3, 2, 4, 5
(c) 1, 2, 4, 3, 5 (d) 1, 3, 2, 4, 5

Answers

1. (b)	2. (c)	3. (b)	4. (b)	5. (c)	6. (c)	7. (c)	8. (c)	9. (a)	10. (c)
11. (b)	12. (a)	13. (b)	14. (a)	15. (a)					

TYPE - 2 Extract Based Questions

16 Marks

Extract 1

Cassius 'O coward that I am, to live so long,
To see my best friend ta'en before my face!
I, that did love Caesar when I struck him,
I kissed his statue and held it to my heart,
I have not left my wife, my country, my children,
For the sake of this noble ambition,
And now to die like a dog-'

(i) What is the emotional tone of Cassius' speech? **(3)**

Ans. The tone is one of regret, guilt and self-loathing. Cassius feels deep sorrow and frustration as he reflects on his actions and the consequences they have led to.

(ii) How does Cassius express his guilt over killing Caesar? **(3)**

Ans. Cassius expresses guilt by referring to his love for Caesar before the assassination highlighting his inner conflict. His self-blame is further emphasised as he calls himself a 'coward' and feels that he is now facing a dishonourable death.

(iii) What is the significance of Cassius saying he 'loved Caesar when I struck him'? **(3)**

Ans. This phrase highlights the complexity of Cassius' emotions. Although he plotted Caesar's murder, he also had personal feelings of affection for him, suggesting that Cassius' motivations were not entirely driven by malice but by his belief in protecting Rome.

(iv) Why does Cassius feel like he is 'dying like a dog'? **(3)**

Ans. Cassius feels degraded and dishonourable because his life, once full of ambition, has come to a bitter end. He compares his death to that of a dog, implying that he feels unworthy of the noble death he had hoped for and sees his life as ending in a shameful manner.

(v) How does Cassius view his sacrifice in the context of his ambitions? **(4)**

Ans. He regrets the sacrifices he made, including leaving behind his family and country, for what now seems like a futile ambition. His personal loss and failure have overshadowed the cause he once believed in leaving him feeling disillusioned and trapped in his own choices.

Extract 2

Messala Is not that he?
Titinius No, this was he, Messala,
But Cassius is no more, O setting sun,
As in thy red rays thou dost sink to night,
So in his red blood Cassius' day is set,
The sun of Rome is set! Our day is gone;
Clouds, dews, and dangers come; our deeds are done!
Mistrust of my success hath done this deed.

(Competency Based Que.)

(i) Where does this scene take place?

What is the nature of the relationship that Titinius and Cassius shared? **(3)**

Ans. This scene takes place on the battlefield near the city of Philippi. Titinius and Cassius share a close and deep friendship. They are comrades-in-arms and fought together against Caesar's forces.

Their relationship is built on mutual respect and trust which is evident in their shared experiences of war and their personal bond.

(ii) **Give two words that would best describe Titinius' mood in the given extract. Justify your choice of words.** **(3)**

Ans. Two words that best describe Titinius' mood are grief-stricken and despondent. Titinius expresses profound sorrow and despair upon realising Cassius is dead, comparing the setting Sun to the end of Cassius' life. His words, 'So in his red blood Cassius' day is set', show his deep mourning and sense of loss.

He also believes that their fate is sealed and that they are now doomed to failure indicating his dejection.

(iii) **Earlier in Act V, Cassius shares some facts about himself with Messala—what are these facts?** **(3)**

Ans. Earlier in Act V, Cassius reveals to Messala that he has had doubts about the outcome of the battle. He speaks of his belief that the gods have turned against them. He also confesses his fear of death referencing the fact that he has never believed in omens but now feels the weight of his fate.

He reflects on how his earlier good luck is running out and that he is facing a difficult and uncertain future.

(iv) **How did Cassius die?**

What were his dying words? **(3)**

Ans. Cassius dies by suicide. He asks his servant Pindarus to help him die by sword after mistakenly believing that Titinius has been captured by the enemy.

His dying words are 'Caesar, thou art revenged, Even with the sword that killed thee' as he sees the death of his friend Titinius as the revenge of Caesar.

However, Titinius was not captured and had in fact killed himself upon hearing of Cassius's death.

(v) **What does the phrase, 'this deed' in the last line of the extract refer to?**

Explain in your own words what Titinius means by, 'Mistrust of my success hath done this deed'. **(4)**

Ans. The phrase 'this deed' refers to Cassius' death which Titinius believes was caused by his own actions. 'Mistrust of my success' refers to Titinius' doubt and fear that the battle would not be successful, which led to Cassius' fatal mistake.

Titinius means that the lack of confidence in his own success, which he believes may have led to the confusion, caused Cassius to wrongly think that Titinius was captured and thus led to his death.

In short, Titinius feels responsible for Cassius' suicide because his own misgivings influenced the tragic outcome.

Extract 3

Thy Brutus bid me give it thee, and I
Will do his bidding.-Brutus, come apace,
And see how I regarded Caius Cassius.-
By your leave, gods, this is a Roman's part.
Come, Cassius' sword, and find Titinius' heart!

(i) **What is the significance of the phrase 'Thy Brutus bid me give it thee'?**

What does it reveal about the relationship between Brutus and his servant? **(3)**

Ans. The phrase 'Thy Brutus bid me give it thee' indicates the servant's loyalty to Brutus, following Brutus' orders to carry out a task, even in the midst of great distress. It highlights the trust and obedience between them.

This line also emphasises the authority Brutus still holds, even in his final moments, and the servant' duty to fulfill his master's wishes, even if it involves death. Moreover it highlights the deepbond between Brutus and Cassius.

(ii) **Why does the speaker mention 'By your leave, gods, this is a Roman's part'? What does this reveal about the speaker's mindset?** **(3)**

Ans. The speaker says 'By your leave, gods, this is a Roman's part' as a final acknowledgment of his actions being in line with Roman ideals of honour and duty.

The reference to the gods suggests that the speaker is seeking divine permission but it also highlights his belief that his death is an act of nobility and patriotism.

It reveals that the speaker sees his suicide as a heroic and honourable act in keeping with Roman values, even in the face of defeat.

(iii) **What does the phrase 'Come, Cassius' sword and find Titinius' heart!' symbolise in this moment of the play?** **(3)**

Ans. The phrase 'Come, Cassius' sword, and find Titinius' heart!' symbolises Titinius's decision to end his own life, perhaps due to the overwhelming grief of Cassius' death. The sword, associated with Cassius' death, is now called upon to carry out the tragic final act.

It underscores the deep bond between Titinius and Cassius and the profound sense of loss and guilt that leads Titinius to suicide. It represents the destructive power of the events that have unfolded.

(iv) **How does the line 'Brutus, come apace, And see how I regarded Caius Cassius' reflect Titinius' emotional state?** **(3)**

Ans. The line 'Brutus, come apace, And see how I regarded Caius Cassius' reflects Titinius' deep grief and sense of loss over the death of his friend and commander, Cassius. He calls for Brutus to witness how he values Cassius, possibly to show that his loyalty and grief are sincere.

This line reveals Titinius' emotional turmoil and his sense of responsibility to honour Cassius, even in death.

(v) **What do these lines reveal about the tragic fate of the characters in Julius Caesar, particularly Brutus, Cassius and Titinius?** **(4)**

Ans. These lines emphasise the tragic nature of the play, where loyalty, honour and friendship lead to death.

The actions of Brutus, Cassius and Titinius reflect the tragic cycle of misunderstanding, guilt and despair that unfolds after Caesar's assassination. Titinius' decision to end his life after Cassius' death shows the depth of the bond between them.

Furthermore, the lines suggest that the characters' idealism and noble intentions ultimately lead to their downfall. It underscores the fatal consequences of their actions and the destruction of their once-promising cause.

ACT 5 : SCENE 4

Summary of Act 5 Scene 4

In this scene, the battle at Philippi rages on. Brutus' forces engage in combat with Octavius' army but they are struggling to maintain their position. Amid the chaos, Brutus orders his men to continue fighting and shows his determination to resist defeat.

Meanwhile, Lucilius, a loyal supporter of Brutus, attempts to protect him. He pretends to be Brutus allowing himself to be captured by Antony's soldiers. This act of loyalty buys Brutus time to escape. When Lucilius is brought to Antony, Antony recognises the ruse but respects Lucilius' bravery. Antony spares Lucilius stating that he would rather have such honourable men as allies than enemies.

This scene highlights the loyalty of Brutus' followers, the honour of Lucilius and Antony's growing sense of benevolence. It sets the stage for the final moments of the play as Brutus faces his ultimate fate.

Characters in the Scene

- **Brutus** The leader of the remaining conspirators, Brutus continues fighting but realizes that the battle is turning against him. He urges his men to keep fighting while he looks for an opportunity to escape.
- **Lucilius** A loyal officer under Brutus. He pretends to be Brutus when captured by Antony's soldiers, attempting to protect the real Brutus.
- **Antony** One of the triumvirs and leader of the opposing forces. When his soldiers bring in Lucilius, thinking he is Brutus, Antony sees through the deception but admires Lucilius' loyalty. Instead of punishing him, Antony orders that Lucilius be treated well.
- **Octavius' Soldiers** They capture Lucilius, believing him to be Brutus, and present him to Antony.

Vocab Vault

Ta'en Captured

Chanc'd Has happened

EXAM ORIENTED QUESTIONS

TYPE - 1 Multiple Choice Questions

01 Mark

Q.1 What is happening on the battlefield during Act 5, Scene 4?
(a) Brutus' army is retreating
(b) Antony and Octavius' forces are defeated
(c) Brutus' forces are engaged in heavy combat/fight
(d) The battle has already ended

Q.2 In Act V, Scene IV, Lucilius pretends to be Brutus and is taken captive. His action reveals his ....
(Competency Based Que.)
(a) loyalty to Octavius (b) desire to escape
(c) loyalty to Brutus (d) youthful folly

Q.3 How does Antony react when Lucilius is captured?
(a) He orders Lucilius to be executed.
(b) He admires Lucilius' loyalty and spares him.
(c) He mocks Lucilius for his failed ruse.
(d) He ignores Lucilius entirely.

Q.4 What does Lucilius' act of loyalty toward Brutus reveal about him?
(a) He is a coward.
(b) He values honour and loyalty over his own safety.
(c) He seeks personal glory.
(d) He is indifferent to the outcome of the battle.

Q.5 What does Antony say about Lucilius after his capture?
(a) He praises him and says he would rather have men like Lucilius as friends than enemies.
(b) He condemns him for siding with Brutus.
(c) He accuses him of cowardice.
(d) He dismisses him as unimportant.

Q.6 What is Brutus doing during the events of this scene?
(a) Hiding from Antony's forces
(b) Rallying his soldiers for a final attack
(c) Preparing to flee the battlefield
(d) Continuing to fight with determination

Q.7 What does this scene primarily emphasise?
(a) The cowardice of Brutus' men.
(b) The strength of Octavius' forces.
(c) The themes of loyalty and honour.
(d) The futility of war.

Q.8 Young Cato died following which of the following ideals proclaimed by his father?
(a) Stoicism (b) Republicianism
(c) Epicureanism (d) None of these

Q.9 Who among the following impersonates Brutus to give him (Brutus) time to flee?
(a) Cato (b) Cassius
(c) Lucilius (d) None of these

Q.10 Lucilius say, "The god defend him from so great shame." What is the shame lucilius is referring to?
(a) Being taken as a prisoner
(b) Being killed by the enemy
(c) Being defeated by the enemy
(d) Being defeated by the tyrants

Q.11 Whom does Antony describe as "a prize no less in worth"?
(a) Brutus (b) Cassius
(c) Lucilius (d) Cato

Q.12 Select the option that shows the correct relationship between statements (1) and (2).
Statement 1 Lucilius pretends to be Brutus and allows himself to be captured by Antony's soldiers.
Statement 2 Lucilius' act of loyalty aims to protect Brutus and give him a chance to escape.
(a) Statement 1 is true and Statement 2 is false
(b) Statement 2 is true and Statement 1 is false.
(c) Statement 2 is the cause for Statement 1.
(d) Both statements are false.

Answers

1. (c) 2. (c) 3. (b) 4. (b) 5. (a) 6. (d) 7. (c) 8. (a) 9. (c) 10. (a)
11. (c) 12. (c)

TYPE - 2 Extract Based Questions

16 Marks

Extract 1

This is not Brutus, friend, but I assure you,
A prize no less in worth. Keep this man safe.
Give him all kindness. I had rather have
Such men my friends than enemies. Go on,
And see whe'er Brutus be alive or dead,
And bring us word unto Octavius' tent
How everything is chanced.

(i) How do Antony's words about Lucilius, 'A prize no less in worth', reflect his understanding of loyalty and honour in the context of war and betrayal? (3)

Ans. Antony's words reflect his deep respect for loyalty. He recognises that Lucilius' self-sacrificial act of impersonating Brutus to protect him holds more value than the betrayal of Caesar's assassination. Antony sees this loyalty as a rare and commendable trait revealing his belief in the nobility of selflessness and his own magnanimity in dealing with enemies.

(ii) In what way do Antony's instructions to 'give him all kindness' and treat Lucilius as a friend demonstrate a contrast to his actions earlier in the play? (3)

Ans. Earlier in the play, Antony is shown as vengeful seeking retribution for Caesar's death, especially when he stirs the Roman crowd against the conspirators. However, his treatment of Lucilius in this scene shows a marked contrast. He now demonstrates mercy and respects the loyalty of an enemy.

This shift highlights Antony's pragmatic leadership and ability to rise above personal animosities when he sees qualities worth admiring.

(iii) What is the significance of Antony preferring men like Lucilius as friends rather than enemies in terms of his broader political strategy? (3)

Ans. Antony's preference for such men as friends rather than enemies indicates a strategic shift toward fostering alliances based on mutual respect, rather than continuing a path of enmity and bloodshed. By valuing loyalty and bravery, even in his enemies, Antony demonstrates wisdom in understanding that allies with such virtues are more useful than adversaries. This attitude also helps to consolidate his power after the defeat of Brutus and Cassius as it establishes a reputation for fairness and generosity which can encourage others to join his cause.

(iv) How does the line 'Go on, And see whe'er Brutus be alive or dead' reflect Antony's leadership style and his view of Brutus at this point in the play? (3)

Ans. Antony's command to check whether Brutus is alive or dead reflects his recognition of Brutus as a worthy opponent. Despite Brutus' role in Caesar's assassination, Antony views him with a certain respect, evident from his earlier praise of Brutus as the 'noblest Roman'. By instructing his men to ascertain Brutus' fate, Antony acknowledges the significance of Brutus in the outcome of the civil war and indicates that he is still a key figure in determining Rome's future.

This shows Antony's leadership style is one of pragmatic engagement, rather than simple revenge.

(v) Analyse how the directive to 'bring us word unto Octavius' tent/How everything is chanced' ties into the themes of fate and control in the play.

Ans. Antony's directive to bring news to Octavius about the outcome of the battle illustrates the theme of fate and the characters' limited control over it. Throughout the play, events seem to unfold due to forces beyond individual control–whether the gods, destiny or personal ambition.

By giving this command, Antony acknowledges the uncertain nature of battle and leadership. The phrase also highlights the division of power between Antony and Octavius suggesting that their partnership is essential to understanding the shifting tides of fate.

Act 5 : Scene 5

Summary of Act 5 Scene 5

The final scene of the play takes place on the battlefield near Philippi. Brutus, now defeated and surrounded by enemy forces, faces the reality of his situation. Recognising that his army is lost and unwilling to be captured by Antony and Octavius, he decides to end his life.

Brutus asks several of his men to assist him in his suicide but they refuse initially, unwilling to participate in their leader's death. Finally, Strato agrees to hold Brutus's sword while Brutus runs onto it, ending his life. As he dies, Brutus declares that he feels more justified in killing himself than he ever did in killing Caesar indicating his deep regret and sense of honour.

When Antony and Octavius arrive, they discover Brutus's body. Antony praises Brutus calling him the 'noblest Roman of them all'. He acknowledges that unlike the other conspirators, Brutus acted not out of envy but for what he believed was the greater good of Rome. Octavius orders that Brutus be given a proper burial with full honour showing respect for his courage and integrity.

The scene concludes with Octavius and Antony victorious marking the end of the civil war and the tragedy of Brutus.

Characters in the Scene

- **Brutus** The leader of the conspirators; he accepts his fate and takes his own life.
- **Clitus** A soldier and servant of Brutus; refuses to kill Brutus when asked.
- **Dardanius** Another soldier of Brutus; also refuses to help Brutus die.
- **Volumnius** A close friend of Brutus; Brutus asks him to hold his sword, but he refuses.
- **Strato** A loyal soldier who finally helps Brutus take his own life by holding his sword.
- **Octavius** The heir of Caesar; he arrives after Brutus' death and offers to take in Brutus' surviving men.
- **Antony** Caesar's loyal friend and general; he honours Brutus as 'the noblest Roman of them all.'
- **Messala** A soldier in Brutus' army; he witnesses Brutus' death.
- **Lucilius** A loyal supporter of Brutus; he survives the battle and joins Octavius' forces.

Vocab Vault

Vessel In the scene, a 'vessel' can be used to describe someone who embodies specific qualities or emotions

List a word Pay attention to a particular statement

Smatch Slight presence of something

The elements The natural forces or qualities that make up the world, such as Earth, air, fire and water

EXAM ORIENTED QUESTIONS

TYPE - 1 Multiple Choice Questions

01 Mark

Q.1 What decision does Brutus make in Act 5, Scene 5?
(a) To continue fighting (b) To surrender to Antony
(c) To flee the battlefield (d) To take his own life

Q.2 Why does Brutus decide to end his life?
(a) He fears capture and humiliation.
(b) He feels guilty about Caesar's death.
(c) He believes his death will save Rome.
(d) He is betrayed by his men.

Q.3 Who holds Brutus' sword as he runs onto it?
(a) Lucilius (b) Strato (c) Volumnius (d) Titinius

Q.4 What does Brutus say about his decision to die?
(a) He regrets killing Caesar.
(b) He feels more justified in his suicide than in killing Caesar.
(c) He curses Antony and Octavius.
(d) He blames his fate on Cassius.

Q.5 How does Antony describe Brutus after finding his body?
(a) As a traitor to Rome
(b) As the 'noblest Roman of them all'
(c) As a coward who avoided capture
(d) As a misguided conspirator

Q.6 Why does Antony call Brutus the 'noblest Roman of them all'?
(a) Brutus acted for the greater good of Rome, not out of envy or ambition.
(b) Brutus never participated in the conspiracy.
(c) Brutus tried to make peace with Antony before the battle.
(d) Brutus showed mercy to Caesar during the assassination.

Q.7 What does Octavius order for Brutus after his death?
(a) A proper burial with full military honours
(b) A public display of his body as a warning
(c) A trial for treason, even in death
(d) Immediate cremation without ceremony

Q.8 What theme is most evident in Brutus' death scene?
I. Revenge II. Honour
III. Loyalty IV. Deception
V. Ambition
(a) I and II (b) II and III
(c) III and IV (d) IV and V

Q.9 What is the significance of the final lines of the play?
(a) They celebrate Octavius' victory.
(b) They highlight the tragic downfall of Brutus as a noble character.
(c) They condemn the conspirators' actions.
(d) They mark the end of the Roman Republic.

Q.10 Brutus does not allow his pain and anguish to interrupt his professional life. This portrays that he practices .... **(Competency Based Que.)**
(a) stoicism (b) cynicism
(c) buddhism (d) epicureanism

Q.11 Who is referred to by clitus as 'noble vessel full of grief?
(a) Brutus (b) Cassius
(c) Antony (d) Lepidus

Q.12 To whom does Brutus refer to as his school fellao?
(a) Strats (b) Volumnius
(c) Dardanius (d) Cato

Q.13 Brutus says that he would attain greater glory than the 'vile conquest' of whom
(a) Octavius and Antony (b) Caesar and Pompey
(c) Old Cato and his son (d) None of these

Q.14 What does Octavius say he would do with all those who were serving Brutus?
(a) Kill them
(b) Take them in his service
(c) Make them prisoner of war
(d) Make them his slaves

Q.15 Select the option that shows the correct relationship between statements I and II. **(Competency Based Que.)**
Statement 1 Brutus was a believer in the stoic philosophy.
Statement 2 Brutus chose to take his life rather than face the humiliation of being taken captive.
(a) Statement 2 illustrates Statement 1.
(b) Statement 2 contradicts Statement 1.
(c) Statement 1 is true, and Statement 2 is false.
(d) Statement 1 is false, and Statement 2 is true.

Q.16 Which of the given options lists the sequence of events in the correct order? **(Competency Based Que.)**

(i) During the battle at Philippi, Brutus's army inflicts an early defeat on Octavius' troops.

(ii) Seeing some troops in the distance, Cassius sends Titinius on horseback to check if they are 'friend or foe'.

(iii) Meanwhile, in another part of the battleground, Cassius learns that his camp has been surrounded by Antony's soldiers and is being attacked.

(iv) Pindarus, seeing Titinius surrounded by horsemen, assumes that he has fallen into enemy hands and reports to Cassius that he (Titinius) has been taken captive.

(v) Next, Cassius instructs his servant Pindarus to climb a hill nearby so that he can give him a detailed account of all that happens to Titinius.

(a) (ii), (iv), (iii), (v), (i)
(b) (iv), (v), (i), (iii), (iv)
(c) (i), (v), (ii), (iv), (iii)
(d) (i), (iii), (ii), (v), (iv)

Answers

1. (d)	2. (a)	3. (b)	4. (b)	5. (b)	6. (a)	7. (a)	8. (b)	9. (b)	10. (a)
11. (a)	12. (a)	13. (a)	14. (b)	15. (b)	16. (d)				

TYPE - 2 Extract Based Questions

16 Marks

Extract 1

Farewell to you-and you-and you, Volumnius.
Strato, thou hast been all this while asleep.
Farewell to thee, too, Strato-Countrymen,
My heart doth joy that yet in all my life
I found no man but he was true to me.
I shall have glory by this losing day
More than Octavius and Mark Antony
By this vile conquest shall attain unto.

(i) How does Brutus' farewell to his companions in these lines reflect his internal state and attitude toward death? (3)

Ans. Brutus' farewell reflects his acceptance of death and his sense of peace about it.

By bidding farewell to each of his companions, he demonstrates a resigned, almost calm demeanour.

His farewell is personal and intimate suggesting he has come to terms with his fate.

He expresses no fear or bitterness, rather a sense of completion. He believes that his loyalty to his ideals is something worth more than the physical life he is about to lose.

(ii) What is the significance of Brutus' statement, 'My heart doth joy that yet in all my life I found no man but he was true to me'? (3)

Ans. Brutus' statement reflects his deep sense of integrity and his satisfaction with the loyalty of those around him.

Despite the betrayal of the conspiracy and his ultimate defeat, Brutus finds solace in the fact that his relationships have been genuine.

It underscores his belief in the goodness of human nature which remains unshaken even as he faces death.

This statement contrasts with the deception and betrayal that marked his life and highlights the theme of loyalty and honour in the play.

(iii) How does Brutus' perception of glory in his death differ from that of Octavius and Antony? (3)

Ans. Brutus believes that his death will bring him greater glory than the victory achieved by Octavius and Antony. He sees his defeat as honourable and consistent with his ideals which contrasts with the 'vile conquest' of Octavius and Antony.

Brutus' sense of glory is tied to his moral integrity and the belief that he acted for the greater good of Rome, even though the outcome was tragic.

He values the nobility of his actions over the physical victory showing his sense of honour and pride in his principles.

(iv) In what ways do these lines reflect Brutus' sense of fatalism and his views on fate? (3)

Ans. Brutus' words reflect his acceptance of fate and the inevitability of his death. He does not seem angry or upset about the outcome of the battle, rather resigned as if he believes his fate was predetermined.

The reference to the 'losing day' suggests that he views his death as an inevitable part of his life's journey and he is at peace with it.

He believes that he will find more glory in his death than his enemies will in their victory. His fatalism underscores the themes of destiny and honour in the play.

(v) What does Brutus' last reflection on loyalty and truth say about his character and motivations throughout the play? **(4)**

Ans. Brutus' final reflection on loyalty and truth reinforces his character as an idealist, someone who is deeply committed to principles of honour and justice.

Throughout the play, Brutus is driven by a sense of duty to Rome believing that he must act in what he perceives to be the greater good. His belief that 'no man but he was true to me' suggests that he values loyalty and integrity above all else, even in the face of betrayal by others.

This highlights his tragic flaw-his naivety in trusting too easily and his commitment to personal virtue over political cunning or self-preservation.

Extract 2

Strato Give me your hand first. Fare you well, my lord.

Brutus Farewell, good Strato.

Caesar, now be still.

I killed not thee with half so good a will.

(i) What is the significance of Brutus' final words, 'Caesar, now be still. I killed not thee with half so good a will'? **(3)**

Ans. Brutus' final words reflect the deep internal conflict and remorse he felt over Caesar's assassination. He expresses that his death is more willingly embraced than the act of killing Caesar indicating that he has come to terms with the consequences of his actions.

This statement shows Brutus' belief that his death is a more honourable and just action, compared to the murder of Caesar, which he carried out reluctantly despite his political reasoning.

(ii) How does Brutus' death scene represent the culmination of his character arc throughout the play? **(3)**

Ans. Brutus' death represents the tragic end of his journey as a noble yet misguided idealist. Throughout the play, he is driven by a sense of duty to Rome and his belief in honour and virtue. In his final moments, he chooses suicide over capture maintaining his integrity until the end.

His death, while tragic, reflects his unwavering commitment to his principles.

(iii) What role does Strato play in Brutus' death?

How does this reflect the nature of their relationship? **(3)**

Ans. Strato assists Brutus in his suicide by holding the sword while Brutus runs onto it. This act of loyalty reflects the deep trust and bond between the two men as Strato respects Brutus' final wish and helps him fulfill it.

Their relationship is one of mutual respect, with Strato being willing to support Brutus in his moment of greatest need, demonstrating the loyalty Brutus cultivated throughout the play.

(iv) Why does Brutus choose to end his life rather than be captured by his enemies? **(3)**

Ans. Brutus chooses suicide over capture because he values his honour and integrity more than his life. He believes that being captured by Antony and Octavius would strip him of his dignity and undermine the noble reasons he had for assassinating Caesar.

By taking his own life, Brutus maintains control over his fate, avoiding the humiliation of being paraded as a prisoner.

(v) What is the symbolic significance of Brutus' death in relation to the themes of honour and sacrifice in the play? **(4)**

Ans. Brutus' death is the ultimate act of honour and sacrifice. Throughout the play, Brutus is portrayed as a man of high principles willing to sacrifice personal relationships for what he believes in. His final act of suicide is the culmination of his dedication to his ideals choosing to die on his own terms rather than surrender.

His death symbolises the tragic cost of maintaining personal honour in a world filled with political turmoil and betrayal.

Extract 3

This was the noblest Roman of them all.
All the conspirators save only he
Did that they did in envy of great Caesar.
He only in a general honest thought
And common good to all made one of them.
His life was gentle and the elements
So mixed in him that nature might stand up
And say to all the world 'This was a man.'

(i) Why does Antony refer to Brutus as 'the noblest Roman of them all'? **(3)**

Ans. Antony refers to Brutus as 'the noblest Roman' because Brutus acted out of a genuine belief that his actions would benefit Rome, rather than out of personal envy or ambition.

Despite being a conspirator, Brutus' motives were rooted in honour and the common good. Antony admires Brutus for his selflessness and the purity of his intentions.

(ii) How does the contrast between Brutus and the other conspirators enhance the tragedy of his character? **(3)**

Ans. The contrast between Brutus and the other conspirators highlights Brutus' tragic flaw. While the other conspirators acted out of personal motives, such as jealousy or fear, Brutus' involvement in Caesar's assassination was driven by a deep sense of duty to Rome.

His integrity makes his eventual downfall even more tragic as he is the only conspirator who believed he was acting for the greater good.

This moral idealism leads to his internal conflict and his ultimate demise which is all the more sorrowful due to his noble intentions.

(iii) What does Antony's description of Brutus' life as 'gentle' suggest about his character and leadership?

Ans. Antony's description of Brutus' life as 'gentle' emphasises Brutus' inherent kindness, moderation and virtue. It suggests that Brutus was not a man of cruelty or tyranny but one who was thoughtful, respectful and measured in his actions.

His leadership, therefore, was not born of aggression or ambition but from a calm and composed desire to serve the common good. It marks him as a tragic figure whose death is especially moving because of his peaceful nature.

(iv) What is the symbolic significance of the phrase 'the elements / So mixed in him that nature might stand up / And say to all the world 'This was a man"?

Ans. The given phrase symbolises the ideal balance of qualities that make Brutus an epitome of humanity.

By saying that 'nature might stand up', Antony implies that Brutus embodied the best attributes of human nature courage, honour and selflessness– so completely that the very forces of nature themselves would recognise him as an exemplary human being.

This metaphor elevates Brutus' character to the level of an ideal making his death even more tragic as it removes a figure of such noble integrity from the world.

(v) How does this tribute to Brutus shape our understanding of his role in the play?

Ans. This tribute by Antony deepens our understanding of Brutus' role as a tragic hero in the play. Despite his involvement in Caesar's assassination, Brutus is portrayed as a fundamentally good man whose intentions were rooted in a sense of justice and the welfare of Rome.

His tragic flaws his inability to recognise the consequences of his idealism– leads to his downfall.

Antony's words help the audience see Brutus as a noble figure caught in a moral struggle whose death is the loss of a man who truly believed in doing what was right for Rome.

TREASURE CHEST: PROSE

1. With the Photographer
2. The Elevator
3. The Girl Who Can
4. The Pedestrain
5. The Last Lesson

WITH THE PHOTOGRAPHER

Satyajit Ray

Introduction

With the Photographer is a humourous story by Stephen Leacock, a Canadian writer known for his humour and satire. This story is about a man's frustrating experience at a photo studio where he wants to get his picture taken. This picture is to be kept by his friend after his demise. The story highlights how photographers focus more on altering a person's appearance rather than capturing them as they are. It is a satire which mocks the unrealistic standards of photography. The story is narrated in a witty tone which makes an ordinary event amusing.

About the Story

The story **With the Photographer** follows a man who visits a photo studio to get his picture taken. The photographer examines his face critically and makes unwanted suggestions for improvement. When the narrator returns to collect the photo, he is shocked to see that his features have been altered beyond recognition. This leads to frustration and disappointment. The story humorously highlights how photographers impose their ideas rather than capturing reality. Through exaggeration and wit, the author makes a simple event entertaining and thought provoking.

Character Introduction

- **The Narrator** A 40-year old man who wants to get his photograph clicked. It could be Leacock himself. He is portrayed as an ordinary individual with simple expectations.
- **The Photographer** A professional who owns a photo studio. He is depicted as a caricature of self-important professional who believed that with his skill he can make people better looking.

Story at a Glance

In the story, the narrator seeks the services of a photographer. He is eager to get his photograph taken. He carefully observes the photographer, who is wearing a gray suit. Without any conversation, the dull stooping man asks the narrator to wait and he is kept waiting for an hour. He reads various magazines in the meantime.

After an hour, the photographer finally calls in the narrator and asks the narrator to sit on a chair. He himself rolled a machine in the middle of the room. Dissatisfied, he wastes a lot of time going in and coming out of the machine to adjust the lighting.

The photographer gets disappointed and finally says that the narrator's face is wrong. He starts humiliating the narrator's facial features and gives him awkward instructions like 'close your mouth', 'droop your ears', 'expand the lungs', etc.

The narrator struggles to follow the complicated instructions. He says that he is aware of his appearance not being attractive but he accepts it as it is. As the narrator is speaking, the photographer pulls the string and a photo gets clicked. He asks to look at the photograph but the photographer asks him to come back on Saturday.

On the designated day, the photographer proudly shows the proof of the image. However, the photograph looks nothing like the narrator as it has been 'improved' by the photographer using his artistic skills and techniques.
The author is disheartened because all he wanted was a photo which looked like him.

He sarcastically comments that the photographer must keep it to show to his family and friends as it is a masterpiece of his skills. As for the author, it is a worthless thing.

Vocab Vault

Dropping Bending
Unwarrantable Unacceptable
Frantic Desperate
Hump Heave
Animation In movement/excitement
Beckoned Called
Splendidly Nicely
Superfices Surface, face
Reconcile Come to terms with
Emboss To bulge
Emboss To bulge up
Bauble A thing of no value

Theme

The story explores themes of professionalism, human vanity, insecurity, appearance and reality of the natural order. The story delves into the conflict between one's self-perception and the perception imposed by others. Leacock also addresses the broader issue of self-perception versus reality.

Message Conveyed by the Story

The story 'With the Photographer' conveys the theme of original self and distorted self. It also gives a message of acceptance and confidence. The protagonist's experience reflects a universal struggle with self-image and the pressure to conform to idealised standards. Through this narrative, Leacock invites readers to reflect on their own perceptions of identity and the impact of societal pressures, all while delivering a story that is both entertaining and thought-provoking.

Style, Tone and Mood

- **Style** Leacock employs humour throughout the story, particularly through exaggeration and irony.
- **Tone** The tone is light-hearted and gets serious towards the end. His use of detailed descriptions and conversational tone draws readers into the comical yet relatable scenario.
- **Mood** The mood is light-hearted and humorous, with elements of satire.

Title

The title with 'The Photographer' is justified as it reflects the central character's role in the story. The photographer's profession and his interactions highlight themes of vanity, appearances, and the gap between how people see themselves and how others perceive them. The title is fitting as it emphasises the photographer's role in capturing moments, while also commenting on society's obsession with appearances.

Figures of Speech

- **Hyperbole** (Exaggeration) "I waited an hour. I read the Ladies Companion for 1912, the Girls Magazine for 1902 and the Infants Journal for 1888."
- **Irony** The narrator expects a simple photograph but receives a heavily altered version. The photographer, instead of capturing the narrator's real appearance, insists on changing it.
- **Sarcasm** "So! I said bitingly, 'Features, eh? You didn't think I could animate them, I suppose"?
- **Personification** "I could see the machine still staggering from the shock."
- **Simile** "The photograph looked like a guinea pig with colic."
- **Metaphor** "The photographer had pulled a string. The photograph was taken."
- **Understatement** "I started to rise from the seat. Snick!"

EXAM ORIENTED QUESTIONS

TYPE - 1 Multiple Choice Questions

01 Mark

Q.1 What magazines did the narrator read while waiting?
(a) The Ladies Companion, Girls Magazine, and Infants Journal
(b) Photographer's Weekly and The Ladies Companion
(c) Infants Journal and Artists' Companion
(d) Girls Magazine and Photographic Techniques

Q.2 What was the first instruction given to the narrator by the photographer?
(a) 'Sit there and wait'.
(b) 'Smile for the camera'.
(c) 'Remove your hat'.
(d) 'Open the door and come in'.

Q.3 In the story, while waiting for the photographer, the narrator spent time ....
(a) examining the studio (b) talking on his phone
(c) writing his diary (d) reading magazines

Q.4 What does the photographer mean when he says, 'The face is quite wrong'?
(a) The narrator's expression was inappropriate.
(b) The narrator's facial features didn't meet the photographer's artistic standards.
(c) The lighting was wrong.
(d) The camera wasn't adjusted properly.

Q.5 Identify the meaning of 'features just in a moment of animation'.
(a) The photograph captured a natural and lively expression.
(b) The narrator was deliberately animated.
(c) The features were adjusted post-click.
(d) The narrator was irritated and animated.

Q.6 The narrator wanted the photograph to reconcile his friends with his ....
(a) flaws (b) face
(c) death (d) absence

Q.7 'I don't care for it. I like to get the hair clear back to the superficies and make out a new brow line'.
(Competency Based Que.)
These lines tell us that the photographer is ....
(a) angry
(b) weak
(c) insensitive
(d) anxious

Q.8 Select the option that shows the correct relationship between statement (1) and (2).
Statement 1 The photographer made changes to the narrator's face to make it more appealing.
Statement 2 The narrator was pleased with the adjustments.
(a) Both statements are true.
(b) Both statements are false.
(c) Statement 1 is true and Statement 2 is false.
(d) Statement 1 is false and Statement 2 is true.

Q.9 What was the narrator's initial request to the photographer?
(a) To edit his features and improve his looks
(b) To take his photograph exactly as he was
(c) To take a group picture with his friends
(d) To capture him in an artistic pose

Q.10 Why does the photographer suggest multiple changes to the narrator's face?
(a) Because he finds the narrator's face unphotogenic
(b) Because he wants to experiment with new techniques
(c) Because the narrator asks for a dramatic look
(d) Because the studio's camera was faulty

Q.11 How does the narrator's reaction to the final photograph show his sense of self-worth?
(a) He accepts the photographer's work without argument.
(b) He firmly rejects the photograph, valuing his unaltered appearance.
(c) He praises the photographer for improving his looks.
(d) He blames himself for not posing properly.

Q.12 The narrator wanted the photograph to look like his ....
(a) ideal self
(b) real self
(c) younger self
(d) imagined self

Q.13 Identify the figure of speech in the line, 'The machine still staggering from the shock'.
(a) Hyperbole
(b) Personification
(c) Simile
(d) Metaphor

Q.14 Choose the option that lists the sequence of events in the correct order from the story 'With the Photographer'. **(Competency Based Que.)**

(i) The photographer hurriedly backs away from the machine and, with a serious expression, comments that there is something wrong with the narrator's face.

(ii) He crawls under the cloth draped over the machine and waits for some time.

(iii) The narrator thinks that the photographer is praying.

(iv) The photographer calls the narrator into the inner room and rolls the machine into the middle of the room.

(a) (i), (ii), (iii), (iv) (b) (iv), (ii), (iii), (i)
(c) (ii), (iii), (iv), (i) (d) (iv), (iii), (i), (ii)

Q.15 'Is it me?', Who said the following words?

(a) The author (b) The photographer
(c) A client (d) None of these

Q.16 What expression does the narrator use to describe his edited photo?

(a) "It looks just like me."
(b) "The photograph looked like a guinea pig with colic."
(c) "This is the best photo I have every seen."
(d) "This is exactly what I wanted."

Q.17 What effect does the photographer's excessive editing have on the narrator?

(a) He laughs and appreciates the changes
(b) He becomes furious and leaves in frustration
(c) He asks for even more modifications
(d) He decides to become a photographer himself

Q.18 Which of the following options contains the same literary device that appears in the following line: '....the machine still staggering from the shock....' **(Competency Based Que.)**

(a) The house roofs seemed to heave and sway.
(b) In the vestibule below was a letter box.
(c) So heavy they were, tidal waves come over the islands.
(d) It became transparent like a thin veil.

Q.19 Select the option that shows the correct relationship between statements (1) and (2). **(Competency Based Que.)**

Statement 1 The author felt that his eyes in the photograph didn't look very much like his.

Statement 2 The photographer had retouched the eyes.

(a) Statement 1 is true, and Statement 2 is false.
(b) Statement 2 is true, and Statement 1 is false.
(c) Statement 2 is the cause for Statement 2.
(d) Statement 1 and Statement 2 are independent of each other.

Q.20 What does the story suggest about art and reality?

(a) Art should always improve on reality.
(b) Reality should never be altered for artistic purposes.
(c) There is often a conflict between artistic vision and true representation.
(d) Photography is a purely realistic art form.

Q.21 How does the photographer's attitude reflect society's obsession with appearances?

(a) By showing indifference to the narrator's feelings.
(b) By attempting to alter the narrator's natural looks.
(c) By ignoring the narrator's requests for authenticity.
(d) All of the above

Q.22 The underlying tone of the story is

(a) comical (b) sensational
(c) sorrowful (d) satirical

Q.23 According to you, the attitude of the photographer was

(a) rage (b) terror
(c) humiliation (d) none of these

Q.24 Of all features, which one remained unchanged in the photograph?

(a) Eyes (b) Lips (c) Ears (d) Hair

Q.25 If the narrator were alive today, how might he react to modern photo-editing apps?

(a) He would embrace them as a necessity
(b) He would reject them for altering reality
(c) He would ask for more extreme modifications
(d) He would become a photographer himself

Q.26 How does Leacock use humour to criticise photography trends?

(a) By using complex words and photography jargon
(b) By showing the narrator's frustration through exaggeration
(c) By praising the photographer's editing skills
(d) By describing the photography studio in great detail

Q.27 If you were the narrator, how would you have responded differently to the photographer?

(a) Politely requested only minor edits
(b) Insisted on clicking the picture himself
(c) Argued more aggressively before the photo was taken
(d) Accepted all the photographer's changes without complaint

Q.28 Which modern-day issue is similar to what the narrator faces in the story?

(a) The rise of artificial intelligence
(b) The widespread use of beauty filters and Photoshop
(c) The decline of professional photography
(d) The popularity of animated movies

Answers

1. (a)	2. (a)	3. (d)	4. (b)	5. (a)	6. (c)	7. (c)	8. (c)	9. (b)	10. (a)
11. (b)	12. (b)	13. (b)	14. (b)	15. (a)	16. (b)	17. (b)	18. (a)	19. (c)	20. (c)
21. (d)	22. (d)	23. (b)	24. (b)	25. (b)	26. (b)	27. (a)	28. (b)		

Explanations

13. The given line uses personification as it attributes human characteristics (staggering) to an inanimate object (the machine).
18. The given line uses personification. Option (a) also uses personification as it attributes human qualities (heaving and swaying) to non-human objects (house roof).
19. In the context of the story, the narrator felt that his eyes in the photograph did not resemble his own eyes. This was because the photographer had retouched the eyes. Therefore, statement (2) explains why statement (1) is true, establishing a cause and effect relationship.

TYPE - 2 Extract Based Questions — 16 Marks

Extract 1

"I waited an hour. I read the Ladies Companion for 1912, the Girls Magazine for 1902, and the Infants Journal for 1888. I began to see that I had done an unwarrantable thing in breaking in on the privacy of this man's scientific pursuits with a face like mine".

(i) From which story has the extract been taken?

What is the overall theme of the story?

Name the author of the story **(3)**

Ans. The extract has been taken from the story 'With the Photographer'.

The overall theme of the story is identity, acceptance of appearance and annoyance.

The name of the author is Stephen Leacock.

(ii) What does the narrator imply the phrase 'an unwarrantable thing'? **(3)**

Ans. The phrase 'an unwarrantable thing' suggests that the narrator feels he is an inappropriate intrusion into the photographer's space. He implies that his face is so unappealing that it was a rude thing to disrupt the photographer's work with his presence.

(iii) What effect does the setting have on the overall tone of the passage? **(3)**

Ans. The setting of the photographer's studio, combined with the outdated magazines and the long wait, creates a sense of absurdity and unease. The narrator passively observes the environment waiting with some outdated magazines.

This suggests a sense of being stuck in an outdated, almost forgotten world. This adds to the humour, as it highlights the contrast between the photographer's disinterest and the narrator's increasing discomfort.

(iv) As you read, there is a sense of exaggeration in the descriptions used by Leacock.

What role does exaggeration play in this passage? **(3)**

Ans. Exaggeration plays a central role in building the humour of the passage. The narrator overstates both his unattractiveness ('an unwarrantable thing') and the outdatedness of the magazines to make the situation feel more absurd.

This over-the-top reaction creates a sense of comedic dissonance, where the narrator's extreme thoughts contrast sharply with the relatively mundane setting of waiting in a studio.

(v) Describe the photographer.

Why does the narrator say that it is not necessary to describe him in detail? **(Competency Based Que., 4)**

Ans. The photographer is a drooping man wearing a grey coat. His body is bent and his eyes are dim. He lacked enthusiasm and interest. He seemed to have a good knowledge of his profession.

The narrator deliberately avoids describing the photographer in detail, to suggest that the photographer's appearance and character are irrelevant to the story. Creating an ironical situation. This choice highlights the photographer's indifference and detachment. He is absorbed in his work to the point of neglecting the narrator's presence.

Extract 2

"The ears are bad", he said, "Droop them a little more. Thank you. Now the eyes. Roll them in under the lids. Put the hands on the knees, please, and turn the face just a little upward. Yes, that's better".

(i) Why did the photographer look at the author without enthusiasm?

What impression did he get of the photographer? **(3)**

Ans. The photographer looked at the author without enthusiasm because he didn't like the face of the author. He viewed him as an, unremarkable subject who is not inspiring for his artistic work.

The impression that he got was that the photographer was an unprofessional man who is rude, unemotional and insensitive.

(ii) Where did the photographer make the author sit? Describe the photographer's initial attempt to take a picture. **(Competency Based Que., 3)**

Ans. He made the author sit in a beam of sunlight filtered through a sheet of factory cotton hung against a frosted skylight. The setup was formal and uncomfortable, designed to control every aspect of the photograph.

In his initial attempt to take the picture, the photographer directed the author to sit still and adjust his posture repeatedly. He gave him various instructions to adjust the pose. However, the photographer was dissatisfied with the narrator's natural posture.

His directions were mechanical and devoid of warmth. This reflected his clinical focus on achieving the perfect shot rather than making the subject feel at ease.

(iii) What instructions did the photographer give the author before taking his photograph? **(Competency Based Que., 3)**

Ans. Before taking the photograph, the photographer gave the author a series of precise instructions to adjust his posture and expression.

He asked the author to tilt his head slightly to one side and then turn it a little more. This was followed by instructions to lower and then raise his chin to achieve the perfect angle.

He emphasised keeping the mouth slightly closed and maintaining a neutral expression. He discouraged any hint of a smile.

(iv) Which feature in the author's photograph had some resemblance to his face?

How did the photographer offer to set this right? **(Competency Based Que., 3)**

Or What was the only part of the narrator's face that seemed original in the photograph?

How did the photographer plan to 'fix' this? **(ICSE Specimen 2025)**

Ans. In the author's photograph, only the author's ears bore some resemblance to his actual face. The rest of the image was heavily altered and distorted due to the photographer's editing, which had drastically changed his natural features.

The photographer offered to 'set this right' by suggesting further retouching and adjustments to the photograph. He proposed to soften the expression, remove the crow's feet, tone down the eyebrows, and even adjust the shape of the mouth.

(v) Comment on the photographer's retouching and altering of the author's photograph.

Mention one modern-day equivalent of what the photographer attempted to do.

Give one reason why the photographer's action was insensitive. **(Competency Based Que., 4)**

Or Which of the narrator's facial features had the photographer altered? **(ICSE Specimen 2025)**

Ans. The photographer's retouching focused on altering the author's natural features to create a perfect but unrealistic image. He proposed changes like softening expressions, removing wrinkles, and reshaping facial features. This made the photo unrecognisable.

A modern equivalent would be using photo-editing apps to create flawless but artificial images.

This was insensitive because it implied that the author's natural appearance was not perfect to an artist's imagination. This may have hurt his feelings and self-esteem.

Extract 3

'Stop', I said with emotion but, I think, with dignity. 'This face is my face. It is not yours, it is mine. I've lived with it for forty years and I know its faults.
I know it's out of drawing. I know it wasn't made for me, but it's my face, the only one I have -'

(i) Who is the speaker? Draw the character sketch of the speaker. **(3)**

Ans. The speaker in the story 'With the Photographer' is the narrator himself, who shares his experience at the photo studio. He is a simple and straightforward man who wants a natural photograph but faces frustration due to the photographer's interference. He has a good sense of humour and uses sarcasm to express his irritation. His witty and observant nature makes the story amusing, as he exaggerates small incidents to create humour.

(ii) How long has the narrator 'lived' with his face? Why does the narrator emphasise, 'This face is my face'? (3)

Ans. The narrator has lived with his face for forty years.

By emphasising 'This face is my face', the narrator asserts his ownership of his appearance. He rejects the photographer's attempts to alter it. He loves and accepts his face as granted by God.

(iii) '....that I caught the features just in a moment of animation.' Explain the quoted line.

What is the significance of this? (3)

Ans. The phrase 'that I caught the features just in a moment of animation' refers to a brief, fleeting moment when the subject's facial expressions appear more alive. This line highlights the contrast between the author's natural, genuine expression and the photographer's idealised vision of the photograph.

The significance of this lies in the photographer's attempt to capture a perfect, static image.

(iv) Comment on the style of the story.

Does the author do justice to the themes it represents? (3)

Ans. The story is written in a lighthearted and humorous style with sarcasm, exaggeration and irony. The author uses everyday situations to create comedy, making the reader laugh while thinking about unrealistic beauty standards. He does justice to the theme by showing how photographers impose their ideas rather than capturing reality. His witty storytelling makes the simple experience both entertaining and meaningful.

(v) Was the photographer satisfied after taking the photograph?

If no, why so? How do you figure out? (4)

Ans. No, the photographer was not satisfied after taking the photograph. He looked at the narrator's face critically and believed it needed many changes. He suggested adjusting the eyebrows, mouth and ears, showing that he was unhappy with the natural look. The photographer believed that his skills could 'improve' the narrator's face. We can figure this out from his expressions and comments, as he kept pointing out flaws and insisted on retouching the image. His dissatisfaction was clear when he edited the photo so much that the narrator could not recognise himself. This shows how photographers often focus on perfection rather than reality.

Extract 4

'The photographer beckoned me in. I thought he seemed quieter and graver than before.

I think, too, there was a certain pride in his manner. He unfolded the proof of a large photograph, and we both looked at it in silence.

'Is it me?' I asked.

'Yes', he said quietly, 'it is you', and we went on looking at it.'

(i) Where was the narrator? Why had he gone there? Why do you think there was a certain pride in the photographer's manner? (ICSE Specimen 2025, 3)

Ans. The narrator was at a photo studio because he wanted to get his photograph taken in its natural form. He went there so his friends could remember him after his death. The photographer showed pride because he believed he had improved the narrator's face through retouching. He thought his editing skills had made the photograph look better.

(ii) What does the word 'proof' mean in this context?

Why did the narrator ask, 'Is it me?' (ICSE Specimen 2025, 3)

Ans. The word 'proof' here means sample of a print before the final printing of the photograph.

The narrator could not recognise himself in the photograph because every feature of his had been altered using editing skills.

It did not look like him. He bore no resemblance to the narrator's real face.

(iii) At the end of the story, the narrator flies into a rage. What makes him angry?

How would you justify the narrator's angry outburst? (ICSE Specimen 2025, 3)

Ans. The narrator becomes angry when he sees his photograph completely changed. The photographer edits his features so much that he looks like someone else. The narrator wanted a natural photo, but his request was ignored. His anger is justified because his identity was altered without his consent. Anyone would be upset if they were not recognised in their own picture.

(iv) Mention any three processes referred to in the story with the help of which the photographer edited facial features. (3)

Ans. The three processes with the help of which the photographer edited facial features are

(a) He retouched the narrator's eyes.

(b) He used the Delphide solution to remove the original eyebrows.

(c) He planned to use the Sulphide solution for removing the ears completely.

(v) **Why did the photographer's 'creativity' appear as a worthless bauble to the narrator?** **(4)**

Ans. The photographer's 'creativity' appeared as a worthless bauble to the narrator because it focused on altering his natural features to fit an ideal image rather than capturing his true self. The narrator saw the photographer's obsession with perfection as superficial and unnecessary. It diminished the value of genuine expression.

To him, the photographer's attempts to create an idealised version of his face were meaningless, as they ignored his identity and personal acceptance. The 'creativity' seemed more like a trivial, shallow pursuit rather than something valuable or artistic.

Extract 5

What I wanted is no longer done. Go on, then, with your brutal work. Take your negative, or whatever it is you call it, – dip it in sulphide, bromide, oxide, cowhide, – anything you like, – remove the eyes, correct the mouth, adjust the face, restore the lips, reanimate the necktie and reconsturct the waistcoat. Coat it with an inch of gloss, shade it, emboss it gild it, till even you acknowledge that it is finished. Then when you have done all that – keep it for yourself and your friends. They may value it. To me it is but a worthless bauble." I broke into tears and left.

(i) **Draw a sketch of emotions that must be flowing in the heart of the narrator.** **(3)**

Ans. In the story, the narrator feels surprised and disappointed when he sees his photograph, because it doesn't match his expectations. He becomes embarrassed and self-conscious about how he looks, realising the gap between his ideal image and reality.

Despite the disappointment, he finds it humorous, reflecting on his own vanity. There's also a sense of irony as he recognises how he has deceived himself about his appearance.

(ii) **Why do you think the photographer and the narrator look at the photograph in silence?** **(3)**

Ans. The photographer and the narrator look at the photograph in silence because both are reflecting on the difference between what the narrator expected and what the photo actually shows.

The silence highlights the awkwardness, as the narrator feels disappointed and embarrassed.

The photographer stays quiet, and does not comment on the situation. It adds to the humour and irony of the moment.

(iii) **Why was there certain pride in the photographer when he received the narrator on Saturday?** **(3)**

Ans. The photographer shows a certain pride when he receives the narrator on Saturday because he likely takes pride in his profession. He is confident in his ability to capture good photographs.

He views the narrator's visit as an opportunity to demonstrate his expertise. The photographer's calm and confident manner reflects his self-assurance in his work.

(iv) **What was the tone of the narrator at the end of the story when he was furiously talking to the photographer?**

Do you sense any sarcasm? Give an example. **(3)**

Ans. At the end of the story, when the narrator is furiously talking to the photographer, the tone is one of frustration and sarcasm. The narrator is angry and upset that the photograph doesn't show his real face. His tone becomes exaggerated and ironic.

Yes, there is a hint of sarcasm.

One example is when the narrator asks the photographer to edit it further and keep it for himself as a proof of his 'excellent' work.

(v) **Did the photo studio look like the one we see today? What were the differences?** **(4)**

Ans. The photo studio in 'With the Photographer' was dark and cramped, with old furniture and bulky equipment, unlike today's modern studios.

The camera used glass plates for negatives and the lighting was dim compared to the bright, adjustable lights we have now.

In the past, photos were formal and required sitting still for longer, while today, they are more casual and taken quickly. Overall, the studio reflected older, slower photography methods compared to the fast, advanced studios we have today.

02

THE ELEVATOR

William Sleator

Introduction

The Elevator is a horror story by William Sleator, an American writer known for his suspenseful and psychological stories. This story is about a twelve-year-old boy, Martin, who is afraid of elevators. His fear grows stronger when he repeatedly encounters a mysterious, heavyset woman in the elevator. The story builds suspense as Martin struggles to escape his fear but ultimately finds himself trapped. Its unique feature is the open-ended and eerie conclusion, leaving readers unsettled.

About the Story

William Sleator's story **The Elevator** is about Martin, a shy boy who feels scared of the old, creaky elevator in his apartment building. His fear grows when a strange, large woman starts appearing in the elevator and makes him feel even more uncomfortable. The story creates suspense and explores Martin's fear and insecurity. The ending is mysterious, leaving readers wondering if Martin's fears are real or just in his mind.

Character Introduction

- **Martin** A shy and insecure twelve-year old boy who is afraid of the old, creaky elevator in his apartment building.
- **Martin's Father** A very indifferent man who is careless and inconcerned towards Martin's fears.

Story at a Glance

The story begins with the introduction of Martin, a 12-year-old boy who lives in an old apartment building with his father. Martin is physically small and fragile. He is timid and insecure.

Martin is terrified of the old elevator in the building. He imagines worst-case scenarios like breaking of the elevator or him being trapped inside it. His father dismisses these fears, often criticising him for being weak and cowardly. Martin's anxiety comes not just from the elevator but also from his father's lack of support.

One day, while Martin is in the elevator, a large, intimidating woman enters. She stands too close, staring at him silently. This makes him feel extremely uncomfortable. Her strange presence starts to haunt Martin, increasing his fear.

Martin starts seeing the woman more often in the elevator. Each time, her silent stare increases his fear. The woman never speaks, but due to her size and constant staring, Martin fears using the elevator. His anxiety grows, and he starts avoiding the elevator whenever possible, even if it means taking the stairs.

Martin is unable to explain his fear to anyone. His father remains unsympathetic and pushes him to face his fears. Martin feels trapped and powerless as he has no choice but to keep using the elevator.

One day, Martin gets injured and is forced to take the elevator with his father. However, his father gets down on another floor. Martin sees that the woman is already inside. She acts more threatening this time and says 'Hello Martin!'. The story ends ambiguously, leaving readers uncertain if the woman poses a real threat or if Martin's fear is purely psychological.

Vocab Vault

Shuddered Shook

Bullied To use power or strength to frighten somebody

Waddled Walked with short steps

Pudgy Fat

Hobbled Limped

Theme

The story explores Martin's strong fears and how they take over his mind. His weakness and low confidence make him feel powerless. His father's harsh words add to his stress and make things worse. The ending is unclear, making readers wonder if Martin's fear is real or imagined. The story shows that fears can only be overcome by facing them.

Message Conveyed by the Story

The story highlights how fear and anxiety can take over our lives if left unchecked. Martin's terror, both real and imaginary, shows how vulnerability can make fears seem overwhelming. It also emphasises the need for empathy.

The dismissive attitude of Martin's father makes his insecurities worse, This shows that lack of support can deepen someone's struggles. The open-ended conclusion reminds us that some fears remain unresolved. This reflects reflecting the uncertainty and complexity of human emotions.

Style, Tone and Mood

- **Style** The style of 'The Elevator' is simple yet suspenseful, focusing on creating a psychological tension that draws the reader into Martin's fears.
- **Tone** The tone is dark and unsettling, as it reflects Martin's fear and vulnerability. The author maintains a sense of unease throughout the story.
- **Mood** The mood of the story is tense and claustrophobic, mirroring the confined space of the elevator and Martin's emotional state.

Title

The title 'The Elevator' by William Sleator is justified because the elevator in the story symbolises both literal and figurative aspects of the plot. It represents the central location where key events unfold, where the main character confront his fear and limitations. As the protagonist, a young boy, imagines the elevator's rise and fall, it mirrors his internal journey of growing up and facing challenges.

Figures of Speech

- **Personification** "The elevator shuddered each time it left a floor, as if it was exhausted."
- **Simile** "It wasn't possible. It was like a nightmare."
- **Imagery** "She had large fleshy cheeks and no chin, just a huge mass of neck."
- **Repetition** "She just kept staring at me. She never stopped looking at me for a minute."
- **Symbolism** "Martin, a thin twelve-year-old, felt nervous in it from the first day he and his father moved into the apartment."
- **Onomatopoeia** "The door slammed shut with a loud clanging noise." "The door slammed."

EXAM ORIENTED QUESTIONS

TYPE - 1 Multiple Choice Questions

01 Mark

Q.1 What aspect of the elevator makes Martin uneasy?
(a) Its speed and noise.
(b) Its size and confined space.
(c) The absence of a mirror.
(d) The lack of emergency buttons.

Q.2 How does Martin's father react to his concerns about the elevator?
(a) He tries to help him overcome his fear.
(b) He ignores him completely.
(c) He mocks and belittles him.
(d) He becomes afraid as well.

Q.3 Whenever Martin tried using the stairs instead of the elevator, he got ....
(a) excited (b) tired (c) breathless (d) fearful

Q.4 The relationship between Martin and his father was ....
(a) affectionate (b) friendly
(c) distanced (d) interactive

Q.5 The detail about the large woman that contributes most to her unsettling presence is ....
(a) her continuous laughter
(b) her silence and direct stare
(c) her habit of following Martin
(d) her conversations with Martin

Q.6 In what way does the story's unresolved ending enhance its impact?
(a) It leaves readers frustrated with the lack of answers.
(b) It creates a sense of closure for Martin's fears.
(c) It reflects the unpredictability of fears and unresolved emotions.
(d) It suggests Martin's fears were imaginary.

Q.7 Based on your understanding, which of the following best describes the large woman?
(a) A symbol of Martin's imagination.
(b) A physical manifestation of his insecurities.
(c) A mysterious but harmless individual.
(d) A direct threat to Martin.

Q.8 What does the large woman do when she gets on the elevator with Martin?
(a) She talks to him.
(b) She smiles at him.
(c) She stares at him silently.
(d) She tries to help him.

Q.9 Martin, in the story, 'The Elevator', is afraid of being trapped in the elevator. What is this fear called? **(Competency Based Que.)**
(a) Hydrophobia (b) Arachnophobia
(c) Claustrophobia (d) Aquaphobia

Q.10 In the story's progression, when does Martin's fear reach its peak?
(a) When his father calls him a coward.
(b) When he realises he must face the elevator alone.
(c) When the large woman steps into the elevator with him.
(d) When the large woman smiles at him in the end.

Q.11 Which of these sentences from the story, 'The Elevator' is not true? **(Competency Based Que.)**
(a) Martin was a thin twelve-year-old boy.
(b) The lady was wearing an old green coat.
(c) Martin was skinny, weak and bad at sports.
(d) The lady had large fleshy cheeks, no chin and brown eyes.

Q.12 Select the option that shows the correct relationship between statement (1) and (2). **(Competency Based Que.)**
Statement 1 Martin backed away from the elevator, ran down the stairs and broke his leg.
Statement 2 In the morning, when the elevator door opened, the fat lady awaited him.
(a) Statement 1 is independent of Statement 2.
(b) Statement 2 is the cause of Statement 1.
(c) Statement 1 is an example of Statement 2.
(d) Statement 1 is a contradiction of Statement 2.

Q.13 "You're afraid," said his father. "When are you going to grow up and act like a man?"
What does this sentence tell us about Martin's father's character? He was **(Competency Based Que.)**
(a) cowardly (b) greedy
(c) insensitive (d) rude

Q.14 Based on the story, how would you analyse the relationship between Martin and his father?
(i) Loving (ii) Caring
(iii) Friendly (iv) Disjointed

(v) Distanced

(a) Only (i) (b) Only (iv)

(c) (iv) and (v) (d) (v) and (i)

Q.15 Choose the option that lists the sequence of events in the correct order

(i) Martin feels uneasy about the elevator.

(ii) Martin's father dismisses his fears.

(iii) Martin encounters the large woman for the first time.

(iv) Martin is left alone with the woman in the elevator.

(a) (i), (iii), (iv), (ii) (b) (i), (ii), (iii), (iv)

(c) (ii), (i), (iii), (iv) (d) (iii), (ii), (i), (iv)

Q.16 Which of the following best describes the sequence of Martin's emotional journey?

(a) Fear → Dismissal → Escalation → Terror

(b) Curiosity → Confidence → Fear → Relief

(c) Fear → Relief → Anger → Defeat

(d) Confidence → Fear → Dismissal → Triumph

Q.17 Martin is the .... in the story.

(a) protagonist (b) antagonist

(c) villain (d) caricature

Q.18 'Hello Martin', who says the following words?

(a) Mrs. Ullman

(b) Martin's Father

(c) The doctor at the hospital

(d) The strange woman

Q.19 Select the option that shows the correct relationship between statements (1) and (2). **(ICSE Specimen 2025)**

Statement 1 Terrified of the fat lady in the elevator, Martin ran down the dark stairs, fell and broke his leg.

Statement 2 Angry and disappointed that his son had behaved like a fool and coward, Martin's father did not talk to him on the way to the hospital.

(a) 1 is true, 2 is false.

(b) 1 is false, 2 is true

(c) 1 is the cause for 2

(d) 1 and 2 are independent of each other

Answers

1. (b)	2. (c)	3. (c)	4. (c)	5. (b)	6. (c)	7. (b)	8. (c)	9. (c)	10. (d)
11. (d)	12. (b)	13. (c)	14. (c)	15. (b)	16. (a)	17. (a)	18. (d)	19. (c)	

TYPE - 2 Extract Based Questions 16 Marks

Extract 1

"It was an old building with an old elevator - a very small elevator, which could carry only three people. Martin, a thin twelve-year-old, felt nervous in it from the first day he and his father moved into the apartment. Of course he was always uncomfortable in elevators, afraid that they would fall, but this one was especially unpleasant. Perhaps this was because of the poor lighting and the dirty walls. Perhaps it was because of the door, which never stayed open long enough, and slammed shut with a loud clanging noise. Perhaps it was the way the elevator shuddered each time it left a floor, as if it was exhausted. Maybe it was simply too small. It seemed crowded even with only two people in it.

(i) Who is the protagonist of the story?

Why is he fearful of elevators?

What kind of building is it? **(3)**

Ans. Martin, a twelve- year old boy is the protagonist of the story.

He is fearful of the elevators because of the poor lighting, dirty walls and door that slammed loudly.

It is an old building with very old elevator.

(ii) What kind of a boy is Martin?

List his few characteristics. **(3)**

Ans. Martin is a sensitive, anxious, and insecure boy who is easily affected by his surroundings and the people around him. He is particularly afraid of elevators, especially the old, small one in his building, which makes him feel trapped and uneasy.

Some of the characteristics of Martin are

- He is physically weak and often out of breath.
- He struggles with activities like climbing the stairs and is made to feel inadequate by his father.
- He is very under confident, vulnerable and cowardly.

(iii) What do you think the description of the elevator suggests about Martin's feelings? **(3)**

Ans. The description of the elevator suggests that Martin feels uneasy, anxious, and trapped in the small, dark old space. The poor lighting, dirty walls and the loud, slamming door make the elevator feel uncomfortable and unsafe, intensifying Martin's fear. The elevator's shuddering motion and cramped size reflect Martin's feelings of claustrophobia and vulnerability.

These details highlight his discomfort and unease, showing how even simple everyday things, like using the elevator, become sources of anxiety for him. It also suggests that Martin feels a lack of control and security, contributing to his overall fear and nervousness.

(iv) **Why was Martin scared of using the elevator?**

List any three possible reasons. **(Competency Based Que., 3)**

Ans. Martin was scared of using the elevator because of the following reasons

- Martin had a general fear of elevators, worrying that they might fall, which made him anxious whenever he had to use one.
- The elevator was old, small, and poorly maintained, with dirty walls, poor lighting, and a noisy door that slammed shut, making it feel unsafe and uncomfortable.
- The elevator was cramped and felt crowded even with only two people inside, which made Martin feel trapped and uneasy in such a confined space.

(v) **Martin disliked using the staircase. Why?** **(Competency Based Que., 4)**

Ans. Martin disliked using the staircase because it was dark and unwelcoming. It had no windows and broken lights, which made it feel eerie and uncomfortable. As he climbed, the silence and the sound of his own footsteps echoed, creating the unsettling feeling that someone else was following him.

Additionally, the physical effort of climbing seventeen floors left Martin exhausted and out of breath. It made the stairs feel like a tiring and overwhelming challenge. All these factors combined made the staircase a place Martin preferred to avoid.

Extract 2

"Martin's father worked at home. He wanted to know why Martin was out of breath. "Why didn't you take the elevator?" he asked, frowning at Martin." You're not only skinny and weak and bad at sports, his face seemed to say, but you are also a coward. After that, Martin always took the elevator. He would have to get used to it, he told himself, just like he got used to being bullied at school.

(i) **How old was Martin? On which floor did he live? What word would you use to describe Martin?** **(Competency Based Que., 3)**

Ans. Martin was twelve years old.

He lived on the 17th floor.

Martin could be described as claustrophobic and vulnerable child.

(ii) **Martin met a strange person in the elevator one day. What did she do that scared Martin? What happened to Martin when he ran away after seeing her?** **(Competency Based Que., 3)**

Ans. One day, Martin met a strange woman in the elevator. She stared at him with sharp eyes, making him feel scared and uncomfortable. He tried to avoid looking at her, but she kept watching him. Terrified, Martin ran away when the elevator stopped at his floor.

However, in his hurry, he fell down the dark stairs and hurt himself. His father was angry, calling him a coward for being afraid and not using the elevator. Martin's fear of the woman led to his injury, making him feel even more vulnerable.

(iii) **Comment on the ending of the story, 'The Elevator'. Identify any two elements of horror in the story.** **(Competency Based Que., 3)**

Ans. The ending of 'The Elevator' is chilling and unsettling, as Martin's fear of the strange woman becomes a nightmare. The open-endedness of 'The Elevator' adds to the sense of suspense and unease, leaving many questions unanswered. The true nature of the strange woman is never fully explained, allowing readers to speculate whether she is simply a bizarre character or a supernatural presence or may be just Martin's imagination.

Two elements of horror in the story are

(a) **The Unseen Threat** The strange woman's continuous, unnerving stare and mysterious actions create a sense of danger without fully explaining her motives.

(b) **Claustrophobia** The small, creaky elevator and the dark, oppressive stairs add to the atmosphere of confinement, making Martin feel trapped and vulnerable.

(iv) **How did the father react to Martin's fears?**

What does it show about his character? **(3)**

Ans. The father reacts dismissively to Martin's fears, calling him a coward and telling him to 'grow up'. He is frustrated by Martin's anxieties and doesn't take them seriously. He brushes off Martin's concerns about the strange woman in the elevator.

This reaction shows that the father is unsympathetic, impatient, and lacks understanding of his son's emotional struggles. He expects Martin to be brave and tough, without acknowledging the real fears that his son is facing.

This highlights the father's inability to provide emotional support, which makes Martin feel isolated and misunderstood.

(v) **In what way does the story reflect universal themes of fear and vulnerability?** **(4)**

Ans. The story 'The Elevator' shows universal themes of fear and vulnerability through Martin's experiences. His fear of the elevator and the strange woman makes him feel trapped and helpless.

Martin is emotionally vulnerable, as he struggles with his fears but feels unable to talk about them, especially with his unsympathetic father. The story highlights how fear can make people feel isolated and weak. Fear affects their sense of safety and control. It shows that fear, whether real or imagined, can deeply impact a person's life.

Extract 3

"She was wearing an old green coat that ballooned around her. As she waddled into the elevator, Martin was sure he felt it sink under her weight. She was so big that her coat brushed against him, and he had to squeeze himself into a corner. There was no room for anybody else. The door closed quickly behind her, and instead of facing it, she turned around and stared at Martin."

(i) **Who is 'she' in the above extract?**

Describe her appearance. **(3)**

Ans. 'She' is a strange, fat lady who Martin encountered in the elevator.

She is described as a fat lady wearing an old green coat that balloons around her. Her face is described as having large fleshy cheeks with no chin, just a large mass of neck. Her blue eyes are tiny but sharp, and they seem to be constantly staring at Martin, making him uncomfortable. This eerie, unsettling appearance contributes to Martin's fear of her.

(ii) **Martin was sure he felt it sink under her weight. Why did he feel so?**

What does it imply? **(3)**

Ans. Martin felt the elevator sink under the woman's weight because he noticed the elevator's movement change when she entered. This likely refers to the feeling of the elevator becoming slightly heavier due to the weight of the Lady or slower as she stepped in.

The implication is that the woman was very large, and her presence made Martin feel the elevator was struggling to carry her. It adds to the sense of discomfort and fear that Martin feels in the confined space, making the elevator seem even more unsafe and claustrophobic.

(iii) **Do you think the title of the story is justified? Give reasons.** **(3)**

Ans. The title 'The Elevator' is justified as it is central to the story's events and themes. The elevator serves as both the physical setting and the metaphorical space where Martin experiences his fears and vulnerability. His discomfort with the elevator mirrors his inner anxieties.

It becomes a place of emotional tension, especially when he encounters the strange woman. The elevator, small and claustrophobic, symbolises Martin's feeling of being trapped, both in the confined space and by his fears.

Additionally, the elevator's movements–shuddering, stopping, and its unsettling atmosphere–heighten the sense of horror.

(iv) **Based on your reading of the story, describe Martin's encounter with the lady in detail?** **(3)**

Ans. Martin's encounter with the lady in the elevator is creepy and frightening. One morning, she enters the elevator, and Martin feels it sink under her weight. Her large coat brushes against him, and he has to squeeze into a corner. The woman turns around and stares at him with sharp eyes, making him uncomfortable.

Despite trying to avoid her gaze, she keeps staring, and Martin feels trapped. When the elevator reaches the first floor, she slowly exits, and Martin runs past her to escape. The encounter leaves him disturbed, and he could not stop thinking about her, feeling nervous about meeting her again.

(v) **Do you think the fat lady is real or is she an imagination of Martin?**

Explain and give reasons. **(4)**

Ans. It is likely that the fat lady is real, but she is perceived by Martin as a source of fear and discomfort. The story describes her in detail, including her green coat and sharp blue eyes, suggesting that she physically exists in the story. Additionally, the lady's actions, like entering the elevator, staring at Martin, and pressing the stop button, all indicate that she is interacting with him in a tangible way.

However, Martin's intense fear and his emotional state might make him overthink her presence. This makes her seem more ominous or supernatural than she actually is. This could explain why Martin is so disturbed by her, even though she may simply be an odd, perhaps socially awkward, woman. The woman's eerie behaviour, combined with Martin's vulnerability, makes her seem more threatening than she might actually be.

Extract 4

"Martin started running down the stairs. The stairs were dark and he fell. His father was silent on the way to hospital, disappointed and angry with him for being a coward and a fool. Martin had broken his leg and needed to walk on crutches. He could not use the stairs now. Was that why the fat lady had smiled? Did she know what would happen? At least his father was with him in the elevator on the way back from the hospital. There was no room for the fat lady to get in, and if she did, his father would see her and maybe he would understand. When he got home, he could stay in the apartment for a few days. The doctor said that he had to rest as much as possible. Martin felt quite safe from the fat lady now."

(i) What causes Martin to run down the stairs? What happens when Martin runs down the stairs? How does Martin's father react to the accident? (3)

Ans. Martin runs down the stairs in panic after encountering the woman again in the elevator.

As Martin runs down the stairs in a fit of fear he falls and breaks his leg, which leads him to use crutches.

Martin's father is silent and disappointed, expressing his anger at Martin for being a coward.

(ii) What does this incident reveal about Martin's relationship with his father? What impact does this event have on Martin's emotional state? (3)

Ans. The incident reveals that Martin's father does not understand or support him. He criticises Martin instead of showing concern for his well-being.

Martin feels further isolated and ashamed, which deepens his fear and internal conflict.

(iii) Do you learn something from the story? What is the central message? (3)

Ans. Yes, we do learn how baseless it is to live with meaningless fears. The central message of the story is about overcoming fear and facing vulnerability. Martin's fear of the elevator and the strange woman symbolises how fear can control us and make us feel trapped.

It also shows how our imagination can amplify our fears, leading to unnecessary anxiety.

The story reminds us that facing our fears, even when they seem irrational, is an important part of growing up.

(iv) What does the story suggest about the role of family support in overcoming fear? (3)

Ans. The story suggests that lack of family support can make overcoming fear even more difficult. Martin's father dismisses his fears, calling him a coward and urging him to grow up. This lack of understanding makes Martin feel isolated, and dejected as his emotional struggles are not validated.

If Martin had received empathy and encouragement from his father, he might have felt more confident in facing his fears. The story highlights that emotional support from family can play a crucial role in helping someone overcome their fears and build resilience.

(v) How does the setting of the elevator contribute to the theme of entrapment? (4)

Ans. The setting of the elevator helps show the theme of entrapment. Its small space makes Martin feel cramped and uncomfortable. The shaky movements and poor lighting make the elevator feel even more eerie.

When the woman enters, Martin feels trapped, unable to escape. The elevator's confined space reflects Martin's feelings of fear and isolation, both physically and emotionally, reinforcing the theme of being stuck or trapped.

Extract 5

Martin hobbled to the buttons and pressed nine, but it didn't do any good. The elevator stopped at ten, where the fat lady was waiting for him. She moved in quickly, and he was too slow to get past her in time to get out. The door closed and the elevator began to move. 'Hello, Martin', she said, and laughed, and pushed the Stop button.

(i) How does the author use the large woman's character to deepen the story's suspense? (3)

Ans. The author uses the large woman's character to deepen the story's suspense by making her mysterious and unsettling. Her size and appearance, with the ballooning green coat and sharp blue eyes, make her seem physically imposing and strange, adding to Martin's sense of discomfort. Her unblinking stare and silent behavior create an eerie, tense atmosphere, keeping Martin (and the reader) on edge.

The woman's odd actions, like pressing the stop button and staring at Martin without speaking, heightens the mystery and makes the reader question her intentions, increasing the overall sense of suspense throughout the story.

(ii) How does the story portray the effects of ridicule on a person's psyche? What is the result of this? (3)

Ans. The story portrays the effects of ridicule on Martin's psyche through his interactions with his father. When Martin expresses his fear of the elevator and the woman, his father ridicules him by calling him a coward and telling him to grow up. This constant mockery makes Martin feel ashamed of his emotions and causes him to believe that his fears are irrational.

As a result, he becomes more isolated and anxious, struggling to cope with his fear on his own. The ridicule affects his confidence, making him feel vulnerable and unable to share his feelings. The story highlights how belittling someone's emotions can negatively impact their mental well-being and self-worth.

(iii) **The tone of the story plays an important role in aggravating the reading experience. Comment.** **(3)**

Ans. The tone of 'The Elevator' is suspenseful, unsettling, and psychologically tense. The author creates a sense of unease by describing Martin's fear of the elevator and the strange woman in vivid detail. The claustrophobic atmosphere of the elevator and the woman's unpredictable behavior build tension, keeping the reader on edge.

(iv) **The fat lady says, 'Hello Martin'. How does this create a feeling of horror? Justify.** **(3)**

Ans. When the fat lady says, 'Hello Martin', it creates a feeling of horror because it reveals that she knows him, even though he has never seen her before. This adds an eerie, unsettling layer to her character, suggesting that she may be watching him or has some sort of control over the situation.

(v) **How would you describe the relationship between Martin and his father?** **(4)**

Ans. The relationship between Martin and his father is distant and emotionally strained. Martin's father dismisses his fears, calling him a coward and telling him to 'grow up'. He ridicules Martin's emotions instead of offering support or understanding.

This lack of empathy leaves Martin feeling isolated and vulnerable, as he cannot openly express his fears. His father's reactions shows that he doesn't acknowledge Martin's emotional struggles. This makes their relationship feel more like a one-sided and disconnected bond, where Martin's emotional needs go unmet.

03

THE GIRL WHO CAN

Ama Ata Aidoo

Introduction

The Girl Who Can is a short story by Ama Ata Aidoo, a Ghanaian writer known for highlighting gender roles in African society. This story is about a young girl, Adjoa, who faces criticism from her grandmother for having thin legs. Despite this, she proves her worth by becoming an outstanding athlete. The story belongs to the genre of realistic fiction and focuses on themes of gender roles and self-worth. Its unique aspect is how it challenges traditional expectations of women in society.

About the Story

The Girl Who Can by Ama Ata Aidoo is about Adjoa, a seven-year-old African girl from a village in Ghana, who struggles with speaking her mind due to discouragement from her elders. Despite criticism of her thin legs, Adjoa is an excellent runner who proves her worth by winning a race – she challenges traditional views about women which reflects on female empowerment. The story reflects feminist themes.

Character Introduction

- **Adjoa** A seven-year-old girl from the village of Hasodzi in Ghana.
- **Nana** Adjoa's grandmother an elder with traditional views.
- **Kaya (Maami)** Adjoa's mother more understanding and supportive of Adjoa's ambitions.

Story at a Glance

Adjoa is a seven-year-old girl from Hasodzi, a village in Ghana, who lives with her grandmother, Nana, and her mother, Maami. She faces challenges at home due to Nana's critical nature, particularly regarding her physical appearance. Adjoa struggles to express herself, as Nana either scolds her or laughs when she speaks, leaving Adjoa feeling uncertain and confused.

The elders in the village reinforce these feelings by reacting negatively to her attempts to speak her mind, making her feel inadequate.

Nana frequently criticises Adjoa's thin legs, insisting that a woman's legs should be strong enough to bear the responsibilities of motherhood. She compares Adjoa unfavourably to other women with 'solid hips' and 'fleshy legs'. This constant criticism pressures Adjoa to conform to traditional expectations of women's bodies.

Determined to prove herself, Adjoa becomes curious about women's legs and secretly plans to observe them. Despite this pressure, Adjoa excels at running and is the fastest runner at school, though she never shares this achievement with her family. The five-kilometer walk to school is long, but Adjoa enjoys it and remains determined.

Adjoa is selected to represent her school at the junior level in the District Sports Week. Adjoa wins the cup for the best athlete in her category. Her family is surprised by her achievement, and Nana, although proud, struggles to show her emotions.

After Adjoa's victory, Nana reflects on her granddaughter's legs. She realises that although they may not be 'fleshy', they are strong enough to run, and that has value. For the first time, Nana acknowledges Adjoa's potential beyond the traditional expectations of women. Nana expresses a soft, tearful pride in Adjoa's accomplishments, while Maami remains silent as usual.

Vocab Vault

Muttering Speaking in a low voice that is difficult to hear, often to oneself.

Creak A high-pitched, squeaky sound made with something stiff.

Sheen A smooth, shiny appearance.

Harbour To keep feelings to oneself

Spindly Thin and weak

Theme

The story explores several interconnected themes that highlight societal norms, personal growth, and the complexities of family relationships. Self-Acceptance and individuality comes to forefront as Adjoa learns to embrace her uniqueness, proving her worth through her athletic achievements. The story also highlights the conflicts between three generations- Nana, Maami and Adjoa. The importance of education is emphasized in the story as a path to enlightenment and progress.

Message Conveyed by the Story

The story conveys that individuality and abilities should be valued over societal expectations and stereotypes. It emphasises that personal worth is not defined by physical appearance or traditional norms, as talents and inner potential can challenge and transform preconceived notions.

Style, Tone and Mood

- **Style** The story is written in first-person narrative with simple, candid language.
- **Tone** The tone of the story is reflective, playful and empowering.
- **Mood** The mood is light-hearted, inquisitive and triumphant.

Title

The title 'The Girl Who Can' by Ama Ata Aidoo is justified because it reflects the central theme of the story. The story revolves around the protagonist, a young girl named Adjoa, who challenges societal expectations and proves her capabilities.

Adjoa defies the traditional belief that girls are less capable than boys, particularly when it comes to physical activities like running. Throughout the story, she demonstrates determination, resilience, and the ability to overcome obstacles, showing that she can succeed just as well as anyone else, regardless of her gender. The title captures her journey of self-discovery and empowerment.

Figures of Speech

- **Metaphor** "I came out of the land of sweet, soft silence into the world of noise and comprehension." "Granddaughter with spindly legs."
- **Personification** "Her mouth moved as though she was going to tell Nana..."
- **Repetition** "Never, never but NEVER to repeat such words."
- **Hyperbole** "She would laugh and laugh and laugh, until tears run down her cheeks..."
- **Irony** "Thin legs can also be useful... Thin legs can run..."
- **Simile** "She carried the gleaming cup on her back like they do with babies."

EXAM ORIENTED QUESTIONS

TYPE - 1 Multiple Choice Questions

01 Mark

Q.1 Where is the story set?
(a) Nairobi, Kenya
(b) Hasodzi, Ghana
(c) Johannesburg, South Africa
(d) Lagos, Nigeria

Q.2 Nana believe that a woman's legs should be ....
(a) long and thin
(b) muscular and capable of running
(c) have meat on them to support solid hips
(d) flexible for dancing

Q.3 The phrase, 'different problems at different stages of life' suggests Adjoa's ....
(a) mature understanding of life
(b) attempt to justify her insecurities
(c) struggle with adulthood
(d) lack of connection with Nana

Q.4 What is one serious problem Adjoa has to face?
(a) She cannot laugh when her grandmother laughs
(b) She cannot express herself
(c) She cannot understand the language of elders
(d) None of the above

Q.5 What does Adjoa's victory in the sports competition symbolise?
(a) Rebellion against tradition
(b) Validation of her abilities despite physical criticism
(c) A shift in her family's financial status
(d) Acceptance of societal norms

Q.6 Which of the following statements is not true of Adjoa in 'The Girl Who Can'? **(Competency Based Que.)**
(a) She has thin and long legs.
(b) She is declared the best all-around junior athlete.
(c) She is seven years old girl from Ghana.
(d) She is proud of her abilities.

Q.7 Assess the impact of education on Adjoa's life as depicted in the story 'The Girl Who Can'. **(Competency Based Que.)**
(a) It has no significant influence.
(b) It is detrimental to her growth.
(c) It empowers her and provides her with a sense of identity.
(d) It creates a rift between her and her family.

Q.8 What does Adjoa mean by 'the land of sweet soft silence'? **(Competency Based Que.)**
(a) Her girlish dreams
(b) Her native village
(c) Her mother's womb
(d) Her entire world

Q.9 Adjoa's grandmother is a representative of **(Competency Based Que.)**
(i) authority (ii) determination
(iii) unconventional approach (iv) patriarchal outlook
(a) (i) and (ii) (b) (ii) and (iii)
(c) (ii) and (iv) (d) (i) and (iv)

Q.10 How does the narrative explores the theme of individuality?
(a) By highlighting Adjoa's defiance of her family's expectations.
(b) Through Nana's insistence on conformity.
(c) By showcasing the uniformity of the village community.
(d) Through Maami's passive support of Adjoa.

Q.11 Evaluate what the story suggests about the relationship between tradition and progress.
(a) Progress is only possible by rejecting tradition.
(b) Tradition can adapt to accommodate progress.
(c) Tradition and progress cannot coexist.
(d) Progress often undermines traditional values.

Q.12 What does Maami's defence of Adjoa's legs indicate?
(a) Her frustration with Nana
(b) Her protective instincts
(c) Her belief in individuality
(d) Her silent rebellion against tradition

Q.13 The sports competition impact Adjoa's self-esteem as ....
(a) it makes her realise her potential
(b) it alienates her from her peers
(c) it reinforces her insecurities
(d) it strengthens her bond with Nana

Q.14 What was Nana's view initially about school?
(a) An idle pursuit
(b) A waste of time
(c) A platform to showcase her talent
(d) None of the above

(iv) Adjoa won the cup for the best-all-round, athlete. What change did this bring about in Nana's perspective?

How did the grandmother feel at the end of the story? Give a reason to justify your answer.

(Competency Based Que., 3)

Ans. Adjoa winning the cup for the best-all-round athlete brought a significant change in Nana's perspective. She realised that Adjoa's thin legs, which she had criticised, were not a weakness but a source of strength and success.

This led Nana to see Adjoa's worth beyond physical appearance and acknowledge her talent and achievements with pride.

At the end of the story, the grandmother feels proud and accepting of Adjoa. This is evident as her attitude shifts from criticism to support, showing that Adjoa's success has helped her challenge traditional views and embrace a broader understanding of value and capability.

(v) How does the story reveal the themes of education and empowerment? Answer in brief. **(4)**

Ans. The story reveals the themes of education and empowerment through Adjoa's journey. Her school provides her the platform to discover and showcase her talent in sports, empowering her to challenge societal and familial expectations. By excelling and winning the sports competition, Adjoa gains confidence and proves her worth beyond physical appearances.

This demonstrates how opportunities and support in education can help individuals realise their potential and overcome societal pressures.

Extract 3

After all, they were my legs ... When I think back on it now, those two, Nana and my mother, must have been discussing my legs from the day I was born. What I am sure of is that when I came out of the land of sweet, soft silence into the world of noise, the first topic I met was my legs.

(i) Who keeps 'discussing' in the extract?

What do they discuss? Why? **(3)**

Ans. Nana, Adjoa's grandmother and Maami, her mother keep 'discussing' in the extract.

They keep discussing about Adjoa' legs.

They discuss it because her legs are too thin.

(ii) How does Adjoa feel about the constant discussion of her legs? **(3)**

Ans. Adjoa feels self-conscious and uncomfortable about the constant discussion of her legs, especially given her grandmother's critical remarks. These comments make her feel like her physical appearance, particularly her legs, is something to be ashamed of. This affects her confidence and self-esteem.

(iii) The story reveals about societal expectations from women.

What are they?

What does it reveal? **(3)**

Ans. The story reveals how societal expectations can place a significant emphasis on women's physical appearances, often promoting certain standards of beauty or attractiveness.

In Adjoa's case, her grandmother's critical focus on her legs reflects a broader societal tendency to judge women's bodies, especially in relation to beauty ideals. Such expectations can lead to feelings of inadequacy or self-doubt, as women may feel pressured to conform to these standards.

(iv) Why might Adjoa's mother remain quiet during these discussions? **(3)**

Ans. Adjoa's mother might stay quiet because of cultural norms, where questioning elders is seen as disrespectful. She may also want to avoid conflict or feel powerless to change her mother's views. This also represents that she is suppressed by her mother and she is not able to speak up openly to stand for her daughter.

(v) Analyse how the story draws a contrast between tradition and modernity. **(4)**

Ans. The story contrasts tradition and modernity through Adjoa and her grandmother. The grandmother represents tradition, valuing physical appearance and old gender expectations.

Adjoa, however, challenges this by winning the sports competition, showing that her worth comes from her abilities, not her looks. This highlights the shift from traditional views to modern ideas about self-worth and gender equality.

Extract 4

"As I keep saying, if any woman decides to come into this world with her two legs, then she should select legs that have meat on them: with good calves. Because you are sure such legs would support solid hips. And a woman must have solid hips to be able to have children."

(i) Who is 'I' in this extract?

Describe her character in brief. **(3)**

Ans. 'I' refers to Nana, Adjoa's grandmother.

Nana is a traditional and strict woman with strong opinions, especially regarding appearances and gender roles. She frequently criticizes Adjoa's legs, believing they are too thin and long for a woman, and this often frustrates Adjoa.

Despite her critical nature, Nana cares deeply for her granddaughter. She is proud of Adjoa when she wins the sports competition. Nana's character reflects a blend of love, concern, and conventional thinking.

(ii) Briefly analyse Adjoa and Nana's relationship. **(3)**

Or

Describe the relationship between Adjoa and her grandmother.

Why was she made to feel inadequate?

(Competency Based Que.)

Ans. Adjoa and Nana's relationship is complex but evolves over time. Nana often criticises Adjoa's thin legs, believing they make her unattractive, which hurts Adjoa, who seeks her grandmother's approval. She is made to feel inadequate due to her thin spindly legs which are not up to the expected beauty standards.

Despite the criticism, there is care in their bond, and Adjoa respects Nana. Their relationship changes when Adjoa proves her worth by winning a running competition, leading Nana to appreciate her for her abilities rather than her appearance.

This shift reflects growth and mutual respect, showing the importance of accepting individuality over prejudice.

(iii) What does this story suggest about the pressures women face in society regarding their physical appearances? **(3)**

Ans. This story suggests that women face significant pressure to conform to societal standards of beauty, which often define their worth based on physical appearance rather than their abilities or character. These pressures can affect self-esteem and limit how women view themselves and their potential.

The story highlights how such expectations are often perpetuated by family and tradition, showing the need to challenge these norms and value women for their achievements and individuality.

(iv) The story draws a contrast between tradition and modernity. Analyse and comment. **(3)**

Ans. The story contrasts tradition and modernity through Adjoa and her grandmother. The grandmother represents tradition, valuing physical appearance and old gender expectations. Adjoa, however, challenges this by winning the sports competition, showing that her worth comes from her abilities, not her looks. This highlights the shift from traditional views to modern ideas about self-worth and gender equality.

(v) Do you think Adjoa is pragmatic in nature?

Why? Justify. **(4)**

Ans. Yes, Adjoa is pragmatic because she focuses on proving her worth through actions rather than dwelling on the criticism about her legs.

Instead of becoming discouraged by her grandmother's remarks, she channels her energy into excelling in sports, showing her ability to rise above negativity.

Adjoa's decision to let her achievements speak for her reflects her practical and solution-oriented mindset, highlighting her maturity and resilience.

Extract 5

You know what she did? She carried the gleaming cup on her back. Like they do with babies. And this time, not taking the trouble to walk by herself. When we arrived in our village, she entered our compound to show the cup to my mother before going to give it back to the headmaster.

(i) What does Nana do with the trophy?

How does the author describe Nana's action with the trophy? **(3)**

Ans. At the end of the story, Nana takes the trophy that Adjoa won for being the best all-round athlete and carries it on her back.

The author uses the simile 'Like they do with babies' to describe Nana's action. This simile makes a comparision between the gleaming cup on Nana's back to a baby.

(ii) Nana's action symbolises something particularly valuable. What do they imply? **(3)**

Ans. Carrying the cup on her back symbolises Nana's newfound pride and recognition of Adjoa's achievements. It shows that Nana now values Adjoa's abilities and no longer focuses solely on her physical appearance.

The act of carrying the cup reflects Nana's acceptance and admiration, signifying a shift from criticism to support and respect for Adjoa's success.

(iii) **Why does Adjoa feel that it was better to prove herself through actions rather than words?** **(3)**

Ans. Adjoa feels it was better to prove herself through actions rather than words because she understands that actions speak louder and are more convincing than mere talk. Given the constant criticism about her legs, she knows that her achievements will be the most effective way to change people's perceptions. She wanted to break the stereotype.

(iv) **How does Adjoa's character grow throughout the story?** **(3)**

Ans. Adjoa's character grows in confidence and self-awareness throughout the story. At the start, she is insecure about her legs, which are constantly criticised by Nana. She feels misunderstood and struggles to express herself.

However, as she excels in running and wins the sports

competition, Adjoa gains a sense of accomplishment. This success challenges Nana's critical views, and Adjoa begins to embrace her physical abilities. By the end of the story, she becomes more confident in herself, and her relationship with Nana transforms as Nana shows pride in her achievements.

(v) **'Thin legs can also be useful', what does this statement suggest about Nana's realisation?** **(4)**

Ans. The statement 'thin legs can also be useful' reflects Nana's realisation and change in perspective about Adjoa. Initially, Nana criticised Adjoa's legs for being too thin and not fitting the ideal standards for a woman.

However, after Adjoa wins the race and proves her abilities, Nana acknowledges that even thin legs can be strong and capable. This marks a shift in Nana's views, as she now sees the value in Adjoa's physical traits, realising that they can be useful in different ways, and not just for traditional expectations of supporting hips for childbearing.

THE PEDESTRIAN

Ray Douglas Bradbury

Introduction

The Pedestrian is a short story by Ray Douglas Bradbury, a famous American writer known for his science fiction and dystopian stories. The story is set in the year 2053, where the main character, Leonard mead, takes a night walk in a lonely city. The story highlights how television has made people stop going out, leading to a lifeless and robotic society. It warns about the dangers of technology controlling human lives. The unique part of the story is how a simple walk becomes an unsual and suspicious act in a future world.

About the Story

The Pedestrian by Ray Bradbury is set in a future society where people stay indoors, absorbed by television and personal interaction is rare. The story follows Leonard Mead, a man who enjoys taking evening walks. One night, while walking, he is stopped by a robotic police car, which is puzzled by his behaviour.

Walking outside is deemed suspicious and abnormal in this controlled, tech-dependent world. Leonard is arrested for his 'crime' of walking without a purpose. The story critiques the dehumanising effects of technology and the loss of individuality, highlighting the dangers of a conformist society.

Character Introduction

- **Leonard Mead** The protagonist of the story, Leonard Mead is an independent, introspective man.
- **The Police Car (Robot)** The robotic police car is the antagonist in the story. It represents the oppressive force of technology.

Story at a Glance

The story is set in a world where people rarely leave their homes, preferring to stay indoors and watch television. The protagonist, Leonard Mead, is an unusual man who enjoys taking evening walks in the city.

In contrast to others, who are content with the passive activity of watching television, Mead finds peace and inspiration in the simple act of walking through the streets alone. One evening, as Mead is out on his walk, he is stopped by a robotic police car. It is an automated car that, drives around the city, ensuring that citizens adhere to societal norms. It questions Mead about why he is outside when there is no clear reason for his walk.

The police car is confused by his behaviour because walking in the streets is considered abnormal in this society, where people are confined to their homes and glued to their screens. The police car, unable to comprehend his desire for freedom and individuality, arrests Leonard Mead. It takes him to a 'psychiatric center' to be processed for his 'crime' of walking in public. In this world, even the most basic act of human independence, like taking a walk, has become an anomaly.

The story ends with Mead being taken away, leaving the reader to reflect on the consequences of a society that has become disconnected from real human interaction and the outside world.

Vocab Vault

Dystopian A fictional society that is undesirable or frightening, often characterised by oppression, control and suffering.

Conformity Behaviour that matches societal norms or, often without individual choice.

Robotic Police Car A machine or automated vehicle that enforces the laws in the story, symbolising the control.

Solitary Existing or living alone, or done alone, without the presence of others.

Autonomous Self-operating or independent

Suspicious Raising doubts or concerns

Isolation Being separated from others

Surveillance The act of watching or monitoring behaviour

Skeletal Outline

Phantoms Ghosts

Puttering Moving out slowly

Theme

In Ray Bradbury's 'The Pedestrian', key themes include technological control and dependence, as the story presents a future where technology dominates and individuality is suppressed. The theme of isolation and conformity is evident as Leonard Mead's evening walks are considered abnormal in a society that values passive entertainment. Dehumanisation is another theme, seen in the cold, mechanical responses of the authorities.

Ultimately, the story critiques a society that sacrifices human connection, individuality, and freedom in favour of technological control. Nature *vs* city is yet another theme where contrast between nature and city life is beautifully depicted with vivid sensory imagery.

Message Conveyed by the Story

The message of 'The Pedestrian' is a warning about the dangers of excessive reliance on technology and its dehumanising effects. Bradbury critiques a society where conformity, passivity, and isolation are enforced.
He emphasised the importance of individuality, human connection, and the value of simple, free experiences like walking.

Style, Tone and Mood

- Style Style is descriptive and concise, with vivid imagery.
- Tone The tone is detached and critical, reflecting the dystopian setting.
- Mood The mood is oppressive with feelings of isolation, fear and loss of freedom.

Title

The title 'The Pedestrian' is justified as it directly relates to the protagonist, Leonard Mead, who enjoys taking solitary walks through the streets. The story is set in a future society where walking has become an unusual activity. In a world dominated by technology, where people are confined indoors, Mead's walking symbolises individuality and freedom.

The title thus highlights the central theme of the story: the clash between personal freedom and a technology-driven, conformist world.

Figures of Speech

- Simile "With only his shadow moving like the shadow of a hawk."
- Metaphor "There was a good crystal frost in the air; it cut the nose and made the lungs."
- Personification "The house were gray and silent."
- Onomatopoeia "Was that a murmur of laughter."
- Alliteration "Stand still. Stay where you are."

EXAM ORIENTED QUESTIONS

TYPE - 1 Multiple Choice Questions

01 Mark

Q.1 Leonard Mead wears sneakers during the night walks to
(a) run faster
(b) keep his feet warm
(c) impress upon the passers by
(d) avoid barking dogs

Q.2 By profession, Leonard is a ....
(a) player (b) writer (c) dancer (d) singer

Q.3 Ray Bradbury's short story 'The Pedestrian', can be best described as .... **(ICSE Specimen 2025)**
(a) utopian (b) dystopian
(c) humorous (d) a fairy tale

Or Which of the following words best describes the world in which Mead lived? **(Competency Based Que.)**
(a) Idyllic (b) Utopian
(c) Dystopian (d) Cheerful

Q.4 What does the author want to convey bay referring to the people in their homes as 'gray phantoms'?
(a) They are old and haggard
(b) They have gray hairs.
(c) They are lifeless
(d) They have no colours in their lives

Q.5 Mead compare his walk to
(a) walk to office (b) a graveyard walk
(c) Both (a) and (b) (d) None of these

Q.6 What does the empty, silent night reflect about Leonard Mead's emotional state?
(a) A sense of loneliness and isolation
(b) A feeling of peace and satisfaction
(c) A lack of purpose
(d) A longing for societal connection

Q.7 What is the societal norm that Leonard Mead does not conform to in 'The Pedestrian'?
(a) Working in an office job
(b) Engaging in nightly walks
(c) Watching television
(d) Reading books

Q.8 Which of the following is reflected by the statement that Leonard Mead was as good as alone?
(a) He was a nonconformist
(b) He was a lonely person
(c) He longed for the company of others
(d) He wished to be like his neighbour

Q.9 How does the police car characterise Leonard Mead's actions when it first encounters him?
(a) Erratic and dangerous
(b) Curious but harmless
(c) A clear violation of societal rules
(d) A threat to society's safety

Q.10 Identify the type of imagery used in the phrase- 'smelling its rusty smell?
(a) Tactile imagery (b) Olfactory imagery
(c) Visual imagery (d) Auditory imagery

Q.11 'He [Mead] was within a block of his destination when the lone car turned a corner quite suddenly ...' means that Mead was .... **(Competency Based Que.)**
(a) blocked by a single car when he suddenly turned the corner
(b) surprised to find a block preventing the single car from turning
(c) destined to be blocked suddenly by a car on a lonely street
(d) close to his home when the car appeared without warning

Q.12 Identify the following best represents the story's critique of technology?
(a) The police car as an unemotional, authoritarian force
(b) Leonard Mead's refusal to use technology
(c) The isolation created by society's dependence on television
(d) All of the above

Q.13 The robotic police car is described as having all of the following except
(a) an emotionless voice
(b) a mechanical nature
(c) a cold, calculating manner
(d) a human like appearance

Q.14 Which of the following statements is not true of Leonard Mead? **(Competency Based Que.)**
(a) He enjoyed walking the streets at night.
(b) He was married to a writer.
(c) He was arrested for being out of his home at night.
(d) He kept all the lights in his home turned on.

Q.15 What does the robotic police car imply about people in the society?

(a) They are all responsible citizens

(b) They are all constantly engaged in meaningful activities

(c) They are all complacent and follow societal rules without question

(d) They are curious about the world around them

Q.16 Select the option which shows the correct relationship between statements (1) and (2).

(Competency Based Que.)

Statement 1 Mead compares walking through the empty, silent streets to walking through a graveyard.

Statement 2 Mead compares the empty street to the dry riverbeds of a windless desert.

(a) Statements 1 and 2 are both true.

(b) Statements 1 and 2 are both false.

(c) Statement 1 is true, and Statement 2 is false.

(d) Statement 1 is false, and Statement 2 is true.

Q.17 What is the final irony of the story?

(a) Leonard Mead is taken away for committing no crime

(b) Leonard Mead escapes unnoticed

(c) The robotic police car realises its mistake

(d) The society eventually changes for the better

Q.18 Explain the significance of the story's title, 'The Pedestrian'?

(a) It highlights the main character's love for walking

(b) It refers to the robotic police car's role in society

(c) It symbolises the passive, mechanical nature of the society

(d) It represents a shift away from individuality towards community

Q.19 Why was Mead's taken away to the Psychiatric centre?

(a) To cure him of his regressive tendencies

(b) To punish him for being a bachelor

(c) To punish him for behaving like a drunkard

(d) None of the above

Q.20 Choose the option that lists the sequence of events from Ray Bradbury's short story, 'The Pedestrian'.

(ICSE 2025)

(i) One night he was nearing home, he was stopped by a police car.

(ii) Since his answer were considered odd and unacceptable, he was forced to enter the car and taken away.

(iv) Leonard Mead loved to walk through the empty sheets at night.

(v) A metallic voice from the car asked him a series of questions.

(a) (ii), (i), (iii), (iv)

(b) (i), (iii), (iv), (ii)

(c) (iii), (i), (iv), (ii)

(d) (iv), (i), (ii), (iii)

Answers

1. (d)	2. (b)	3. (b,c)	4. (c)	5. (b)	6. (a)	7. (c)	8. (b)	9. (c)	10. (b)
11. (d)	12. (d)	13. (d)	14. (b)	15. (c)	16. (a)	17. (a)	18. (c)	19. (a)	20. (c)

TYPE - 2 Extract Based Questions

16 Marks

Extract 1

"The streets were silent and long, with only the faintest whisper of a breeze. He turned back at the intersection, moving slowly. He had walked for an hour, and there was a slight chill in the air. He walked through empty neighbourhoods, streets filled only with the faint smell of burning leaves."

(i) How does Bradbury use symbolism in the story to convey the desolation of the society in which Leonard Mead lives? **(3)**

Ans. Bradbury uses the symbolism, 'eyes of th dead' to describe the dull, lifeless glow of TV screens inside homes. It emphasises the emotional emptiness and passive existence of people in the story's society. Like the dead, they are physically present but mentally and spiritually unengaged, consumed by technology and detached from real life.

(ii) What is the significance of Leonard Mead being the only one walking in this deserted world? **(3)**

Ans. Mead's solitary walk highlights his isolation from the rest of society. His decision to walk in a world where no one else does suggests that he is out of sync with the conformist, technology-dependent world around him. This reinforces the theme of individuality versus conformity.

(iii) What do the 'empty houses' symbolise in the context of the story? **(3)**

Ans. The 'empty houses' symbolise a society that has retreated into passivity, where individuals are metaphorically and physically absent from the world around them. People are no longer engaged in real-life activities or relationships, preferring to be isolated and absorbed by the passive entertainment of television.

(iv) Why does the description of the street as 'empty' have a strong connection to the protagonist's mental state? (3)

Ans. The emptiness of the street mirrors Leonard Mead's mental and emotional state. His loneliness is reflected in the deserted world he walks through. Mead is disconnected from others and lives in a society that has chosen comfort over meaningful interaction or intellectual pursuit, much like the empty homes around him.

(v) How does Bradbury's description of the streetlamps contrast with Leonard Mead's individualism? (4)

Ans. The streetlamps, described as 'eyes of the dead', contrast with Mead's individuality because while he seeks life and engagement through his walks; the streetlamps represent a lifeless society that sees no value in such activity.

Mead's desire to walk, a human activity, stands in stark contrast to the passive, controlled existence represented by the streetlamps.

Extract 2

"He would stand upon the corner of an intersection and peer down long moonlit avenues of sidewalk in four directions, deciding which way to go, but it really made no difference."

(i) What was Leonard Mead's occupation?

What did he love to do?

When is the story set? (ICSE Specimen 2025, 3)

Ans. Leonard Mead's occupation is not explicitly mentioned in the story, but it is implied that he is a writer, as he has the time and inclination to walk around the city at night and enjoy solitary activities. Moreover during the interrogation he claims himself as a writer.

He loves to take long, solitary walks through the city, especially at night, enjoying the quiet and empty streets.

The story is set in a futuristic, dystopian society, possibly in the mid-to-late 21st century, where technology dominates and people have become isolated from each other.

(ii) To what does Mead compare his walk through the empty streets?

Mention two reasons he gives for making this comparison? (3)

Ans. Mead compares his walk through the empty streets to walking through a graveyard.

Two reasons for this comparison are

(a) The streets are empty, silent, and lifeless, just like a graveyard.

(b) There is no human presence, and everything is eerie and still, adding to the feeling of desolation.

(iii) Elaborate on the atmosphere of the story. (3)

Ans. The atmosphere of the story is one of silence and isolation. The protagonist, Leonard Mead is alone on the empty streets during his night walks in the world of AD 2053. The city has a deserted, graveyard look.

(iv) What happened quite suddenly as he was making his way home?

What was Mead's immediate reaction? (3)

Ans. As Mead was making his way home, a robotic police car appeared quite suddenly, turning a corner.

Mead was immediately startled and confused by its appearance, as he did not expect to be confronted by any authority while simply walking.

(v) Why was Mead taken away by the police car? Would you call this a horror story or a piece of science fiction? Give reasons for your answer. (4)

Ans. Mead was taken away by the police car because he was considered suspicious for walking alone at night in a society where people are expected to stay indoors, watching television. The authorities could not understand why anyone would choose to be outside for no reason.

This is a piece of science fiction, not a horror story. It depicts a dystopian future where technology and conformity dominate, and individual freedom is suppressed. The story explores the consequences of a highly controlled society rather than focusing on supernatural or horrific elements.

Extract 3

"... he [Mead] was alone in this world of A.D. 2053, or as good as alone, and with a final decision made, a path selected, he would stride off sending patterns of frosty air before him like the smoke of a cigar."

(i) What was the thing that Leonard Mead 'most dearly loved to do'? (Competency Based Que., 3)

Ans. Mead most dearly loved to go for walks in the streets, especially at night. This activity brings him joy and peace, as it allows him to be alone and think freely.

(ii) Why did Mead switch to wearing sneakers when he went for a walk? **(Competency Based Que., 3)**

Ans. Mead switched to wearing sneakers so that he could walk quietly without making a sound, ensuring he wouldn't be heard and to avoid the barking dogs, lights being switched on, or people peeping out startled.

(iii) What are Mead's neighbours and fellow citizens doing when Mead is out walking?

What can you conclude about Mead from this? **(Competency Based Que., 3)**

Ans. Mead's neighbours and fellow citizens are all inside their homes, watching television. This suggests that society in this future world is isolated and disconnected. People prefer passive activities rather than engaging in anything as active or stimulating as taking a walk.

Mead, in contrast, stands out as an individual who values personal reflection and physical activity. This makes him somewhat of an outsider in this society.

(iv) What reasons does Mead give for being out alone on the street at night?

Why is this viewed with suspicion? **(Competency Based Que., 3)**

Ans. Mead explains that he is out for a walk because he simply enjoys it and finds peace in it. He has no destination in mind and does not engage in any crime or mischief.

However, this is viewed with suspicion because, in a society where everyone is glued to their screens, such behaviour is considered odd or even dangerous. It doesn't fit with the prescribed norms of passivity and conformity.

(v) Where is Mead taken at the end of the story?

Why is he taken to this place? If you had to describe this story in a single word, what word would you use? Give a reason for your choice of word. **(Competency Based Que., 4)**

Ans. At the end of the story, Mead is taken to a psychiatric center because he is considered abnormal for walking alone at night. In this future society, where people are expected to stay indoors and passively consume media, his behaviour is deemed suspicious and mentally unstable.

If I had to describe this story in a single word, I would choose 'conformity'. This word encapsulates the central theme of the story, which explores how a highly controlled society suppresses individuality and punishes anyone who does not conform to its rigid expectations.

Extract 4

"He turned his head, and there was the faintest smile on his lips as he stared up at the enormous face of the empty television screen. There were no other faces but those of the dead."

(i) What is the significance of the 'enormous face of the empty television screen' in this passage? **(3)**

Ans. The 'enormous face of the empty television screen' represents the pervasive influence of technology in society, overshadowing all other forms of interaction or human connection. The fact that it is 'empty' highlights the hollowness and emptiness of the lives of those who are engrossed in their passive consumption of media, reinforcing the dystopian theme of disconnection.

(ii) What do the 'faces of the dead' represent in the context of the story? **(3)**

Ans. The 'faces of the dead' symbolise the metaphorical death of individuality and human engagement in the society. People are so absorbed in their screens that they no longer engage with life in a meaningful way, resulting in an emotional and social death. This is a critique of a society where technology replaces human interaction and fulfillment.

(iii) How does Mead's reaction to the television screen (a smile) contrast with the rest of society? **(3)**

Ans. Mead's faint smile may indicate his awareness of the absurdity of a society consumed by television, or it could reflect his recognition of his role as an outsider.

While others in society may be passively engaged with the screen, Mead retains a semblance of individuality and thought, making him stand out from the passive masses.

(iv) What role does television play in reflecting the society's values and mindset? **(3)**

Ans. Television represents a society that has prioritised passive entertainment over intellectual engagement, creativity, or human connection. It symbolises the societal control mechanisms that keep people disengaged and docile, reinforcing the themes of conformity and isolation in the story.

(v) What might the fact that there are no living 'faces' on the screen suggest about the future of human interaction in this society? **(4)**

Ans. The fact that there are no living faces on the screen suggests that human interaction in this society has disappeared. People no longer talk to each other or connet in real life. Instead, they are isolated, spending all their time watching television. The screen is empty, just like their lives, showing that technology has replaced real relationships. This also hints at a world where emotions and conversations no longer matter. The reference to 'faces of the dead' suggests that people are physically alive but socially and emotionally lifeless, trapped in a world controlled by screens and routines.

Extract 5

" 'What are you doing out here?' asked the officer. 'Just walking,' said Leonard Mead. 'What's wrong with that?' "

(i) What does the interaction between Leonard Mead and the officer reveal about the nature of the society in which Mead lives? (3)

Ans. The interaction highlights a society where deviation from the norm is met with suspicion and interrogation. Mead's innocent activity of walking is perceived as abnormal, showing how the society has become over-regulated and controlled. Even simple, harmless behaviour like walking at night is questioned.

(ii) What does the officer's question imply about societal expectations and the role of individuality? (3)

Ans. The officer's question implies that walking alone at night is suspicious in this society, where everyone is expected to stay indoors and conform to the established routines, particularly watching television.

Individuality is seen as an anomaly or even a threat, and the officer's questioning reflects the societal need for conformity and control.

(iii) How does Leonard Mead's response to the officer, 'just walking', reflect his attitude toward societal norms? (3)

Ans. Mead's response, simple and direct, indicates his disinterest in justifying his actions to a society that has lost its sense of individuality.

He does not see his walk as anything extraordinary or suspicious, showing his resistance to the societal pressures that demand conformity and discourage independent thought or action.

(iv) Where was Mead when he saw a lone car? What was the lone car in actuality? (3)

Ans. While walking Mead was circling around towards his home and was within a block of his destination when the lone car came. The lone was actually a Robotic car.

(v) How does this exchange contribute to the dystopian tone of the story? (4)

Ans. The officer's questioning and the suspicion surrounding Mead's harmless action emphasise the dystopian nature of the society, where conformity is strictly enforced.

Anything outside the norm is treated as suspicious or criminal.

This highlights the oppressive control and the lack of freedom in the world Bradbury has created.

THE LAST LESSON

Alphonse Daudet

Introduction

The Last Lesson is a short story by Alphonse Daudet, a French writer known for his simple yet emotional storytelling. This story highlights the importance of one's mother tongue and the pain of losing it due to foreign rule. The story belongs to the historical fiction genre and stands out for its emotional depth and patriotic theme. Through Franz's experiences, the story reminds readers to value their language and culture before it is too late.

About the Story

The Last Lesson by Alphonse Daudet is set during the Franco-Prussian War when Germany took over Alsace. Franz, a young boy, narrates the story. Initially uninterested in his schoolwork, Franz realises the importance of his native language when he learns that French will no longer be taught.

M. Hamel, the teacher, gives an emotional final lesson, stressing the value of language and culture. Franz feels regret for neglecting his studies and finally understands the significance of education and heritage.

Character Introduction

- **Franz** The story's young narrator, a schoolboy from Alsace, initially indifferent to his studies, especially French.
- **M. Hamel** A dedicated and emotional French teacher, who is delivering his final lesson.
- **The Villagers** Other people from the village who attend the lesson.

Story at a Glance

The story is set in a small village in Alsace, a region annexed by Germany after the Franco-Prussian War. As a result the use of French in schools is banned, and German is imposed as the new language of instruction.

Franz, the protagonist, is a young schoolboy. One day, he arrives late to class, expecting a scolding from his teacher, M. Hamel. However, to his surprise, M. Hamel announces that this will be the last French lesson he will ever teach, as German will be taught from the next day. Some villagers, who once studied under M. Hamel, also attended the class to show respect and to witness this significant moment.

During the lesson, Franz feels regret for not valuing his education earlier. He begins to understand the importance of his mother tongue and feels a deep sense of loss. M. Hamel teaches with great dedication, knowing it is his last chance to instruct in French. At the end of the lesson, as an act of patriotism, he writes ('Long Live France!') on the blackboard.

Franz is deeply moved. He realises that the French language is not just a tool for communication but a link to his culture, identity, and heritage. Reflecting on the lesson, he feels regret for the lost opportunities to learn and a renewed appreciation for his language.

M. Hamel's last lesson is more than a class—it is a powerful reminder of how language embodies a people's identity, culture and pride.

Vocab Vault

Participles Participles are verb forms that function as adjectives, describing or modifying nouns

Drilling Improve skills, or perform tasks with precision

Thunder-clap Something startling

Anxious Feeling worried, nervous, or uneasy about something

Annexed Taken over or added to another country

Dismay Sudden and complete loss of courage due to an unexpected event

Berets A type of traditional French hat

Parchment A type of material used for writing, often used in reference to official documents

Apprentice Trainee

Saar A river in N.E. France

Cranky Ill-tempered

Primer A small book

Solemn Formal

Theme

The central theme of 'The Last Lesson' by Alphonse Daudet is the importance of language as a symbol of identity, culture, and freedom. The story highlights how language connects individuals to their heritage and expresses their collective identity.

Through M. Hamel's last French lesson, the narrative reflects on themes of loss, regret, patriotism, and the value of education.

Message Conveyed by the Story

The message of 'The Last Lesson' by Alphonse Daudet is about the importance of language and culture and the value of education. The story shows how a language is not just a tool for communication but a symbol of identity and freedom. The story reminds us to cherish our language, culture and education before it is too late.

Style, Tone and Mood

- **Style** Daudet uses clear and detailed language to make readers feel the emotions of the characters, like their regret and sadness.
- **Tone** The tone is serious and thoughtful.
- **Mood** Mood is sad and reflective. It becomes very solemn.

Title

The title 'The Last Lesson' is meaningful because it refers to the final French lesson taught by M. Hamel before the Prussian rulers ban the language. It shows the loss of freedom and culture. The title also symbolises regret, realisation and the importance of one's language and identity.

Figures of Speech

- **Metaphor** "What a thunderclap these words were to me!"
- **Personification** "The pigeons cooed very low and I thought to myself, Will they make them sing in German, even the pigeons?"
- **Simile** "Everything had to be as quiet as Sunday morning."
- **Hyperbole** "He had never explained everything with so much patience."
- **Symbolism** "Vive La France!"

EXAM ORIENTED QUESTIONS

TYPE - 1 Multiple Choice Questions

01 Mark

Q.1 Who do you think is the protagonist of the story 'The Last Lesson'?
(a) M. Hamel (b) Franz
(c) The villagers (d) None of these

Q.2 Why did the narrator feel afraid of going to school
(a) He had not learnt Nouns
(b) He had not studied about participles
(c) He had forgotten his assignment at home
(d) None of the above

Q.3 What lesson did Franz have to recite that day?
(a) Tenses (b) Participles (c) Voice (d) Verbs

Q.4 The thought that came to the narrator's mind when he started school was ....
(a) spending the day outside
(b) playing outside
(c) going back to home
(d) None of the above

Q.5 What was Franz expecting when he arrived late to the class?
(a) To be praised by the teacher
(b) To be scolded by M. Hamel
(c) To be sent home
(d) To be allowed to leave school early

Q.6 What was the usual thing that was missing, when the narrator entered the school?
(a) Absolute silence (b) Great bustle
(c) Guards at the door (d) No students

Q.7 Which of the options contains the same literary device that appears in the following line?
"Besides, the whole school seemed so strange and solemn." **(Competency Based Que.)**
(a) The boom of the fireworks scared the baby.
(b) The daffodils were tossing their heads in a sprightly dance.
(c) While I nodded, nearly napping.
(d) Her smile is a ray of sunshine.

Q.8 M. Hamel wears his best clothes on the day of the last lesson ....
(a) to celebrate a personal achievement
(b) to show respect for the occasion
(c) to impress the villagers
(d) to mark the end of his teaching career

Q.9 What important announcement does M. Hamel make in the class?
(a) The school will be closed
(b) The teacher is retiring
(c) French will no longer be taught in the school from the next day
(d) The school will be moving to a new building

Q.10 Why did M. Hamel have to leave the school after forty years of service? **(ICSE 2025)**
(a) He was not allowed to teach French any longer.
(b) He had grown tired of his job as a school teacher.
(c) He was thought to be too strict in his ways.
(d) He wanted to retire and take up farming.

Q.11 Describe the tone of M. Hamel's voice during the lesson.
(a) Angry and loud (b) Soft and gentle
(c) Serious and emotional (d) Humorous

Q.12 How does Franz initially react to the news?
(a) He is indifferent
(b) He becomes sad and regretful
(c) He becomes angry
(d) He is relieved

Q.13 Name the figure of speech used in the line given below. "Besides, the whole school seemed so strange and solemn".
(a) Simile (b) Personification
(c) Metaphor (d) Alliteration

Q.14 'The new master comes tomorrow'. Who was supposed to be the new master?
(a) The teacher who teach them German language.
(b) The Prussian administrators
(c) The new Principal of the school
(d) None of the above

Q.15 The villager's presence at the last lesson contributes to the story's theme as ....
(a) they are attending as a form of protest
(b) they are showing their respect for the teacher and the language
(c) they are there to collect their children's homework
(d) they are excited to learn French

Q.16 How does Franz feel as he listens to M. Hamel's final lesson?

(a) He feels excited

(b) He feels embarrassed

(c) He feels regretful for not learning the language earlier

(d) He feels happy

Q.17 Franz was quite .... to his learning of French language. **(Competency Based Que.)**

(a) serious (b) attentive

(c) indifferent (d) focused

Q.18 Franz's regret was so strong during the lesson because ....

(a) he never enjoyed learning

(b) he was realising how important French is

(c) he has missed his chance to learn German

(d) he is afraid of being punished

Q.19 The atmosphere in the classroom was

(a) cheerful and energetic

(b) tense and argumentative

(c) quiet, somber and reflective

(d) confused and chaotic

Q.20 Choose the option that lists the sequence of events in the correct order. **(Competency Based Que.)**

(i) Every time the young boy looked up from writing, during the last lesson, he found M. Hamel sat motionless in his chair.

(ii) He had put on his fine Sunday clothes as he was delivering his last lesson.

(iii) M. Hamel had also brought new copies written in a beautiful round hand to the class that day.

(iv) The boy noticed that M Hamel, their teacher, was wearing his beautiful green coat, frilled shirt, and the little black silk cap.

(a) (iv), (ii), (iii), (i) (b) (ii), (iii), (iv), (i)

(c) (ii), (iii), (i), (iv) (d) (iii), (i), (ii), (iv)

Q.21 Select the option that shows the correct relationship between statements (1) and (2). **(Competency Based Que.)**

Statement 1 My children, this is the last lesson I shall give you.

Statement 2 The order has come from Berlin to teach only German in the schools of Alsace and Lorraine.

(a) Statement 1 is true, and Statement 2 is false.

(b) Statement 2 is true, and Statement 1 is false.

(c) Statement 1 and Statement 2 are independent of each other.

(d) Statement 2 is the cause for Statement 1.

Q.22 Describe M. Hamel feelings about the imposition of the German language.

(a) He is angry and upset

(b) He feels a sense of loss and sorrow

(c) He is indifferent

(d) He welcomes it

Q.23 M. Hamel writes "Vive La France!" on the blackboard to express ....

(a) love for French language

(b) his anger towards the Germans

(c) his sense of regret for not teaching adequately

(d) his gratitude towards the villagers

Q.24 What does M. Hamel's final lesson teaches the students about language?

(a) Language is just a tool to pass exams

(b) Language should be learned only for practical purposes

(c) Language is a vital part of a person's identity and culture

(d) Language can easily be replaced by any other language

Answers

1. (b)	2. (b)	3. (b)	4. (a)	5. (b)	6. (b)	7. (c)	8. (b)	9. (c)	10. (a)
11. (c)	12. (a)	13. (d)	14. (a)	15. (b)	16. (c)	17. (c)	18. (b)	19. (c)	20. (b)
21. (d)	22. (b)	23. (a)	24. (c)						

Explanations

7. The literary device used in the given line is alliteration. It is the repetition of initial consonant sounds in closely placed words. Similarly, in option (c), there is a repetition of the 'n' sound also demonstrating alliteration.

17. Franz was initially indifferent to learning French. He did not take his studies seriously and often avoided schoolwork. He showed little interest in the language until he realised its importance during M. Hamel's last lesson.

TYPE - 2 Extract Based Questions

16 Marks

Extract 1

Usually, when school began, there was a great bustle, which could be heard out in the street, the opening and closing of desks, lessons repeated in unison, very loud, with our hands over our ears to understand better, and the teacher's great ruler rapping on the table. But now it was all so still! I had counted on the commotion to get to my desk without being seen; but, of course, that day everything had to be as quiet as Sunday morning

(i) But now it was all so still! what does this phrase symbolise in the context of the story? **(3)**

Ans. The absence of the usual village noises is indicated by the given phrase. It symbolises the end of normalcy and the onset of a profound change. It reflects the seriousness of the situation, where the loss of the French language is about to take place, creating a somber and emotional atmosphere that is different from the everyday life of the village.

(ii) How does the setting contribute to the mood of the story? **(3)**

Ans. The stillness and quietness described in the extract contributes to the mood of sadness, loneliness, and introspection.

The lack of normal noise and the quietness in the school mirrors the sense of loss and the emotional weight of the day. It is the last time the children will hear French spoken in class. The silence adds to the feeling of the finality of the event.

(iii) Why does the narrator specifically mention having "without being seen"? How does this affect the reader's understanding of the narrator's state of mind? **(3)**

Ans. The narrator specifically mentions getting to his desk "without being seen" because he is late for school and feels nervous and guilty about it. This detail shows that he is anxious and hopes to avoid punishment or embarrassment in front of his teacher and classmates.

By including this line, the reader understands that the narrator is not only worried about being late, but also about the consequences of it. It reveals his uneasy state of mind—he is tense, self-conscious, and perhaps a little regretful.

(iv) Evaluate the reader's perception of Franz's emotional state. **(3)**

Ans. Franz is experiencing a sense of isolation and sorrow. It indicates that he is beginning to recognise the gravity of the moment—he is emotionally alone in his realisation that this is the last French lesson. It underscores the narrator's growing awareness of the loss of his language and the impact of this cultural shift on his identity.

(v) How does the silence in the classroom contrast with the usual environment?

Analyse what it reveals about the significance of the day. **(4)**

Ans. The silence contrasts sharply with the usual noise of the classroom, which would normally be filled with chatter, laughter, and the sounds of everyday school activities.

This silence emphasises the gravity of the situation–this is not a typical school day, but a moment of historical change.

The silence reveals that something important is happening, marking the end of French instruction and the imposition of German as the language of education.

Extract 2

"My children, this is the last lesson I shall give you.

The order has came from Berlin to teach only German in the schools of Alsace and Lorraine. The new master cames tomorrow. This is your Last French Lesson. I want you to be attentive."

What a thunderclap were there words to me!

Oh the wretches; that was what they had put up at the town-hall! **(ICSE 2025)**

(i) What does the word 'that' in the extact refer to?

What other 'bad-news' had the villagers received from the bulletin board outside the town-hall? **(3)**

Ans. 'That' refers to the notice put at the town-hall by the German government.

The other 'bad news' were, the lost battles, the draft, the orders of the commanding officers.

(ii) How does the narrator describes the daily bustle at the start of a typical schoolday? **(3)**

Ans. Usually, when the school began, there was a great bustle which could be heard in the screats *i.e.*, the opening and closing of the desks, lesson repeated in unison, very loud, with their hands over their ears to understand better, the teacher's great ruler rapping on the table.

(iii) What was different on the morning when he arrived late for school? **(3)**

Ans. That morning when he arrived, it was all so still, there was no usual commotion in the class, everything was as quiet as Sunday morning, classmates were already in their places.

(iv) **What filled the narrator's head when he heard the above announcement?** **(3)**

Ans. The narrator was startled on hearing the announcement. He could now realise that why the bulletin-board was crowded. He was filled with regret and guilt and realised that he could not learn his native language anymore. He regretted for missing his lessons for sake of seeking birds eggs or going sliding on the Saar. All his books and lessons what he considered burden seemed to be his friends now. He also had forgotten Mr. Hamel's ruler and beating.

(v) **What does M. Hamel urge his listeners never to forget?**

M. Hamel writes a few words on the board at the end of the lesson what were they?

What does he hope to inspire through his words and actions on that day? **(4)**

Ans. M. Hamel urged his listeners that French is the most beautiful language and they should always guard it because when people are enslaved, as long as they hold fast to their language it is as if they had the key to their prison.

The words what Hamel wrote were "Vive La France!" Through his words Hamel hoped to convey that Long Live France and the French people should never give up. They should educate themselves to gain freedom.

Extract 3

Poor man! It was in honour of this last lesson that he had put on his fine Sunday clothes, and now I understood why the old men of the village were sitting there in the back of the room. It was because they were sorry, too, that they had not gone to school more. It was their way of thanking our master for his forty years of faithful service and of showing their respect for the country that was theirs no more.

(i) **What does the silence in the classroom and the presence of the villagers suggest about the atmosphere during M. Hamel's last lesson?** **(3)**

Ans. The silence and the presence of the villagers create a deeply emotional and respectful atmosphere. It shows that everyone—young and old—truly values this final lesson. The quietness reflects their shared sorrow and regret, as they realise what they are about to lose. This moment is not just about a lesson, but about saying goodbye to their language and identity.

(ii) **What is the significance of the old men sitting at the back of the classroom during the last lesson?** **(3)**

Ans. The old men's presence at the back of the room symbolises their regret for not valuing school and learning when they were younger. It also shows their deep respect for M. Hamel, who had served the community for forty years. By attending this last lesson, they honour the teacher and show their sorrow for the loss of the French language. It is their way of quietly expressing gratitude and grief.

(iii) **How does the narrator's realisation about the old men's presence affect our understanding of the emotional depth of the scene?** **(3)**

Ans. When the narrator notices the old men and understands why they are there, it changes the way we see the whole moment. It's not just a classroom scene anymore–it becomes a powerful image of a whole village mourning a loss. The narrator's growing awareness helps the reader feel the sadness more deeply, and shows how the moment affects everyone, not just the students.

(iv) **What literary device is used in the phrase "the country that was theirs no more," and how does it enhance the meaning?** **(3)**

Ans. The phrase uses metaphor, suggesting that losing their language means losing their connection to their country and identity. It's not only about territory, but about the heart and soul of who they are as a people. This device adds emotional power and helps the reader understand how deeply the villagers feel the loss of their language and nation.

(v) **How does the image of M. Hamel wearing his "fine Sunday clothes" contribute to the theme of respect and farewell?** **(4)**

Ans. M. Hamel's decision to wear his best clothes shows how seriously he takes this final lesson. He dresses not just with pride, but with a quiet dignity, as though he is marking the day like a special ceremony. It reflects his deep love for teaching and his language, and it helps us see this day as a respectful, heartfelt farewell to both.

Extract 4

"I think, too, that I had never listened so carefully, and that he had never explained everything with so much patience."

(i) **Who are 'I' and 'he' in the above extract?**

What kind of a teacher was 'he'?

(Competency Based Que., 3)

TREASURE CHEST: POETRY

01

HAUNTED HOUSES

Introduction

Haunted Houses is a poem by Henry Wadsworth Longfellow, a famous American poet known for his simple and heartfelt poetry. The poem belongs to the genre of meditative and philosophical poetry. Its central idea is that while the material world is temporary, the spirit world is everlasting. The poem's unique feature is its comforting message that our loved ones never truly leave us but stay with us in our thoughts and memories.

About the Poem

The poem **Haunted Houses** is about the idea that houses where people have lived and died are 'haunted' by memories or spirits of those who once lived there. These 'harmless phantoms' are not scary but are peaceful and quiet, moving silently through the house.

Despite the human occupants, the houses continue to have a subtle presence of these spirits. The spirits represent the memories of those who have lived and died in the house. This establishes a connection between the past and the present.

Exploring the Stanzas

All houses .... upon the floors.

In the first stanza, the poet claims that every house where people have either lived or died is a haunted house. They are not haunted in a horrific sense but they are gentle presences, silently moving through the house. They leave no trace of their presence.

The word 'haunted' does not represent the ghostly quality. It refers to the remains of the past. The imagery of 'harmless phantoms' suggests that the past continues to exist alongside the present. This stanza sets the tone for the poem's exploration of the connection between the material and spiritual worlds.

We meet .... to and fro.

In this stanza, the poet describes the movement of the spirits in various parts of the house like doorways, stairs and hallways. These presences cannot be seen or touched but their movements from one place to another can be felt.

This stanza presents the idea that the spirits are an inseparable part of the house. Usage of words like 'impalpable' and 'impressions' suggest that they exist more as feelings or memories. This reinforces the poem's theme of the past quietly coexisting with the present.

There .... on the wall.

In this stanza, the poet suggests that during gatherings, there are always more 'guests' present than those actually invited. These include quiet, harmless ghosts who are present in the surroundings, as unnoticed and silent as the pictures on the walls.

This stanza highlights the poet's idea that the spirits of the past remain present in the daily life, even in joyful moments like celebrations. Comparing the ghosts to 'pictures on the wall' highlights their stillness and invisibility.

The stranger .... and clear.

In this stanza, poet states that stranger around the fireplace cannot see or hear the presence of ghosts like the poet does. However, he can recognise their presence. The stranger might be aware of the presence of these ghosts at the fireside but the poet is aware of the history of his surroundings.

This stanza emphasises the poet is more sensitive to his surroundings. He can sense the invisible connections between the past and the present. The contrast between the stranger and the poet highlights the theme of a dual reality—one seen by ordinary eyes and another perceived by the introspective or imaginative mind.

We have .... old estates.

In this stanza, the poet states that the living survivors have no legal ownership over the houses or land. Instead, the ownership is held by previous inhabitants or the dead ancestors of the house.

This stanza highlights the impermanent nature of human ownership and the permanent presence of the past.

The phrase 'dusty hands' refers to those who lived before, while 'mortmain' refers to the idea that the dead still influence the living world.

The spirit-world .... ethereal air.

In this stanza, the poet describes that the spirit world moves around us like an atmosphere and brings out a more refined and purer air. The ethereal life which enters our perceptive mind enriches our understanding and experience. This stanza introduces the spiritual realm as something coexisting with the physical world.

Our little .... that aspires.

In this stanza, the poet states that there is a balance in human life, which is maintained by opposing forces of our desires for pleasure and our more noble aspirations. These instincts create a constant inner struggle, shaping our lives.

However, this balance of basic instincts gives us both enjoyment and spiritual experience. The struggle between these instincts is central to human experience as it shapes the choices that people make in their life.

These perturbations
.. in our sky.

In this stanza, the poet suggests that the constant conflict between earthly desires and higher aspirations is caused by the influence of an unseen force like an undiscovered star or planet in the sky. This force creates the tension in human life.

The mention of something 'undiscovered' suggests that the source of this conflict is mysterious and not fully understood. This reinforces the theme of the tension between the earthly and the spiritual.

And as the .... and night.

In this stanza, the poet describes that the moonlight throws a bridge of light over the sea.

It is compared to a spiritual bridge connecting the world of spirits with the physical world. This bridge allows our thoughts to enter the mysterious realm of the unknown.

So from .... dark abyss.

In this stanza, the poet states that the world of spirits is far away yet it is reachable. This world also descends a bridge of light which connects us to it. This shows that the dead never really die and they live around us. They also influence our present lives.

Through this stanza, the poet shows the search for meaning and understanding. It also shows the interplay between what is known and what is unknown.

Theme of the Poem

The central theme of 'Haunted Houses' is the lasting influence of the past on the present. The poem shows how the physical and spiritual worlds exist together and affect each other. It reassures us that the spirits of our loved ones remain with us. Their presence brings comfort, reminding us that they are never truly gone. The poem highlights the connection between the seen and unseen worlds.

Message Conveyed by the Poem

The poem conveys a message that the past is never truly gone. The memories, experiences and influences of those who are dead continue to shape our lives. Longfellow urges readers to acknowledge the presence of these 'ghosts' as important parts of the journey of life. They remind us that the material world and the spiritual realm are interconnected.

Style, Tone and Mood

- **Style** The poem consists of several stanzas, each contributing to the development of the central theme. Longfellow employs a simple yet effective rhyming scheme - ABAB throughout the stanzas.
- **Tone** The tone of the poem is reflective and meditative, marked by a sense of quiet reverence for the past.
- **Mood** The mood is calm, yet it carries an underlying sense of mystery as the poet contemplates the invisible presence of spirits.

Title

The title 'Haunted Houses' is justified because it reflects the poem's theme of how homes are 'haunted' by the lingering memories and influences of those who have lived and died there. The poem connects the physical world with the spiritual realm. Thus, the title captures the essence of the poem, emphasising the permanence of the spiritual world.

Literary Devices

- **Metaphor** 'Haunted Houses' is an extended metaphor for remnants of past ***[Stanza 1]***
  - And as the moon from some dark gate of cloud
  - Throws o'er the sea a floating bridge of light.
  - The comparison of the spirit world to an 'atmosphere' ***[Stanza 6]***
  - This perpetual jar/Of earthly wants and aspirations high denoting the immortal soul ***[Stanza 8]***
  - The descent of a "bridge of light" ***[Stanza 9/10]***
- **Personification** The concept of houses being 'haunted' personifies the dwellings, attributing human-like qualities of being influenced or marked by the spirits of those who lived and died within them. ***[Stanza 1]***
  - From graves forgotten stretch their durty hands.
  - Wander our throughts above the dark abyss.
- **Simile** "Inoffensive ghosts, As silent as the pictures on the wall." ***[Stanza 3]***
  - Floats like and atmosphere
- **Alliteration** Haunted Houses ***[Title, Stanza 1]***
  - A sense of something moving to and fro
  - From graves forgotten.
  - Our little lives.
- **Assonance** "Impalpable impressions on the air," ***[Stanza 2]***
- **Enjambment** "All houses wherein men have lived and died/Are haunted houses."

  ["Through the open doors/The harmless phantoms on their errands glide, /With feet that make no sound upon the floors."]

REVISION NOTES

Vocab Vault

Phantoms Something that can be sensed but has no real existence

Errands To do a task that involves going somewhere

Impalpable Unable to be felt by touch

Title-deeds Legal documents that prove ownership of property, such as land or a house.

Mortmain A legal term which refers to property that is controlled or held by the dead, symbolising the ongoing claim the dead have over their former possessions, even after death.

Wafts Moves gently through the air, like a soft breeze or fragrance.

Ethereal Light, delicate, or heavenly, often used to describe something beyond the physical world.

Equipoise A state of balance or equality between opposing forces.

Perturbations Disturbances or in a state of calm; disruptions.

Fancies Imagination or thoughts, representing the human mind's ability to wander into the unknown.

Realm A domain or kingdom, used here to represent the world of mystery and the unknown.

Abyss A deep, seemingly bottomless space, symbolising mystery, danger or the unknown.

EXAM ORIENTED QUESTIONS

TYPE - 1 Multiple Choice Questions

01 Mark

Q.1 Which of the following does H.W Longfellow use to describe the movement of the phantoms in his poem?

(a) Slide (b) Glide
(c) Noiseless (d) Invisible

Q.2 How does the imagery of 'feet that make no sound' enhance the portrayal of the phantoms?

(a) It suggests their subtle, ethereal nature.
(b) It implies they are afraid of being noticed.
(c) It highlights their skill in sneaking.
(d) It makes them seem menacing and stealthy

Q.3 The ghosts/phantoms in H.W Longfellow's Haunted Houses are described as

(a) harmless (b) mischievous
(c) malevolent (d) vengeful

Q.4 The poet uses the phrase 'open doors' in describing the house ....

(a) to show that the ghosts are free to come and go.
(b) to imply the house is abandoned and desolate.
(c) to suggest that the living are welcoming the ghosts.
(d) to highlight the physical state of the house.

Q.5 Who enter through the open doors of houses?

(a) Ancestors (b) Phantoms
(c) Ethereal air (d) Thoughts

Q.6 When the ghosts cannot be seen or heard, how are they perceived in the house

(a) A gleam of light
(b) A gust of wind
(c) A sense of something
(d) A shadow on the wall

Q.7 Which of the following is not true about the 'Haunted Houses?

(a) They are visited by spirits
(b) They are visited by guests
(c) They are deserted
(d) Strangers are entertained

Q.8 What mood is created by the description of 'harmless phantoms on their errands'?

(a) Ominous and eerie (b) Calm and reflective
(c) Tense and suspenseful (d) Joyful and lighthearted

Q.9 Ghosts are compared to .... in the illuminated hall?

(a) shadows on the walls (b) quiet whispers
(c) pictures on the wall (d) flickering lights

Q.10 Which of the following options contains the same literary device as the given verse from the poem?

'As silent as the pictures on the wall'

(Competency Based Que.)

(a) Because I could not stop for death. He kindly stopped for me.
(b) Where the mind is without fear, and the head is held high.
(c) Soon, the sun's warmth makes them shed crystal shells, shattering and avalanching on the snow crust
(d) Some are like fields of sunlit corn.

Q.11 Why do you think the poet describes the ghosts as 'inoffensive'?
(a) To emphasise their harmless and peaceful nature.
(b) To highlight their frustration with the living.
(c) To suggest that they are trying to blend in with the living.
(d) To show that they are powerless to act.

Q.12 The theme that the phrase 'A sense of something moving to and fro' conveys is ....
(a) the cyclical nature of life and death
(b) the disruption caused by the supernatural
(c) the inevitability of forgetting the past
(d) the tangible presence of spirits in the living world

Q.13 How does the poet's use of the term 'illuminated hall' juxtapose the presence of the ghosts?
(a) It highlights the ghosts' transparency against the brightness.
(b) It contrasts the ghosts' quiet nature with the lively light.
(c) It symbolises how ghosts bring darkness into the light.
(d) It reflects the tension between the living and the dead.

Q.14 The phrase 'title-deeds to house or lands' brings in a sense of
(a) ethereal quality (b) philosophy
(c) materialism (d) None of these

Q.15 What does the phrase 'while unto me, all that has been is visible and clear' suggest about the poet's perception?
(a) The poet has a heightened sensitivity to the past.
(b) The poet is haunted by unresolved issues.
(c) The poet is indifferent to the presence of ghosts.
(d) The poet is imagining events that never happened.

Q.16 What mood does the description of 'graves forgotten' and 'dusty hands' evoke?
(a) Nostalgic and sorrowful
(b) Haunting and eerie
(c) Reflective and somber (d) Joyful and serene

Q.17 Why might the poet describe the ghosts as holding their old estates in 'mortmain'?
(a) To suggest that the past's grip on the present is unyielding.
(b) To imply the ghosts actively haunt the living.
(c) To show that the estates are no longer significant.
(d) To argue for the legal ownership of the dead.

Q.18 Human lives are in 'equipoise', according to the poet. What keeps them so?
(a) The balance of physical and spiritual desires
(b) The guidance of the spirit world
(c) The struggle between enjoyment and aspiration
(d) The influence of the unseen star

Q.19 What tone does the poet adopt while discussing the spirit world and its influence on life?
(a) Mournful and despairing
(b) Reflective and contemplative
(c) Hopeful and optimistic
(d) Skeptical and questioning

Q.20 The poet uses the metaphor of 'an undiscovered planet in our sky' to describe the spiritual influence on life ....
(a) to emphasise its mystery and inaccessibility
(b) to critique human ignorance of the divine
(c) to suggest that spirituality is separate from physical life
(d) to highlight its visibility to the spiritually awakened

Q.21 Which theme is central to the poet's use of the metaphor of 'a bridge of light'?
(a) The connection between the physical and spiritual worlds
(b) The fleeting nature of spiritual enlightenment
(c) The unattainable ideal of human balance
(d) The isolation of the spiritual realm from human existence

Q.22 How do the 'realm of mystery and night' and 'dark abyss' contribute to the mood of the poem?
(a) They create a tone of fear and foreboding.
(b) They evoke a sense of wonder and curiosity about the unknown.
(c) They highlight the poet's skepticism about the spiritual world.
(d) They emphasise the poet's longing for understanding.

Q.23 Which of the following is not associated with the spirits in the poem?
(a) They glide (b) They throng
(c) They waft (d) They wail

Q.24 What are needed to be kept in balance in our little lives?
(a) Divine justice
(b) The presence of the spirits of ancestors
(c) Opposite attractions and desires
(d) None of the above

Q.25 Who among the following can cross the 'Bridge of light'?
(a) Earthly beings (b) The spirits
(c) The Holy men (d) None of these

Q.26 The poet uses tone and imagery to portray the spiritual connection described in the stanza. How does he do so?
(a) By using mysterious and reflective imagery to evoke a contemplative tone
(b) By creating fearful and dark imagery to evoke dread
(c) By employing direct and simple language to clarify the connection
(d) By using lighthearted and optimistic imagery to inspire hope

Q.27 The atmosphere created in the poem 'Haunted Houses' is **(Competency Based Que.)**
(a) melancholic (b) eerie
(c) peaceful (d) unsettling

Q.28 Select the option that shows the correct relationship between statements (1) and (2).
Statement 1 The poet perceives ghosts and sounds that others cannot see or hear.
Statement 2 The stranger at the fireside shares the poet's experience of the spirit world.
(a) Statement 1 is true and Statement 2 is false.
(b) Statement 1 is false and Statement 2 is true.
(c) Both statements are true.
(d) Both statements are false.

Q.29 What is the correct sequence that best reflects the movement of thought in the poem?
1. The poet contemplates the invisible spiritual realm
2. The poet describes the presence of ghosts in a house The poet reflects on the balancing forces in human lives
3. The spiritual world and the material world are connected by a bridge of light.

(a) 1, 2, 3 (b) 2, 3, 1
(c) 1, 3, 2 (d) 3, 1, 2

Q.30 Which of the following lines contains the same literary, device as, 'From graves forgotten stretch their dusty hands'.
(a) Ten thousand saw I at a glance
Tossing their heads in springhtly dance.
(b) Last week in someone's place we saw
A dozen eyeballs on the floor.
(c) Lustrous tokens of radian lives
For happy daughters and happy wives.
(d) In triumphs, people have dropped down dead.

Answers

1. (b)	2. (a)	3. (a)	4. (a)	5. (b)	6. (a)	7. (d)	8. (b)	9. (c)	10. (d)
11. (a)	12. (b)	13. (c)	14. (c)	15. (a)	16. (c)	17. (a)	18. (c)	19. (b)	20. (a)
21. (a)	22. (b)	23. (d)	24. (c)	25. (b)	26. (a)	27. (c)	28. (a)	29. (a)	30. (a)

Explanations

10. The given verse from the poem, 'As silent as the pictures on the wall' uses simile as it compares 'silent' to 'pictures on the wall' using 'as'. The phrase 'some are like fields of sunlit corn' uses simile as it compares something to 'fields of sunlit corn' using the word 'like'.

19. The poet's tone is reflective and contemplative which suggests a thoughtful exploration of the topic.
It encourages readers to ponder over the relationship between the spiritiual and physical realms.

30. The given line from the poem uses personification, using human qualities for graves. The line 'Ten thousand ...... dance' also uses personification as it attributes human qualities to daffodils.

TYPE - 2 Extract Based Questions

16 Marks

Extract 1

All houses wherein men have lived and died
Are haunted houses.Through the open doors
The harmless phantoms on their errands glide
With feet that make no sound upon the floors.

(i) **What is the significance of the phrase 'haunted houses' in the context of the poem?** **(3)**

Ans. In the context of the poem, the phrase 'haunted houses' does not refer to ghostly, vengeful spirits but to the lingering presence of memories and past experiences. Longfellow suggests that all houses where people have lived and died are 'haunted' because they are filled with the invisible, subtle 'phantoms' of the past.

We derive our values and traditions from the memory and influence of our dead ancestors.

(ii) **How does the poet use the imagery of 'harmless phantoms' and 'feet that make no sound' to convey his message?** **(3)**

Ans. The poet uses the imagery of 'harmless phantoms' and 'feet that make no sound' to suggest that the presence of the past is not frightening or intrusive but gentle and subtle.

The 'phantoms' glide silently, symbolising the quiet, persistent influence of memories and experiences left behind by those who have passed.

This emphasises that the spirits of the past are not to be feared but are simply an ever-present part of life that continues to affect the living in a silent, non-threatening way.

(iii) **What role do the 'open doors' play in the poem? What do they imply?** **(3)**

Ans. The 'open doors' in the poem symbolise the gateway between the physical world and the world of memories and spirits. They are an entry point through which the 'harmless phantoms' glide, suggesting that the past is always accessible and continues to influence the present.

The open doors also imply that these memories and experiences are not shut out but are allowed to enter and remain with the living, constantly shaping their lives.

(iv) **Give any three characteristic features of the phantoms as mentioned in the poem Haunted Houses.** **(ICSE Specimen 2025, 3)**

Ans. Three characteristic features of the phantoms in the poem Haunted Houses are

(a) **Harmlessness** The phantoms are 'harmless', causing no fear or harm.

(b) **Invisibility** They are described as 'impalpable impressions on the air', meaning they cannot be seen, only sensed.

(c) **Silent Movement** The phantoms glide 'with feet that make no sound', emphasising their quiet, ghostly nature.

(v) **What does the silence of the phantoms contribute to the overall tone of the poem?**
How does it portray a different view of the poet about memory and identity? **(4)**

Ans. The silence of the phantoms contributes to a tone of calmness and serenity. The lack of sound emphasises the gentle and unobtrusive nature of the ghosts, portraying them as peaceful and non-threatening.

This enhances the contemplative mood of the poem, suggesting that the presence of the past is felt subtly rather than through loud or disruptive means. This silence reflects the poet's view of memory and identity as something that subtly and quietly persists over time.

Rather than being loud or overwhelming, memories and identities are 'harmless' and often 'glide' in and out of our lives. This portrayal implies that our past experiences and the people who shaped us remain an indelible part of our identity. They are part of the ongoing flow of life, quietly shaping who we are without overwhelming us.

Extract 2

We meet them at the doorway,on the stair,
Along the passages, they come and go
Impalpable impressions on the air
A sense of something moving to and fro.

(i) **How does the poet's use of the term 'impalpable impressions' contribute to the thematic depth of the poem, particularly in relation to memory and the past?** **(3)**

Ans. The term 'impalpable impressions' refers to something that cannot be physically touched or grasped, emphasising the intangible nature of memory and the past. This choice of words deepens the theme of the poem by highlighting how the past cannot be easily perceived through the senses.

Instead of being a physical presence, the memories or 'phantoms' are felt through subtle impressions. The use of 'impalpable' thus underscores the idea that the influence of the past remains ever-present like an invisible force that is constantly at work.

(ii) **Analyse how the line 'A sense of something moving to and fro' contributes to the central motif of continuity in the poem.** **(3)**

Ans. 'A sense of something moving to and fro' evokes the idea of constant, uninterrupted motion, symbolising the ongoing and cyclical nature of memories, thoughts, and spirits. The 'to and fro' motion suggests that the past is not fixed or final but remains in flux, continuously re-entering the present in various forms. This continuous movement reinforces the poem's central motif of continuity—how the influence of the past persists, fluctuating between presence and absence.

(iii) **Discuss the significance of the locations mentioned in the stanza— "the doorway, on the stair, along the passages"—in terms of their symbolic representation in the poem.** **(3)**

Ans. The locations mentioned 'the doorway,' 'on the stair', and 'along the passages'—are symbolic of transitional spaces. A doorway represents a threshold between different states of human mind, suggesting the point where the past enters the present.

The stair signifies movement, metaphorically representing the flow between the physical and the spiritual realms.

Passages are symbolic of a journey or transition over time, highlighting the idea that the past is ever-present, moving through different stages and spaces in one's life.

Collectively, these locations symbolise the fluidity of time and the idea of continuity the material world and the spiritual world.

(iv) **How does the poet's choice of the word 'meet' in "We meet them at the doorway" reflect the interaction between the living and the past in the poem?** **(3)**

Ans. The word 'meet' is significant because it implies a deliberate or conscious encounter with the past.

This suggests that the presence of memories or spirits is not passive but something that the speaker actively experiences.

It evokes a sense of transience and adds to the poem's contemplative tone, highlighting the impermanence of life and the quiet persistence of memories or spirits within our daily lives.

(v) **In your opinion, why might the poet have chosen to describe the ghosts as part of the everyday setting of the hall rather than depicting them as other worldly beings? What theme does this choice highlight?** **(4)**

Ans. The poet likely chose to describe the ghosts as part of the everyday setting to show their connection to the familiar, rather than as distant, supernatural beings.

By placing them in ordinary spaces like the 'doorway' and 'passages', the poet blurs the line between the living and the dead, suggesting that spirits are part of the environment.

This highlights the theme of the persistence of the past and the continuity of life, making the supernatural feel less frightening and more reflective.

Extract 3

There are more guests at table than the hosts
Invited; the illuminated hall
Is thronged with quiet, inoffensive ghosts,
As silent as the pictures on the wall.

(i) **What does the phrase 'more guests at table than the hosts invited' suggest?** **(3)**

Ans. The phrase suggests that there are more guests on the table than expected and invited by the host for the party. The 'guests' are not physical, living people, but rather spirits of all dead ancestors who have joined in the celebrations.

(ii) **How does the description of the hall as 'illuminated' affect the tone of the poem?** **(3)**

Ans. The description of the hall as 'illuminated' creates a sense of light and openness, which contrasts with the ghostly presence that fills it.

The tone of the phrase is reflective, where the warmth of the present is intertwined with the ever-lasting but non-threatening influence of past memories. Symbolically, the illuminated hall is our mind which is charged with the memories of the dead.

(iii) **What is the significance of describing the ghosts as 'quiet' and 'inoffensive'?** **(3)**

Ans. Describing the ghosts as 'quiet' and 'inoffensive' highlights their non-threatening nature. Instead of being scary or disruptive, the ghosts represent the lingering presence of the past, which is gentle and not intended to cause harm.

(iv) **Which figure of speech is used in the last line of the extract? Explain and Analyse.** **(3)**

Ans. The comparison of ghosts to 'pictures on the wall' in the last line uses simile. In a simile, two different things are compared to each other with the use of the word 'as'. Just as pictures remain fixed and unmoving, the ghosts symbolise the past that is not actively changing the present but rather remains silently in the background.

This comparison enhances the overall theme of the poem.

(v) **How do the poet's views of ghosts differ from the traditional perception of ghosts? How would you describe the mood that the poem evokes? Give one reason for your answer.** **(ICSE Specimen 2025, 4)**

Ans. The poet's view of ghosts differs from the traditional perception by portraying them as harmless and silent, rather than frightening. Instead of scaring, these ghosts represent the continuity of the past and memory, gently influencing the present. The mood of the poem is calm and reflective, with a touch of melancholy.

The ghosts are described as part of the natural setting, not menacing, creating an atmosphere of peaceful contemplation rather than fear. This contrasts with the usual eerie portrayal of ghosts.

Extract 4

The stranger at my fireside cannot see
The forms I see, nor the sounds I hear
He but perceives what is; while unto me
All that has been is visible and clear

(ICSE Specimen 2025)

(i) **What makes the poet-narrator different from the stranger at the 'fireside'?**

Or How is the speaker's perception different from that of the stranger? **(Competency Based Que., 3)**

Ans. The poet-narrator differs from the stranger at the 'fireside' in their perception of reality. The poet-narrator sees the past as vivid and clear, integrating it into their present understanding, while the stranger only perceives the immediate, present reality.

This gives the poet-narrator a deeper emotional and historical connection to the world, unlike the stranger, who has a more shallow, limited view.

(ii) **What, according to the poet, turns a house into a haunted house?**

Or Why does the poet feel that all houses are haunted? **(Competency Based Que., 3)**

Ans. According to the poet, a house becomes a haunted house because it holds the memories and legacies of those who have lived and died there.

The influence of past owners and occupants lingers in the house, even after their deaths, as their 'harmless phantoms' continue to glide through the space.

The past, through memories and the presence of the deceased, makes the house feel alive with the spirits of those who once lived there, turning it into a haunted place.

(iii) **Where is one likely to meet the phantoms in the house?**

Or Where in the house do we meet these phantoms? **(Competency Based Que., 3)**

Ans. One is likely to meet the phantoms in everyday places around the house, such as at the doorway, on the stair, and along the passages. The poet suggests that the phantoms move freely throughout the house, gliding silently and subtly, often in places where one would expect to encounter others, blending seamlessly with the surroundings.

(iv) **What are the poet's views on owning property?** **(3)**

Ans. The poet's views on owning property suggest that ownership is not permanent or solely in the hands of the living. Through the idea of 'harmless phantoms' and 'mortmain', the poet emphasises that even after death, the influence of past owners and occupants persists, symbolising that property is never truly owned outright by the living.

The dead continue to hold sway over the land or house, implying that ownership is a temporary, passing concept, while the past remains connected to the present.

(v) **Who is 'I' in the above stanza, and who is referred to as 'he' in the third line of the stanza?**
Who is the present occupant of the house?

(Competency Based Que., 4)

Ans. 'I' refers to the poet-narrator, who sees and hears the presence of the past, such as memories, ghosts, or forms that others cannot perceive. 'He' refers to the stranger who is unfamiliar with the house and its history.

The present occupant of the house is the poet-narrator, who is aware of both the past and the present. The stranger, in contrast, represents someone disconnected from the history and deeper memory of the house, focusing only on the immediate, visible reality.

Extract 5

We have no title-deeds to house or lands;
Owners and occupants of earlier dates
From graves forgotten stretch their dusty hands,
And hold in mortmain still their old estates.

(i) **Who are the 'owners and occupants of earlier dates' referred to in the poem?** **(3)**

Ans. The 'owners and occupants of earlier dates' refer to the people who lived in the past and owned or occupied the land before the current generation. These individuals have passed away, yet their influence or claim to the land continues to persist in the form of memories, traditions or legal claims.

(ii) **What is the significance of the phrase 'stretch their dusty hands' in the context of the poem?** **(3)**

Ans. The phrase 'stretch their dusty hands' conveys the idea that the past reaches out to the present. The word 'dusty' emphasises death and decay, while 'hands' symbolises the ever-lasting, omnipresent influence of those who have passed.

This suggests that the dead still have a hold on what they once owned, even though they are forgotten, highlighting the permanence of history and the past.

(iii) **What figure of speech is used in the phrase 'hold in mortmain still their old estates,' and how does it enhance the poem's theme? (3)**

Ans. The figure of speech here is metonymy. 'Mortmain' refers to property that is held by a deceased person or their heirs, symbolising the continuing influence of the dead on the land.

By using 'mortmain' in place of the more direct reference to death or inheritance, the poet highlights the idea that the past–through legal or ancestral means–still controls or holds sway over the present. It enhances the theme of the persistence of the past and its control over the present.

(iv) **How does the idea of the past holding sway over the present relate to the overall theme of the poem? (3)**

Ans. The idea that the past holds sway over the present is central to the poem's overall theme. The poem explores how the deceased continue to influence the present world, especially in the context of property and memory.

The ghosts are not frightening but 'inoffensive' and 'silent', suggesting that the past lingers quietly in the present. This highlights the poet's view that history, memory, and legacy are not easily erased and continue to shape current reality.

(v) **What is the mood created by this stanza? (4)**

Ans. The mood created by this stanza is one of melancholy and reflection. The poet reflects on the idea that ownership of land or property is not permanent, as the influence of the dead still lingers.

The phrase 'stretch their dusty hands' evokes a sense of decay and the passage of time, while the mention of 'graves forgotten' creates a feeling of loss and absence.

This mood suggests that the past, though forgotten, continues to hold sway over the present, giving the stanza a reflective, somewhat somber tone.

Extract 6

The spirit-world around this world of sense
Floats like an atmosphere, and everywhere
Wafts through these earthly mists and vapours dense
A vital breath of more ethereal air.

(i) **What figure of speech is used in 'floats like an atmosphere'?**

How does it contribute to the overall meaning of the poem? (3)

Ans. This is a simile, where the spirit-world is being compared to an atmosphere using the word 'like'.

The comparison suggests that the spirit-world surrounds the physical world in a subtle, invisible manner, similar to the way air surrounds us.

It contributes to the poem's theme of the unseen forces that exist beyond the material world, emphasising the idea that the spirit-world is always present, but only perceptible through deeper, non-sensory understanding.

(ii) **What role do the 'earthly mists and vapours dense' play in the poet's view of the relationship between the physical and spiritual worlds? (3)**

Ans. The 'earthly mists and vapours dense' serve as symbols of the obstacles that hinder our perception of the spiritual realm. The poet suggests that the physical world, with its distractions and material concerns, clouds our understanding of the deeper, spiritual forces that exist around us.

This highlights the theme of the poem that the spiritual world is ever-present but not always accessible to the human senses, encouraging a more intuitive or reflective approach to understanding it

(iii) **How does the poet describe the air of the spirit-world? (3)**

Ans. The poet describes the air of the spirit-world as a 'vital breath of more ethereal air'. This suggests that the air of the spirit-world is not only more delicate and intangible (as indicated by the word 'ethereal') but also life-giving and pure, in contrast to the dense and material nature of the physical world.

The use of the word 'vital' emphasises the importance and energy of the spirit-world's air, highlighting its difference from the mundane, earthly realm.

(iv) **In what way does the contrast between the 'earthly mists' and the 'ethereal air' reflect the central theme of the poem? (3)**

Ans. The contrast between the 'earthly mists' and 'ethereal air' underscores the theme of the poem that the material and spiritual realms are distinct yet interconnected.

The 'earthly mists' represent the dense, often limiting nature of the physical world, while the 'ethereal air' symbolises the purity and transcendence of the spiritual world.

This duality reflects the poet's view that the material world may obscure our awareness of the spiritual, yet the two realms coexist and influence each other.

(v) **What is the theme reflected in this stanza? (4)**

Ans. The stanza talks about the spirit-world existing around our physical world, just like an atmosphere surrounding the earth. It suggests that beyond what we see and feel, there is a deeper, unseen reality. This spirit-world is present everywhere, even though our world is often covered in mist and vapours, symbolizing confusion or lack of awareness. The stanza also describes a vital breath of ethereal air, which means that this unseen world brings life, energy and purity beyond the material world. The theme reflects the connection between the spiritual and physical realms, emphasising their coexistence and influence.

Extract 7

Our little lives are kept in equipoise
By opposite attractions and desires;
The struggle of the instinct that enjoys,
And the more noble instinct that aspires

(i) How does the phrase 'Our little lives are kept in equipoise' reflect the poet's views on life and its balance? (3)

Ans. The phrase 'Our little lives are kept in equipoise' reflects the poet's view that life is fragile and delicately balanced. The word 'equipoise' suggests a state of equilibrium or balance, implying that human lives, though seemingly insignificant or small ('little'), are held in a delicate harmony between different forces, possibly between the material and spiritual realms.

This view implies that life is precarious and dependent on a subtle, often invisible equilibrium, encouraging reflection on the fragility and transient nature of human existence.

(ii) Explain the significance of the 'opposite attractions and desires' mentioned in the poem. (3)

Ans. The 'opposite attractions and desires' symbolise the conflict within human nature. On one hand, there is the instinct for pleasure and enjoyment (represented by the enjoyment instinct) and on the other, there is the noble instinct for higher ideals, such as ambition, self-improvement or moral growth.

These opposing forces keep a person in balance and create inner tension, shaping the complexity of human experience.

(iii) What do you think the poem symbolises? Is there any deeper meaning involved? (3)

Ans. The poem 'Haunted Houses' symbolises the connection between the material and spiritual realms, exploring the lasting impact of the past. The ghosts in the poem represent memories and past lives that continue to influence the present, suggesting that the spirit-world subtly affects our lives.

It reflects the fragility of human existence, with the balance of life maintained by invisible forces, as seen in the idea of 'ethereal air'.

The poem also comments on the impermanence of material wealth, emphasising that ownership is temporary, as the past lingers through memory and legacy.

(iv) What can bring about the superior state of mind according to the poet? (3)

Ans. According to the poet in 'Haunted Houses', a superior state of mind can be achieved through an awareness of the spiritual realm and the continuity of life beyond the physical world.

The poet suggests that understanding the presence of memories, past lives, and spiritual influences can elevate one's perception and lead to a deeper, more balanced state of mind.

(v) What theme does the extract highlight in terms of human nature? (4)

Ans. The extract highlights the conflict within human nature between desire and aspiration. On one side, people have an instinct to seek pleasure and enjoy life's comforts. On the other, they have a higher instinct that pushes them toward growth, nobility and self-improvement. These opposing forces create a balance in life, shaping decisions and actions. The struggle between immediate satisfaction and long-term goals is a key part of being human. This duality keeps life in equipoise, meaning a delicate balance. The poem suggests that both instincts are important and life is about managing these contrasting forces wisely.

Extract 8

These perturbations, this perpetual jar
Of earthly wants and aspirations high,
Come from the influence of an unseen star
An undiscovered planet in our sky.

(i) What is meant by the 'perturbations' and 'perpetual jar'? (3)

Ans. 'Perturbations' and 'perpetual jar' refer to the constant struggles and inner conflicts in life. People feel unsettled because of the clash between earthly desires and higher aspirations. This restlessness is compared to the pull of an unseen force, like a hidden planet, influencing human thoughts and emotions without being fully understood.

(ii) How does the poet link the inner conflict of human life to celestial forces in the poem? (3)

Ans. The poet suggests that the inner conflict between earthly wants and aspirations is influenced by an 'unseen star' or an 'undiscovered planet'.

This metaphor implies that external, cosmic, or spiritual forces beyond human understanding play a role in shaping the inner turmoil and struggles humans face.

(iii) **How do the 'earthly wants' and 'aspirations high' relate to the central themes of the poem? (3)**

Ans. The 'earthly wants' and 'aspirations high' represent the dual nature of human existence-the tension between material desires and spiritual or moral goals.

The struggle between these opposing forces is a central theme in the poem, as it reflects the inner conflict people experience in their efforts to achieve balance in life.

The contrast between immediate gratification and higher, noble aspirations mirrors the poem's broader exploration of how individuals navigate the challenges of maintaining equilibrium between the physical and spiritual realms.

(iv) **What is the metaphysical aspect reflected in the extract? (3)**

Ans. In this stanza, imagination is connected to the supernatural world in a seamless manner. It feels as if both the worlds are blending into each other.

(v) **Why are we affected by these perturbations? (4)**

Ans. We are affected by these perturbations because of the constant conflict between our earthly desires and higher aspirations. Humans struggle between satisfying material needs and seeking spiritual or intellectual growth. The poet compares this inner struggle to the gravitational pull of an unseen star or undiscovered planet, suggesting that an unknown force influences our actions and emotions. This hidden influence keeps us in a state of restlessness, always torn between immediate wants and greater goals. The poem implies that this mystery is a natural part of life, shaping our choices and direction without us fully understanding it.

Extract 9

And as the moon from some dark gate of cloud
Throws o'er the sea a floating bridge of light,
Across whose trembling planks our fancies crowd
Into the realm of mystery and night,-

(i) **What natural image is described in the extract of the poem? (3)**

Ans. The extract describes the moon shining through a gap in the clouds, casting a bridge of light on the sea. The shimmering reflection looks like a pathway across the water. The poet compares this to imagination crossing into the unknown, symbolising a journey into mystery and night, where dreams and thoughts freely wander.

(ii) **What does the 'floating bridge of light' symbolise in the poem, and how does it contribute to the overall atmosphere? (3)**

Ans. The 'floating bridge of light' symbolises the connection between the known world and the unknown, representing a passage into the realm of mystery. It also reflects the transient nature of beauty and wonder, as the light is 'floating' and the planks are 'trembling.'

(iii) **How does the poet describe the movement of the light across the sea? (3)**

Ans. The poet describes the movement of the light as a 'floating bridge of light' that stretches across the sea. The light seems to hover gently over the water, with 'trembling planks' giving the impression that the bridge is unstable and fragile.

(iv) **Why do you think the poet uses the words 'trembling planks' in the description of the bridge of light? (3)**

Ans. The use of 'trembling planks' suggests fragility and impermanence, which could symbolise the fleeting nature of beauty and the mysterious quality of the scene.

The trembling of the planks might also represent the uncertainty and unpredictability of life or the unknown, inviting the reader to imagine a journey into the mysterious realm that lies beyond the visible world.

(v) **Do you think the poet uses the moonlight to evoke a particular emotional response in the reader? Explain. (4)**

Ans. Yes, the poet uses moonlight to create a sense of mystery and wonder. The image of the moon emerging from a dark cloud and casting a bridge of light over the sea makes the scene feel dreamlike and magical. The phrase 'trembling planks' suggests uncertainty and curiosity, as if our thoughts and imagination are drawn into the unknown. The poet evokes deep emotions, encouraging the reader to explore the mysteries of life and night. The use of light and darkness symbolises the contrast between clarity and the unknown, making the scene both beautiful and thought-provoking.

Extract 10

So from the world of spirits there descends
A bridge of light, connecting it with this,
O'er whose unsteady floor, that sways and bends,
Wander our thoughts above the dark abyss

(i) In what way do the ghosts make their house their own despite forsaking the physical world? (3)

Ans. The ghosts make their house their own by maintaining a spiritual connection to it, even after leaving the physical world.

Their presence lingers, marking the house with memories and emotions, making it a lasting part of their identity. This reflects the idea that the past persists beyond death, with the ghosts 'owning' the space in a symbolic, emotional or spiritual sense.

(ii) How do the verbs 'sways' and 'bends' contribute to the overall tone of the poem? (3)

Ans. The verbs 'sways' and 'bends' contribute to a tone of instability and vulnerability. These actions evoke a sense of movement and unpredictability, reinforcing the fragility of the bridge of light.

The tone becomes more tense and uncertain, as the swaying and bending suggest that the journey across this bridge is not secure, but rather filled with the possibility of falling or losing balance.

(iii) What does the 'dark abyss' symbolise in the poem, and how does it contribute to the meaning of the extract? (3)

Ans. The 'dark abyss' likely symbolises the unknown, the unconscious, or perhaps the realm of death the infinite. It represents a vast, mysterious space that is separate from the tangible world.

The 'dark abyss' serves to heighten the sense of danger and uncertainty surrounding the bridge of light, implying that the journey of the thoughts or spirit is fraught with peril. It contrasts with the illumination of the bridge, emphasising the tension between light and darkness, knowledge and mystery, safety and risk.

(iv) Mention any three descriptions to show the house is haunted by harmless ghosts? (3)

Ans. Three descriptions to show that the house is haunted by harmless ghosts are

(a) **Gentle Presence** The ghosts are not menacing or aggressive, but their presence lingers in a peaceful or subtle way, implying they are not harmful.

(b) **Faint sounds or Whispers** The ghosts may create soft noises, like faint footsteps or whispers, suggesting a benign, non-threatening existence in the house.

(c) **Unseen but Felt** The house may feel slightly different, with objects shifting gently or an ethereal glow, indicating the ghosts are harmless and merely present, rather than disruptive.

(v) Comment on the ending of the poem in brief. What tone does the poet use? (4)

Ans. The ending of the poem creates a reflective and contemplative tone. The poet uses soft, gentle imagery to suggest the peaceful, lingering presence of the ghosts.

The tone is not one of fear or horror, but rather one of quiet acceptance and serenity, as the ghosts, despite being in the afterlife, seem to peacefully inhabit their former space without harming anyone (harmless).

This calm and reflective tone encourages the reader to think about the continuity of existence beyond physical life, focusing on the emotional and spiritual connection to the past.

02

THE GLOVE AND THE LIONS

Leigh Hunt

Introduction

The Glove and the Lions is a narrative poem by Leigh Hunt, an English poet and essayist known for his vivid storytelling. The poem is set in medieval times when animal fights entertained the royal court. The poem highlights how pride and vanity can overshadow true love. It tells the story of a lady who dangerously tests her lover's bravery. The poem's unique feature is its strong message that love should not be proven through reckless challenges.

About the Poem

The Glove and the Lions by Leigh Hunt is a humorous narrative poem. It tells the story of dangerous games of love played in the royal court of King Francis. The poem highlights the dangers of playing games in the royal court. These games are played to express one's love for their beloved and the result of going to the extremes for love.

During a show at the king's arena, where lions are part of the spectacle, the lady throws her glove into the lion's den deliberately and asks the Count de Lorge to retrieve it as proof of his love. The Count bravely retrieves the glove. However, to express his disapproval, he throws the glove back at her and walks away. The poem emphasises true courage and the importance of integrity over shallow displays of affection.

The poem has following characters

- King Francis The king is a good-natured man who loves and enjoys dangerous sports.
- The Lady The woman in the poem is confident, beautiful, and somewhat manipulative. She is not concerned with the actual love her lover feels but with the public display of devotion. She is also portrayed as attention seeker.
- Count de Lorge The Count loves the lady. Though he is brave, but he finds the lady's act very offensive. Therefore he throws the glove at her face and leaves the arena.

Exploring the Stanzas

King Francis .... royal beasts below.

This stanza opens with the poet describing to King Francis and the courtiers seated for an extraordinary sports show. The king is a passionate and robust monarch who is enjoying watching his lions fight with each other. This cruel yet grand display was a form of entertainment for the nobles and royalty of the time.

The arena is filled with nobles, who sit on benches, and elegantly dressed ladies, proud of their appearance and status. Among them is the Count de Lorge, a nobleman deeply in love with a lady.

The scene emphasises the grandeur and magnificence of the event.

Ramped and .... here than there."

This stanza describes the atmosphere of the fight in the court. It is a ferocious, terrifying atmosphere where lions roaring with their mouths wide open. They are quite angry and are baring their horrible teeth.

Their powerful blows stirred the air, and they rolled over attempting to tear each other. This created chaos and the pit became a noisy, violent mess, with bloody foam flung into the air everywhere. The king is impressed by the majesty of the events and he is enjoying the experience safely. He humorously says that he and the nobles are better off watching from their seats than being in the midst of the lions' fight.

The stanza vividly portrays the ferocity of a lion fight in an arena, emphasising the raw power, chaos, and violence of the scene.

De Lorge's .... will be mine.

In this stanza, De Lorge's love (a beautiful and lively woman) overhears the King. She turns and smiles at him. She is described as having a radiant appearance with a smile and sharp, bright eyes that always seem the same. She is confident and assured in her thoughts and decides to test her lover.

She believes her lover, the Count, is courageous and brave, convinced that he would go to great lengths to prove his love for her. Her plan is to drop her glove, expecting that her lover will perform a brave and remarkable act to retrieve it. She thinks that by doing so, she will gain glory and attention. She thinks that this a godsend opportunity to show that lovers can perform acts of bravery for love.

She dropped .... task like that."

In this stanza, the lady executes her plan by dropping the glove and her lover does what she expected. He chivalrously bows before her and leaps headlong into the pit of lions.

He quickly regains his seat before anyone has any time to react to his actions. This also shows that he did not perform the task out love.

However, the unexpected happens when rather than returning the glove with affection or admiration, the Count throws it directly at the woman's face in a dismissive manner.

The king exclaims in agreement with what the Count did as what the lady had done out of her vanity was not right. He believes that such a dramatic test of love is more about showing off than about genuine affection. There has not been any love in her heart when she decides to test the lover.

Theme of the Poem

The central themes of the poem are love, vanity, and human nature. The poem explores how love can be manipulated and tested in public. It highlights the difference between true devotion and a superficial act of bravery for attention.

The poem satirises romantic heroism, mocking the idea that grand gestures prove love when done for the wrong reasons. It also reflects traditional gender role, showing how women were portrayed as expecting men to prove their devotion througt extraordinary acts. This highlights societal expectations in love and relationships.

Message Conveyed by the Poem

The message of the poem is based on the idea that love cannot be proven through grand gestures or acts designed to impress others. True love is not about vanity or the desire for recognition, but about sincerity and depth of feeling. The poem criticises the tendency to test love through public challenges. It highlights how these tests are often more about personal pride and appearance than genuine affection.

Style, Tone and Mood

- **Style** It is a four-stanza narrative ballad which uses vivid imagery and descriptive language to bring the dramatic scene to life.
- **Tone** The tone of the poem is both dramatic and satirical.
- **Mood** The mood of the poem is a mix of dramatic tension, irony and satire.

Title

'The Glove and the Lions' is an appropriate title for the ballad as it tells the story of a medieval event. It aptly reflects the central elements and themes of the poem. The glove symbolises the woman's test of her lover's devotion and the lions represent the danger and public spectacle of the situation.

The title also carries irony, as the Count's actions are driven by vanity, not love. Thus, the title effectively captures the themes of superficiality, vanity, and the contrast between true love and public displays of bravery.

Literary Devices

- Personification With horrid laughing jaws ***[Stanza 2]***
- Metaphor The sand and tangle of mane said to be thunderous ***[Stanza 2]***
- Alliteration Ramped and roared the lions ***[Stanza 2]***
- Repetition The leap was quick, return was quick ***[Stanza 4]***
- Symbolism The glove: represents test of chivalry
  - The lions: danger
- Simile Gave blows like beams ***[Stanza 2]***
  - Brave as brave can be ***[Stanza 3]***
- Internal Rhyme Love and king above ***[Stanza 1]***
  - Dropped her glove to prove his love ***[Stanza 4]***

Vocab Vault

Hearty Lively, energetic

Court Enclosed area for sports

Gallant Dignified

Crowning Ultimate, extraordinary

Valour Bravery, courage

Ramped Prowled

Horrid Dreadful

Wallowing might Immense power

Thunderous smother Deafening loud roars

Whisking Spraying

O'erheard Heard accidentally or without intention; overheard.

Beauteous lively dame A woman of exceptional beauty and liveliness

Wondrous Wonderful

Regained Sat back in his seat

Quoth Archaic word for said

Vanity Pride, arrogance

EXAM ORIENTED QUESTIONS

TYPE - 1 Multiple Choice Questions

01 Mark

Q.1 King Francis is described as 'hearty'. What does the word 'hearty' mean?
(a) Generous (b) Soft-hearted
(c) Good-natured (d) Jealous

Q.2 How does the poem describe the scene at the court?
(a) It is a chaotic scene filled with tension.
(b) It is a peaceful scene with no excitement.
(c) It is a regal and grand event where valour and love are on display.
(d) It is an ordinary scene with no special significance.

Q.3 The phrase 'ladies in their pride' means
(a) The females of the pride of lions
(b) The wives of king
(c) Jealous maids
(d) Ladies dressed in extraordinary clothes and ornaments

Q.4 And 'mongst them sat the Count de Lorge, with one for whom he sighed.' What can be inferred about Count's emotions for the lady?
(a) The Count de Lorge is indifferent to the lady beside him.
(b) The Count de Lorge is admiring the lions.
(c) The Count de Lorge is emotionally invested in the lady sitting next to him.
(d) The Count de Lorge is focused solely on the king.

Q.5 Which of the following is not the theme of the poem 'The Glove and the Lions'? **(Competency Based Que.)**
(a) Vanity (b) Chivalry (c) Pride (d) Cruelty

Q.6 From the description of the nobles and ladies in the court, what can we infer about the nature of the gathering?
(a) It was a casual, informal meeting with no sense of grandeur.
(b) It was a prestigious and a formal event where nobility and royalty were gathered.
(c) It was a secret meeting that the public was unaware of.
(d) It was a quiet gathering without much attention paid to the participants.

Q.7 What was the attitude of the king towards the 'royal beasts'?
(a) Apathy (b) Disgust (c) Fearful (d) Empathy

Q.8 Why was it a 'gallant thing to see that crowning show'?
(a) It required courage to see such a ferocious act.
(b) There was love, valour and royalty in the scene.
(c) It was the most brutal fight ever fought.
(d) It was being held for the first time in the kings court.

Q.9 What was the attitude of the king and his noble towards the 'royal beasts'?
(a) Apathy (b) Empathy (c) Disgust (d) Fearful

Q.10 Who is the 'one for whom' 'he' sighed?
(a) Count de Lorge
(b) King Francis
(c) Count de Lorge's beloved
(d) The Queen

Q.11 What happens to the sand and mane in the pit during the fight?
(a) They remain undisturbed.
(b) They are scattered in the air.
(c) They are caught in a 'thunderous smother'.
(d) They are cleaned up by the nobles.

Q.12 "The lions roared with horrid laughing jaws."
Which of the following uses the same literary device as given in the above line from the poem, 'The Glove and the Lions'? **(Competency Based Que.)**
(a) The snowflakes glittered like diamonds.
(b) The caged bird sings with a fearful trill.
(c) My hands were icicles because of the cold weather.
(d) The smell of freshly brewed coffee woke me up.

Q.13 According to you, the state of the lion pit from the description of it being in a 'thunderous smother' represents that ....
(a) the pit is orderly and calm, with no disturbance
(b) the pit is filled with noise, chaos, and confusion due to the lions' struggle
(c) the lions are being carefully controlled by the king
(d) the pit is being cleaned by the nobles after the fight

Q.14 Which poetic device is used in the following line?
'The bloody foam above the bars came whisking through the air'
(a) Hyperbole (b) Metonymy
(c) Irony (d) Simile

Q.15 Which of the given options contains the figure of speech that appears in the following line from Leigh Hunt's poem 'The Glove and the Lions': 'ramped and roared the lions'? **(ICSE Specimen 2025)**

(a) 'Your eyes are like the diamond bright'

(b) 'Suddenly the black night showed its teeth in a flash of lightning'

(c) 'Rich gifts of raiment, grain or gold'

(d) 'pack up the moon and dismantle the Sun'

Q.16 Who is the 'beauteous lively dame' in the poem?

(a) The Count de Lorge's friend.

(b) The woman the Count de Lorge is in love with.

(c) The king's daughter.

(d) A noble lady sitting beside the king.

Q.17 Why does the lady smile after dropping her glove in the arena?

(a) To show her love for the count

(b) To grab king Francis' attention

(c) To suggest that de Lorge would do as she wants him to do

(d) None of the above

Q.18 Why did de Lorge throw the glove 'right in the lady's face'?

(a) To show his love for her

(b) To prove his bravery

(c) To show how significant she is

(d) To show his annoyance at her vanity

Q.19 What is the lady's perception of the Count de Lorge?

(a) She believes he is timid and unworthy of admiration.

(b) She thinks he is brave and capable of performing wondrous feats for her.

(c) She thinks he is indifferent to her.

(d) She believes he is not interested in proving his love.

Q.20 What does the phrase 'great glory will be mine' suggest about the lady's attitude?

(a) She is humble and does not seek attention.

(b) She believes the test will prove her own worth and elevate her status.

(c) She thinks that the Count's actions will be a failure.

(d) She is indifferent to the outcome of the situation.

Q.21 Which of the following lines reflects Count de Lorge's valour?

(a) Then threw the glove, but not with love.

(b) And 'mongst them sat Count de Lorge, with one for whom he sighed.

(c) He bowed, and in a moment leaped among the lions wild.

(d) I'll drop my glove, to prove his love

Q.22 What aspect of medieval age can be figured out from the poem?

(a) Medieval ignorance

(b) Medieval penchant for horror

(c) Cultural elegance

(d) Noble lifestyle

Q.23 According to the king, what prompted lady's actions?

(a) Deep love (b) Pride (c) Vanity (d) Faith

Q.24 Choose the option that lists the sequence of events in the correct order.

(i) Retrieving the glove, the angry Count flung it in her face.

(ii) While the lions were engaged in a vicious battle, the count's beloved threw her glove into the arena.

(iii) The Count realised that it was her vanity which prompted her to do this.

(iv) The king was enjoying the fight of the royal beasts.

(a) (i), (ii), (iii), (iv) (b) (iv), (ii), (iii), (i)

(c) (ii), (iii), (iv), (i) (d) (iv), (iii), (i), (ii)

Q.25 And 'mongst them sat the Count de Lorge, with one for whom he sighed:/ And truly 'twas a gallant thing to see that crowning show,/ Valour and love, and a king above, and the royal beasts below.

Pick out the assonance from the above lines.

(a) He sighed

(b) Crowning show/valour

(c) Love, and king above

(d) Royal beasts below

Q.26 'He surely would do wondrous things to show his love for me.'

The line given above shows the primary characteristic of the lady character is ....

(a) superciliousness

(b) self-depreciation

(c) superstitious nature

(d) confidence in oneself

Q.27 Select the option that shows the correct relationship between statements (1) and (2).

Statement 1 The lady's declaration that 'great glory will be mine' suggests a deep belief in her own importance and an expectation of public admiration.

Statement 2 Her intention to use the Count de Lorge's love as a means of elevating her own status aligns with the theme of vanity in the poem.

(a) Both Statement 1 and Statement 2 are true.

(b) Statement 1 is true, but Statement 2 is false.

(c) Statement 1 is false, but Statement 2 is true.

(d) Both Statement 1 and Statement 2 are false.

Q.28 Select the option that shows the correct relationship between statements (1) and (2).

Statement 1 The lady's actions were motivated by her love for the Count.

Statement 2 She wanted to publicly test his devotion to gain personal glory.

(a) Both are true and Statement 2 explain statement 1.
(b) Statement 2 is true, but Statement 1 is false.
(c) Statement 1 is true, but Statement 2 is false.
(d) Both statement 1 and statement 2 are false.

Q.29 Select the option that shows the correct relationship between statements (1) and (2).

Statement 1 The lions in the pit fought fiercely, creating a chaotic and terrifying scene.

Statement 2 Francis remarked that the gentlemen were safer outside the pit than within.

Which of the following is correct about Statement 1 and Statement 2?

(a) Both Statement 1 and Statement 2 are true.
(b) Statement 1 is true, but Statement 2 is false.
(c) Statement 1 is false, but Statement 2 is true.
(d) Both Statement 1 and Statement 2 are false.

Answers

1. (c)	2. (c)	3. (d)	4. (c)	5. (d)	6. (b)	7. (c)	8. (a)	9. (d)	10. (c)
11. (c)	12. (b)	13. (b)	14. (a)	15. (c)	16. (b)	17. (c)	18. (d)	19. (b)	20. (b)
21. (c)	22. (b)	23. (c)	24. (b)	25. (b)	26. (d)	27. (a)	28. (b)	29. (a)	

Explanations

14. Hyperbole is the use of exaggeration for emphasis or dramatic effect. In the given line, the imagery of 'bloody foam' is an exaggerated description intended to heighter the drama and evoke strong emotions.

15. The line 'ramped and roared the lions' employs alliteration as it repeats the 'r' sound for poetic effect. The phrase 'Rich gifts of raiment, grain or gold' also employs alliteration (repetition of 'g' and 'r' sounds).

TYPE - 2 Extract Based Questions

16 Marks

Extract 1

King Francis was a hearty king, and loved a royal sport,
And one day as his lions fought, sat looking on the court;
The nobles filled the benches, and the ladies in their pride,
And 'mongst them sat the Count de Lorge, with one for whom he sighed:

(i) Describe the physical and literal setting of the poem. **(3)**

Ans. The poem 'The Glove and the Lions' by Leigh Hunt is set in a royal court during a dramatic event where King Francis and his nobles watch lions fighting in a pit. The arena is chaotic and intense, with the lions roaring, biting, and thrashing, creating a dangerous and wild atmosphere.

Literally, the poem is set in a medieval setting. This signifies the grandeur and ritual of courtly life. The setting symbolises power, prestige, and the interplay of human emotions such as love, vanity, and courage in a highly public and dramatic context.

(ii) According to the poet, how is the king described? What are his characteristics? **(3)**

Ans. According to the poet, King Francis is described as a good-natured, jovial and kind, just ruler who enjoys grand displays of power and spectacle. His love for 'royal sport', such as lion fights, reflects his appreciation for majestic events.

The king although, a powerful monarch, comes across as a humorous leader, observing the funny side of events. His behaviour suggests confidence, control, and a sense of pride in the traditions and rituals of his court. These characteristics portray him as an example of a medieval monarch who relishes displays of valour and loyalty within his realm.

(iii) Who is the Count de Lorge? Why is he significant in this scene? **(3)**

Ans. Count de Lorge is a nobleman seated among the court audience, notable for being in love with one of the ladies. He is significant because his presence sets the stage for the later events, as his actions will serve to test his courage and loyalty in the eyes of the court.

(iv) How does the poet's tone contribute to the depiction of the courtly scene? **(3)**

Ans. The poet's tone is grand and celebratory, emphasising the splendour of the event and the gallantry of the participants. Words like 'royal sport', 'gallant thing' and 'crowning show' create an atmosphere of majesty and drama, aligning with the court's formal and ceremonial nature.

His comment reinforces the moral lesson that genuine love should not be proven through dramatic displays, but through sincerity and selflessness.

(v) **What do we infer about the traditions and values of the medieval setting of the poem?**
What message does it convey? **(4)**

Ans. The medieval setting of the poem 'The Glove and the Lions' reflects the chivalric ideals and values of the time, where bravery, honour, and valour were highly revered.

Chivalry demanded that knights demonstrate their courage and loyalty through acts of bravery, often in public displays.

The poem conveys a message that true love and valour should come from sincere emotion and integrity, rather than from seeking public recognition or glory. It critiques the idea of using dramatic, outward acts to prove one's worth, suggesting that such tests of character can be empty and misguided.

Extract 5

And truly 'twas a gallant thing to see that crowning show,
Valour and love, and a king above, and the royal beasts below.

(i) **Justify the title of the poem.** **(3)**

Ans. The title of the poem, 'The Glove and the Lions', is highly significant and reflects the central elements of the poem. The glove acts as a symbol of test for love.

The title captures both the literal action-the glove being dropped and the lions' fierce behaviour-and the underlying themes of the poem, such as vanity, pride. Thus, the title encapsulates the central conflict of the poem: the challenge of love tested through a dangerous, outward show of courage.

(ii) **The poet uses vivid imagery in the poem. List out one example from each of the following categories.** **(3)**

- Sight (Visual Imagery)
- Sound (Auditory Imagery)
- Smell (Olfactory Imagery)

Ans. The poet uses vivid imagery to describe the chaotic nature of fight between the two beasts. Here are the examples

Sight (Visual Imagery) The whole scene of the fight in Stanza 2 of the poem creates vivid visual image of the fierce lions' fight, with the foam flying through the air, painting a graphic picture of the chaos and violence.

Sound (Auditory Imagery) 'Ramped and roared the lions, with horrid laughing jaws'

This line uses auditory imagery to convey the loud, terrifying sounds of the lions roaring and ramping, which heightens the drama and intensity of the scene.

Smell (Olfactory Imagery) The mention of 'bloody foam' could evoke the smell of blood in the reader's mind, adding to the vivid sensory experience of the fight.

(iii) **Do you think the lady's challenge was justified? Justify your answer.** **(3)**

Ans. No, the lady's challenge was not justified because it intentionally tested the Count's love in a superficial and dangerous way. Instead of fostering genuine affection, the test turned into a public spectacle, revealing the vanity and pride rather than love. True love should not be based on such dramatic and hazardous gestures but should come from a deeper, sincerer emotional connection.

(iv) **What impression do we get about** **(3)**

- **The Lady**
- **The Count**
- **The King**

Ans. The characters in the ballad are interestingly unique.

The Lady is portrayed as vain and calculating, seeking to prove her lover's bravery through a public challenge. She values glory and display over genuine love, using the glove to test the Count's devotion.

The Count is brave warrior, motivated by the desire to impress others rather than by true affection for the lady. His quick actions and the way he throws the glove back at her highlight his anger on being tested.

King Francis is wise and pragmatic, recognising that the Count's actions were driven by vanity, not love. His comment adds insight into the poem's critique of false heroism and superficial bravery.

(v) **Comment on the genre of the poem.**
Explain and justify your answer. **(4)**

Ans. The poem 'The Glove and the Lions' can be classified as narrative poetry with elements of ballad. It tells a story with characters, a clear plot, and a moral lesson, which are key characteristics of narrative poetry. The poem follows a structured plot-the lady drops her glove to test her lover's bravery, the Count's reaction, and the King's commentary-leading to a clear resolution.

Moreover, the poem's rhyming pattern, along with the dramatic action and dialogue between the characters, aligns with the traditional style of a ballad. Ballads often focus on themes of heroism, romantic love, and adventure, and include elements of chivalric values and moral lessons. In this case, the poem critiques superficial displays of bravery and vanity, reflecting on the true nature of love and courage.

03

WHEN GREAT TREES FALL

Maya Angelou

Introduction

When Great Trees Fall is a touching poem by Maya Angelou, a famous American poet, writer and civil rights activist. It talks about the impact of losing great people in our lives. It belongs to the genre of elegy, as it expresses grief and remembrance. The poem shows that death is natural but leaves a deep mark on those left behind. Its unique feature is the hopeful message that, over time, memories bring strength and inspire us to be better.

About the Poem

The poem **When Great Trees Fall** metaphorically compares the deaths of great individuals to the falling of trees in a forest. The poem effectively captures the complex emotions and far and wide consequences associated with the death of influential figures.

Just as the fall of massive trees shakes the Earth and leaves animals in confusion and fear, the loss of these influential figures vibrates throughout the world, leaving a sense of grief and uncertainty. However, over time, this sorrow transforms into the realisation that the world is better for having been touched by these 'great souls'.

Exploring the Stanzas

When great .... lumber after safety.

In this stanza, the poet is describing the fall of great trees. She states that when these trees fall, the impact is felt by the distant hills which start shaking in resonance. There is also a feeling of uneasiness and fear in animals. Lions crouch under the tall grasses to portect themselves and elephants slowly run towards a safe place. The animals and the natural world reacts to the fall of the 'great trees'.

The stanza uses vivid imagery to convey the impact of the loss of great individuals. The fall of great trees is a metaphor for the death of influential figures. The shuddering rocks, hunkering lions, and lumbering elephants represent the widespread disruption and grief that such a loss causes.

When great .... eroded beyond fear.

In this stanza, the poet continues the description of what happens when the great trees fall. When they fall, the small creatures in the forests silently move back. They experience a sense of emotion beyond fear when their senses go numb. This shows that the creatures of the natural world are sad and fearful at the fall of the trees. The lines evoke a sense of mourning that is universal and deeply felt when someone close to us leaves. The imagery of small things recoiling into silence symbolises how the vulnerable and insignificant parts of life are profoundly affected by such loss.

When great .... never taken.

In this stanza, the poet reflects on the emotional aftermath of losing great souls, capturing the profound sense of absence and regret that follows their passing. The effect of the death of great souls is described in detail. It gets difficult to breathe because the air is no longer rich, fresh and vibrant.

It is rare and sterile and we feel lifeless.

REVISION NOTES

Our eyes are filled with tears but the vision becomes clearer as we start to see the unfulfilled moments and lost opportunities with the departed. This means that recollection of grief brings in acute nostalgia. This stanza poignantly explores the themes of regret, reflection, and the bittersweet nature of memory sharpened by loss.

Great souls .... dark, cold caves.

In this stanza, the poet further delves into the profound impact of losing great souls. Their death creates a void in the lives of those who depended on their guidance and presence. The loss is deeply personal and transformative, leaving those left behind feeling diminished and untethered. We feel undernourished and drained out. Their radiant influence takes away the light from us and we become like creatures who live in dark caves. Without the great souls, we seem disoriented and we are ignorant of ourselves.

This stanza represents a return to ignorance and isolation, emphasising how their departure strips the world of light, warmth, and understanding. Angelou captures the profound disorientation and sense of loss that follows the death of those who profoundly shape and elevate the lives of others.

And when .... they existed.

In this stanza, the poet moves from despair to hope. The poet reflects on the eventual healing and transformation that follows the loss of influential individuals. With time, the idea of peace and reconciliation settles in the sense of void is filled with positive energy and understanding. The positivity starts resonating in life. We move on but our lives are forever changed without the presence of such great souls.

The fact that these great people existed keeps on coming back in our life, making it fuller and more meaningful. This reinforces the enduring significance of their lives, serving as a reminder of their influence. The poem concludes with a powerful affirmation, a call to action, urging individuals to honour the memory of the departed. It is a hopeful and uplifting message, celebrating the transformative legacy of great souls.

Theme of the Poem

Maya Angelou's When Great Trees Fall explores the loss of a loved one and the deep grief that follows. The poem shows how this loss affects both people and nature, emphasising the pain and emptiness it brings. However, it also highlights grief and acceptance, showing that, with time, memories help in healing. Angelou stresses individual greatness and cultural change, encouraging people to honor the legacy of those who have passed by growing and improving themselves. The poem carries a message of hope, resilience, and the interconnectedness of life and death, making it meaningful for everyone.

Message Conveyed by the Poem

The poem conveys that the lives of 'great souls' leave an indelible mark on the world, inspiring us to carry forward their legacy. Angelou reminds readers that even though great souls may die, their influence continues to shape and inspire those who are left behind. The poem ultimately suggests that through this loss, we can find strength, growth, and a deeper understanding of our own potential. This affirms that the legacy of great individuals allows us to 'be and be better'.

Style, Tone and Mood

- **Style** The poem is characterised by rich imagery, metaphor, and rhythmic flow. It is written in free verse.
- **Tone** The tone of the poem shifts as it moves from sorrow to hope. Initially, the tone is somber and reflective. However, by the end, the tone becomes more uplifting.
- **Mood** The mood of the poem fluctuates consistently. At the outset, the mood is one of sadness, confusion, and loss. However, as the poem progresses, the mood transitions to one of hope and renewal.

Title

The title of Maya Angelou's poem 'When Great Trees Fall' serves as a profound metaphor for the impact of losing extraordinary individuals, or 'great souls'. Just as a fallen tree disrupts the environment, the death of remarkable people creates a deep void in our lives. The title reflects the universal experience of grief, the enduring influence of their legacy, and the journey towards healing. It encapsulates the poem's exploration of grief, memory, and resilience, making it a filting and evocative representation of its message.

Literary Devices

- Metaphor Angelou employs the central metaphor of 'great trees falling' to symbolise the loss of influential individuals. This metaphor is extended throughout the poem.
- Personification Our souls shrink wizened ***[Stanza 4]***
- Alliteration Fall-forest ***[Stanza 2]***
  - Silence-senses ***[Stanza 2]***
  - Breathe-briefly ***[Stanza 3]***
  - Suddenly-harpened ***[Stanza 3]***
  - Cold-caves ***[Stanza 4]***
- Repetition They existed. They existed ***[Stanza 5]***
- Anaphora When great souls die
  - Great souls die
  - And when great souls dies
  - When great trees fall ***[Stanza 1 and 2]***
- Enjambment Slowly and always irregularly spaces fill with a kind of soothing electric vibration
  - When great trees fall, /rocks on distant hills shudder, ***[Stanza1]***
  - We breathe, briefly. /Our eyes, briefly, /see with/ hurtful clarity. ***[Stanza 3]***

Vocab Vault

Shudder Tremble in fear
Hunker Crouch or cover
Lumber Move slowly
Recoil Move back because of fear
Erode Wear away slowly
Sterile Completely clean and free from bacteria
Hurtful Clarity an acute sense of hurt and pain

Gnaws Tortures
Nurture Care and protection
Wizened Dried up
Radiance Brilliance
Unutterable Beyond words or description
Electric vibrations Positive energy
Restored Brought back

EXAM ORIENTED QUESTIONS

TYPE - 1 Multiple Choice Questions

01 Mark

Q.1 Identify the figure of speech that the phrase 'rocks on distant hills shudder' primarily uses.
(a) Personification
(b) Simile
(c) Oxymoron
(d) Irony

Q.2 The poet use animals like lions and elephants to convey the theme of loss. What could be the probable reason?
(a) To show their dominance in nature despite disruptions.
(b) To highlight their vulnerability in the face of great changes.
(c) To compare their strength to that of falling trees.
(d) To emphasise the insignificance of the trees' fall to wildlife.

Q.3 How does the line 'elephants lumber after safety' contribute to the poem' s tone?
(a) It adds a sense of urgency and movement.
(b) It contrasts the stillness of the trees with the activity of animals.
(c) It conveys a feeling of hopelessness and fatigue.
(d) It emphasises the resilience of life in times of loss.

Q.4 The lions and elephants react to the death of great personalities by
1. running here and there
2. lumbering
3. roaring and making sounds
4. crouching

(a) 1 and 2 (b) 2 and 3
(c) 2 and 4 (d) 3 and 4

Q.5 The broader theme does the poet hint at through the reactions of nature and animals to the falling trees is ....
(a) The inevitability of destruction and its universal impact.
(b) The cyclical nature of life and death in ecosystems.
(c) The chaos caused by the loss of foundational figures.
(d) The harmony and balance maintained despite great loss.

Q.6 What does the phrase "small things recoil into silence" suggest about the reaction of smaller creatures?
(a) They become cautious to avoid predators.
(b) They experience a deep sense of shock and stillness.
(c) They find comfort in silence amidst chaos.
(d) They actively hide to protect themselves.

Q.7 How does the poet create a tone of solemnity in the second stanza?
(a) By using vivid imagery of destruction and chaos.
(b) By focusing on the silence and sensory depletion of small beings.
(c) By describing the loudness of the falling trees.
(d) By portraying a balance between life and death in nature.

Q.8 Which words from the stanza 2 reflect that the senses are numb?
(a) Recoil into silence
(b) Erode beyond fear
(c) Small things
(d) Fall in forests

Q.9 We see atmospheric changes when great souls die. Complete the phrase based on this inference.
The air around us becomes light, ... and ....
(a) rare and sterile (b) purer and fresh
(c) polluted and silent (d) rare and sceptic

Q.10 The poet suggests that after great souls die, our memories
(a) focus on joyful moments shared.
(b) become overwhelmed by unspoken regrets and missed opportunities.
(c) fade away to ease the pain.
(d) provide us comfort through their permanence.

Q.11 'We breathe, briefly. /Our eyes, briefly, /see with/a hurtful clarity.'
Which figure of speech is used in the above lines?
(a) Personification
(b) Anaphora
(c) Assonance
(d) Enjambment/Epistrophe

Q.12 The poet uses the phrase 'kind words unsaid'. What does it symbolise?
(a) The power of silence during grief.
(b) Missed chances to express love or gratitude.
(c) The indifference of the speaker towards the departed.
(d) The futility of communication after loss.

Q.13 The repetition of the word 'briefly' in the poem suggests
(a) the fleeting nature of grief and its emotions.
(b) the immediate and overwhelming shock of loss.
(c) the temporary clarity and reflection brought by grief.
(d) the insignificance of loss in the broader context of life.

Q.14 Poet uses the line 'our reality, bound to them...' What does it signify?
(a) Relief that great souls are gone
(b) Dependence on influential figures.
(c) Immediate sense of loss
(d) Emotional imbalance

Q.15 The line "Our minds, formed and informed by their radiance, fall away" implies that
(a) the influence of great souls is temporary.
(b) the guidance of great souls is vital for intellectual and emotional growth.
(c) minds cannot function independently of others.
(d) loss completely destroys one's ability to think and reason.

Q.16 The poet compares the state of being after great souls die to
(a) a life full of light and hope.
(b) an existence in dark, cold caves of ignorance.
(c) a gradual return to normalcy and joy.
(d) a journey through radiant memories.

Q.17 The use of the words 'cold caves' represent the ....
1. our ignorance   2. our stupefaction
3. our despair   4. our agony
(a) 1 and 2   (b) 1, 2 and 4
(c) 2, 3 and 4   (d) 1, 2, 3 and 4

Q.18 Identify the figure of speech in 'peace blooms, slowly and always irregularly'.
(a) Simile   (b) Metaphor
(c) Personification   (d) Hyperbole

Q.19 The poet concludes that the existence of great souls
(a) serves as a constant reminder of human limitations.
(b) offers hope and motivation to strive for improvement.
(c) creates a burden of living up to their standards.
(d) leaves us yearning for their physical presence.

Q.20 How does the poet suggest that the legacy of great souls inspires us?
(a) By stating that their lives lead to despair and reflection.
(b) By encouraging us to live better and honour their memory.
(c) By showing the impossibility of matching their greatness.
(d) By advocating for forgetting and moving on quickly.

Q.21 The line 'They existed. They existed' is an example of
(a) anaphora
(b) epiphora
(c) repetition/epizeuxis
(d) antithesis

Q.22 Which theme is most prominent in the poem's conclusion?
(a) The inevitability of death.
(b) The resilience of humanity in the face of loss.
(c) The permanence of grief and sorrow.
(d) The futility of remembering the past.

Q.23 The poet explores the relationship between grief and inspiration. How does she do so?
(a) By showing how grief erases memories of the deceased.
(b) By portraying grief as a transformative and motivating force.
(c) By emphasising the struggle to recover from loss.
(d) By stating that grief leads only to despair.

Q.24 The tone of the poem as it transitions from grief to hope can be described as
(a) gradually uplifting and reflective.
(b) abruptly celebratory and jubilant.
(c) consistently mournful and somber.
(d) hesitantly critical and skeptical.

Q.25 Select the option that shows the correct relationship between (1) and (2). **(Competency Based Que.)**
Statement 1 The falling of a great tree shocks both big and small creatures.
Statement 2 The death of a great person maddens their loved ones.
(a) Statement 1 is true, and Statement 2 is false.
(b) Statement 1 is false, and Statement 2 is true.
(c) Statement 1 is an analogy for Statement 2.
(d) Statement 1 is the reason for Statement 2.

Q.26 The five stages of grief are described as shock, anger, bargaining, depression and acceptance. Which of these stages is expressed in the following lines? **(Competency Based Que.)**

"And when great souls die,
after a period peace blooms,"

(a) Shock
(b) Anger
(c) Depression
(d) Acceptance

Q.27 The central idea of Angelou' s poem When Great Trees Fall is that .... **(Competency Based Que.)**

(a) when a gigantic tree falls, it affects all the trees in the jungle
(b) the death of an ancient tree disturbs all the animals in the jungle
(c) the impact of the death of a loved one on those struggling to cope with the loss
(d) life will never be the same after the loss of a loved one

Q.28 The theme of Maya Angelou's poem 'When Great Trees Fall' is **(ICSE Specimen 2025)**

(a) the impact of the death of a loved one on those left behind.
(b) the effect of felling trees on the environment.
(c) how the death of trees affects humanity.
(d) the impact of natural calamities on a forest.

Q.29 Arrange the following events from the poem in the correct sequence.

1. Our senses, restored, never to be the same, whisper to us.
2. Peace blooms, slowly and always irregularly.
3. They existed. They existed.
4. Great souls die, and our reality takes leave of us.
5. We can be. Be and be better.

Options

(a) 4, 2, 1, 3, 5 (b) 2, 4, 1, 5, 3
(c) 4, 1, 3, 2, 5 (d) 4, 2, 3, 1, 5

Answers

1. (a)	2. (b)	3. (a)	4. (c)	5. (c)	6. (b)	7. (b)	8. (b)	9. (a)	10. (b)
11. (d)	12. (b)	13. (c)	14. (b)	15. (b)	16. (b)	17. (d)	18. (c)	19. (b)	20. (b)
21. (c)	22. (b)	23. (b)	24. (a)	25. (a)	26. (d)	27. (c)	28. (a)	29. (a)	

Explanations

11. The given line uses enjambment which is the continuation of a sentence or phrase across multiple lines without a pause or punctuation at the end of a line.
18. The phrase 'peace blooms, slowly and always irregularly' attributes human–like qualities to 'peace' by describing it as if it could 'bloom'. This is a clear example of personification where an abstract idea is given characteristics of a living being.
21. The given line is an example of repetition where the same phrase is repeated for emphasis. Repetition is used to underline the importance of the statement or an idea.

TYPE - 2 Extract Based Questions

16 Marks

Extract 1

When great trees fall,
rocks on distant hills shudder,
lions hunker down
in tall grasses,
and even elephants
lumber after safety.

(i) How does the poetic genre enhance the expression of ideas in these lines? (3)

Ans. The poetic genre allows for the use of rich imagery and symbolism, which deepen the emotional response of the ideas. Here, the poet uses free verse to evoke an understanding of the majesty of loss and its consequences. The conciseness of poetry emphasises the weight of each image, making the message more impactful.

(ii) Why does the poet use animals like lions and elephants in these lines? (3)

Ans. The poet uses animals such as lions and elephants to symbolise strength and majesty. They seek safety which illustrates that the repercussions of falling of 'great trees' are felt by all. Even the strongest and most powerful creatures are rendered vulnerable, highlighting the magnificence of the fall.

(iii) Evaluate the effectiveness of the imagery in conveying the gravity of loss. (3)

Ans. The imagery is highly effective in conveying the gravity of loss. By comparing the fallen great souls to 'great trees,' the poet draws a parallel between their importance and the essential role.

The reactions of rocks, lions, and elephants further emphasise the widespread and profound effects of their absence, making the idea of loss relatable and universal.

(iv) What can be inferred about the poet's perspective on loss from these lines? (3)

Ans. The poet views loss as a powerful, all-encompassing force that affects not just individuals but the world at large. The poet sees the fall of great souls as a disruption in the natural order, with widespread and long-lasting consequences.

(v) Describe the effect on the people when great souls die, according to the poet. (4)

Ans. According to the poet, when great souls die, their absence causes a deep sense of loss and disruption. People feel disconnected, as their souls shrink and their minds fall into ignorance.

However, after the initial sorrow, peace gradually returns, though irregularly. As people reflect on the deceased, their memories become sharper, and they regret missed opportunities. Over time, the legacy of the great souls inspires others to 'be and be better', motivating them to live more meaningfully. The effect is both sorrowful and transformative, ultimately leading to personal growth.

Extract 2

When great trees fall in forests,
small things recoil into silence,
their senses eroded by fear.

(i) What effect does the falling of 'great trees' have on distant hills and animals in the jungle? (Competency Based Que., 3)

Or

What effect does the falling of a 'great tree' have on the creatures of the forest? (ICSE Specimen 2025)

Ans. The falling of 'great trees' causes a profound effect on the distant hills and animals in the jungle. The poet describes how the rocks on distant hills 'shudder', indicating that even the most solid and immovable elements of nature react to the loss.

Animals, like lions and elephants, seek safety, with lions hunkering down in tall grasses and elephants lumbering away. This suggests that the loss of great souls has a universal and far-reaching impact, affecting even the strongest and most stable forces in nature.

(ii) Explain in your own words the line, 'small things ... eroded by fear'. (Competency Based Que., 3)

Ans. The line 'small things ... eroded by fear' suggests that the smaller, more vulnerable aspects of life-whether it be people, emotions, or elements of nature-become overwhelmed and weakened by the fear caused by the loss of great souls.

The small creatures withdraw into silence and they are too terrified to make a sound.

The word 'eroded' conveys the idea of something gradually worn down or destroyed. In this context, it implies that their senses are eaten up by fear. They are overwhelmed at the magnitude of the loss.

(iii) How is one's memory affected by the death of a great soul? (Competency Based Que., 3)

Ans. The death of a great soul sharpens one's memory. According to the poet, after the death, people become more aware of things they may have overlooked before, such as 'kind words unsaid' or 'promised walks never taken'. The loss brings sudden clarity, making one reflect on the unspoken and the unfulfilled, often leading to regret.

This heightened awareness and emotional reflection cause the memory to become more vivid and intense, as people revisit moments and feelings they may have taken for granted when the great soul was alive.

(iv) What analogy does Angelou use to describe the death of a great soul?

Give two reasons to show that this analogy is appropriate. **(Competency Based Que., 3)**

Ans. Angelou uses the analogy of the fall of 'great trees' to describe the death of a great soul. This analogy is appropriate for two main reasons

(a) The fall of a tree, like the death of a great soul, creates a significant and lasting impact on the surrounding environment.

(b) The poet highlights that when great trees fall, even distant hills and animals in the jungle are affected. Similarly, the death of a great soul disrupts not only the immediate circle but also has far-reaching consequences on the lives of many others, symbolising the universal impact of such a loss.

(v) Trace the stages of grief and coming to terms with the loss of a loved one that Maya Angelou describes in her poem 'When Great Trees Fall'. **(Competency Based Que., 4)**

Ans. In Maya Angelou's poem, the stages of grief are

- **Shock** The loss causes immediate disruption, symbolised by rocks shuddering and animals seeking safety.
- **Fear/Denial** People retreat into silence, overwhelmed by fear and struggling to accept the reality of the loss.
- **Regret/Remorse** There is reflection on 'kind words unsaid' and missed opportunities, leading to feelings of regret.
- **Sense of Loss** The loss creates a deep emptiness, with reality feeling distant and people feeling diminished.
- **Acceptance** Over time, peace slowly returns, and the memory of the departed inspires others to live better lives in their honour.
- These stages represent the emotional journey from shock to eventual acceptance.

Extract 3

When great souls die,
the air around us becomes
light, rare, sterile.
We breathe, briefly.
Our eyes, briefly,
see with
a hurtful clarity.

(i) How does the death of a great soul affect the lives of those left behind in the immediate aftermath of their passing? **(ICSE Specimen 2025, 3)**

Ans. In the immediate aftermath of a great soul's passing, those left behind experience a deep sense of loss and disruption.

The poet describes how their reality seems to 'take leave' of them, suggesting a feeling of disorientation and emptiness.

The death causes a profound shift, leaving those affected feeling smaller and more vulnerable, as if their minds fall into ignorance and their souls shrink.

There is a moment of clarity but it brings with it regret for things left unsaid and promises unfulfilled. The immediate effect is sorrow and confusion.

(ii) What long term effect does the death of a 'great soul' have? **(ICSE Specimen 2025, 3)**

Ans. The long-term effect of the death of a 'great soul' is a gradual return of peace and inspiration. While the immediate aftermath is filled with grief and loss, over time, a sense of calm begins to emerge, though it is slow and irregular.

The memory of the departed soul sharpens one's awareness and motivates the living to improve themselves.

People are inspired to be better as the legacy of the great soul continues to guide and influence them.

(iii) What feeling is being expressed by the following lines/phrases? **(ICSE Specimen 2025, 3)**

(a) Small things recoil into silence

(b) Kind words/unsaid

(c) Be and be/better. For they existed

Ans. (a) '**Small things recoil into silence**' This line expresses a feeling of fear and shock. It suggests that, in the face of loss, those who are vulnerable or sensitive retreat into silence, overwhelmed by the magnitude of the grief.

(b) '**Kind words unsaid**' This phrase expresses a feeling of regret or remorse. It reflects the sorrow and self-blame felt by individuals when they realise that they did not express their feelings or appreciation when they had the chance.

(c) '**Be and be better. For they existed**' This line expresses a feeling of inspiration and renewed purpose. It conveys the idea that the legacy of the departed great soul motivates the living to strive for personal growth and to live better lives in honour of their memory.

(iv) What is 'Great tree' a metaphor for?

What is the central message of Angelou's poem, 'When Great Trees Fall'? **(ICSE Specimen 2025, 3)**

Ans. In the poem, the 'great tree' is a metaphor for a great soul or an influential, exceptional individual whose presence profoundly impacts the world and the lives of those around them. The fall of a 'great tree' represents the death or loss of such an individual.

The central message of Maya Angelou's poem, 'When Great Trees Fall', is about the far-reaching impact of the loss of a great soul.

The poem explores the emotional journey through grief, reflecting on the sorrow, regret, and sense of disorientation experienced by those left behind. It also conveys that, in time, peace and healing slowly return, and the legacy of the departed soul continues to inspire and encourage others to live better lives in their honour.

(v) Can the experiences of the poet be related to personal loss?

What differences can you notice in the two situations? **(4)**

Ans. Yes, the experiences described by the poet in 'When Great Trees Fall' can be related to personal loss. The emotions expressed in the poem, such as shock, grief, regret, and a sense of emptiness, are common feelings experienced when one loses a loved one.

The difference is that the poem focuses on the loss of a 'great soul', affecting many, whereas personal loss typically impacts an individual's immediate circle.

In the poem, healing is slow and irregular, with inspiration from the departed. In personal loss, healing can be unpredictable, and not everyone may find renewal or motivation.

Extract 4

Our souls,
dependent upon their
nurture,
now shrink, wizened.
Our minds, formed
and informed by their
radiance, fall away.

(i) How does the genre of free verse help convey the emotions in the poem 'When Great Souls Die'? **(3)**

Ans. The use of free verse in 'When Great Souls Die' allows the poet to express emotions and ideas without the constraints of a regular rhyme or meter.

This free-flowing style mirrors the chaos, confusion, and emotional turbulence that follows the loss of a great soul.

The lack of structure reflects the disorientation and loss of stability experienced by those mourning the death, allowing the poet to capture the raw, unfiltered emotions tied to grief and remembrance.

(ii) What is the significance of the phrase, "reduced to the unutterable ignorance of dark, cold caves"? **(3)**

Ans. The phrase "reduced to the unutterable ignorance of dark, cold caves" metaphorically suggests that the loss of a great soul leaves individuals in a state of confusion and ignorance. The 'dark, cold caves' represent a place of emotional and intellectual darkness, where understanding, clarity, and guidance are lost.

The phrase underscores the feeling of being cut off from enlightenment and wisdom, leaving the mourner in a state of helplessness and despair, unable to fully comprehend or navigate life without the great soul's influence.

(iii) The poet uses several words and phrases to establish the dependence of the bereft on great souls in the poem. What are such words? **(3)**

Ans. In the poem, the poet highlights the dependence of the bereft on great souls through phrases like 'bound to them', which suggests an inseparable connection, and 'dependent upon their nurture', which indicates an emotional and spiritual reliance.

Additionally, 'formed and informed by their radiance' shows how the great souls shape and enlighten the minds and spirits of those around them. These expressions convey that the bereft are deeply reliant on the influence of great souls, and their absence creates a profound sense of loss.

(iv) How does Maya Angelou use the concept of 'light' and 'radiance' in the poem to depict the influence of a great soul on the lives of others? **(3)**

Ans. Maya Angelou uses the concepts of 'light' and 'radiance' to symbolise the wisdom, guidance, and moral clarity provided by a great soul.

These qualities illuminate the lives of those around them, shaping their thoughts and actions. When the great soul passes away, the 'radiance' fades, leaving a void in the lives of those left behind.

(v) The poem has been carefully crafted to make it reflective and philosophical.

How does the language enhance the understanding of grief and loss? **(4)**

Ans. The reflective and philosophical genre of the poem allows Maya Angelou to explore grief and loss on a deep, intellectual level. The use of introspective language invites readers to consider the profound emotional and spiritual effects of losing a great soul.

It faltered: .... accorded it of fate.

In this stanza, the mite hesitates and accepts whatever happens to it. Frost shows how the tiny creature recognises its vulnerability and must face its fate. This moment reflects themes of weakness, mortality and it prompts the reader to think about life's fragility.

I have none .... I hope it slept.

In this stanza, the poet says that he personally does not have a sentimental or gentle nature. However, he still feels sympathy and admiration for the tiny mite and its efforts. He does not go 'overboard' with love which he sees as currently in the modern world. He is against the desire and will to control other person's actions as this can kill the creativity. He lets the mite decide its own fate and let it sleep there.

I have a .... display of mind.

In this stanza, the poet expresses an appreciation for intellect. He values the presence of 'mind' in all its forms. He takes joy in recognising even the smallest display of thought. He is immensely happy to see even the smallest display of intelligence. This is worthy of admiration. This stanza shows that the poet prefers intelligence over societal norms, highlighting the importance of consciousness and creativity.

Theme of the Poem

Robert Frost's 'A Considerable Speck' explores deep ideas through the poet's observation of a tiny living mite. The poem highlights awareness and purposeful behavior even in the smallest creatures. It shows the importance of keen observation and finding something special in ordinary moments.

The poem also reflects on the human mind, its imagination, and creativity. Frost compares the mite's natural instincts with human intelligence, suggesting that people often take their thinking abilities for granted. He encourages respect for all living beings and reminds us to stay humble. Through this simple yet meaningful encounter, Frost gives a thoughtful message about life, awareness, and perspective.

Message Conveyed by the Poem

The central message of 'A Considerable Speck' by Robert Frost is that even the smallest forms of life possess consciousness, intelligence, and value. They deserve recognition and respect. Through the poet's observation of a tiny mite, the poem emphasises the importance of attentiveness, empathy, and humility in acknowledging the significance of all living beings. It also critiques human thoughtlessness, urging readers to reflect on the true essence of intellect and the interconnectedness of life.

Style, Tone and Mood

- Style The poem is composed in blank verse, giving it a rhythm that looks like natural speech. The poem's conversational style makes it easily readable, but it has layered meanings which invite deeper analysis.
- Tone The tone of 'A Considerable Speck' is playful yet reflective which blends light-hearted humour with deeper philosophical insights.
- Mood The mood of the poem is curious and reflective.

Title

The title 'A Considerable Speck' is both literal and metaphorical, perfectly capturing the essence of the poem. Literally, it refers to the tiny mite that the poet notices on his paper. Despite its small size, the speck is 'considerable' because it exhibits intelligence, purpose and life. Metaphorically, the title highlights the poet's message even the seemingly insignificant things can hold profound meaning. Frost highlights the value of observation, consciousness, and empathy, making the title a fitting reflection of the poem's themes.

Literary Devices

- Anthropomorphism Human activities like imagination and creativity have been attributed to the mite.
- Hyperbole It seemed too tiny to have room for feet, Yet must have had a set of them complete To express how much it didn't want to die. It ran with terror and with cunning crept ***[Stanza 4]***
- Metaphor Mite is a metaphor for intelligence.
- Oxymoron A Considerable Speck **(Title)**
- Imagery The poet has used visual imagery to describe how an insignificant spect turns into a living, considerable speck.

Vocab Vault

Speck A tiny spot/dust particle
Poised Ready to take an action any moment now
Period Full-stop
Inclinations Instincts
Suspicion Distrust
Manuscript Text which is hand-written or typed
Loathing To hate somebody or resentment
Faltered Lost momentum or balance
Cower down Bend down
Desperation Hopelessness
Tenderer than thou Extreme concern
Collectivistic regimenting Group orientation
Microscopic Very tiny
Guise Form
Least display Little evidence

EXAM ORIENTED QUESTIONS

TYPE - 1 Multiple Choice Questions

01 Mark

Q.1 "A speck that would have been beneath my sight" What does the phrase suggest about the poet's perspective?
(a) The speck was too insignificant to notice elsewhere.
(b) The poet deliberately ignored the speck.
(c) The poet usually observes all small details.
(d) The speck had a special purpose on the paper.

Q.2 Why does the poet mention the paper as being 'so white'?
(a) To emphasise the purity of the paper.
(b) To show contrast and make the speck visible.
(c) To highlight the significance of his writing.
(d) To explain why the speck moved across it.

Q.3 Which of the following options contains the same literary device that appears in the following line.
".....On any but a paper sheet so white....."
(Competency Based Que.)
(a) Silver and blue as the mountain mist.
(b) He names the sky his own.
(c) The fir trees dark and high.
(d) Song and mother-croon of bird.

Q.4 What did the mite drink or smell?
(a) Ink
(b) Water
(c) Sweat
(d) None of these

Q.5 What does the poet's ability to notice the speck reveal about his character?
(a) He is easily distracted.
(b) He values the finer details of life.
(c) He is highly critical of imperfections.
(d) He struggles to focus on his work.

Q.6 How are the words of title 'A Considerable Speck' connected?
(a) Oxymoron
(b) Personification
(c) Paradox
(d) Assonance

Q.7 What does the phrase 'idly poised my pen in air' suggest about the poet's initial reaction?
(a) He was determined to destroy the speck.
(b) He hesitated out of curiosity.
(c) He was unsure whether the speck was alive.
(d) He was contemplating his next line of writing.

Q.8 The poet observes the speck closely and realises that ....
(a) it is simply a speck of dust
(b) it is moving due to his breathing
(c) it is a living creature with agency
(d) it is irrelevant to his writing

Q.9 Arrange the following in the correct order as they occur in the lines.
1. The poet realises the speck has its own inclinations.
2. The poet notices a speck on the white paper.
3. The poet prepares to stop the speck with his pen.
4. The poet identifies the speck as a living mite.

(a) 2, 4, 3, 1
(b) 3, 2, 1, 4
(c) 4, 2, 3, 1
(d) 2, 3, 4, 1

Q.10 The poet's realisation progresses in a specific way. How does it progress?
(a) From curiosity to recognition of life to admiration.
(b) From frustration to curiosity to dismissal.
(c) From ignorance to destruction to regret.
(d) From observation to irritation to action.

Q.11 Which of the following poetic devices is used in the title of the poem?
(a) Paradox (b) Metaphor
(c) Persainification (d) Oxymoron

Q.12 Which characteristic trait of the speaker is revealed in the line uttered by him? 'Whatever I accorded it of Fate'.
(a) Arrogance (b) Annoyance
(c) Superiority (d) None of these

Q.13 Which figure of speech is used in the line given below? 'I have none of the tenderer-than-thai.'
(a) Personification (b) Metaphor
(c) Simile (d) Alliteration

Q.14 Why does the poet believe he is dealing with 'an intelligence'?
(a) The mite's movements are random but quick.
(b) The poet assumes all living things are intelligent.
(c) The mite's actions show purpose and awareness.
(d) The mite reacts unpredictably to the ink.

Q.15 The mite's reaction to the ink reflect its intelligence in a way that ....
(a) it flies away immediately without hesitation
(b) it carefully examines and rejects the ink, showing discernment
(c) it ignores the ink entirely, focusing on its path
(d) it shows curiosity but lacks awareness

Q.16 What does the phrase 'paused as with suspicion of my pen' suggest about the speck's behaviour?
(a) It was aware of the poet's pen as a potential threat.
(b) It admired the pen's design.
(c) It was confused about its surroundings.
(d) It wanted to rest before continuing its journey.

Q.17 The creature's movement is described as 'with terror and with cunning crept'. What do you think it captures?
(a) It used both speed and stealth to survive.
(b) It was unable to move without panicking.
(c) It hesitated before escaping.
(d) It relied on deception to outsmart predators.

Q.18 The literary device in the phrase 'ran with terror and with cunning crept' is
(a) Oxymoron
(b) Antithesis
(c) Personification
(d) Imagery

Q.19 The actions of the mite represent a certain idea. What does the following action represent?
Cunningly creeping ....
(a) confidence
(b) fear
(c) intelligence
(d) relief

Q.20 To express how much it didn't want to die.
It ran with terror and with cunning crept.
What mood do the given lines represent?
(a) The mood is optimistic, highlighting survival.
(b) The mood is tense, focusing on fear and desperation.
(c) The mood is indifferent, showcasing the creature's apathy.
(d) The mood is triumphant, emphasising the creature's success.

Q.21 The word 'faltered' suggests that the creature ....
(a) moved quickly and confidently
(b) was momentarily unsure or hesitant
(c) was physically injured
(d) gave up immediately

Q.22 The poet juxtaposes the creature's 'hesitation' with 'desperation' in the poem. This serves to
(a) Create suspense regarding the creature's next move.
(b) Highlight the inevitability of submission.
(c) Emphasise the cruelty of the speaker's actions.
(d) Contrast the creature's vulnerability with its cunning.

Q.23 Which of the following statements reflects the same theme as 'whatever I accorded it of fate'?
(a) 'The king decides the destiny of his subjects.'
(b) 'The bird flew freely, away from danger.'
(c) 'Nature is both nurturing and unforgiving.'
(d) 'The Sun rose again, marking a new day.'

Q.24 The speaker's attitude in the lines 'I have none of the tenderer-than-thou collectivistic regimenting love' can best be described as
(a) romantic and nostalgic
(b) cynical and detached
(c) compassionate and empathetic
(d) indifferent and apathetic

Q.25 What do you think the term 'collectivistic regimenting love' refer to?
(a) Genuine love shared in small communities.
(b) Overwhelming, forced displays of affection in society.
(c) The nurturing care found in traditional families.
(d) The speaker's personal philosophy of love.

Q.26 What does the phrase 'Since it was nothing I knew evil of' reveal about the speaker's actions?
(a) The speaker is protective of anything unfamiliar.
(b) The speaker is reluctant to make moral judgements.
(c) The speaker seeks to avoid responsibility.
(d) The speaker's decision is based on a lack of prejudice.

Q.27 From the speaker's perspective, 'modern world' is portrayed as
(a) a place filled with sincere love and genuine compassion.
(b) a progressive society guided by collectivistic ideals.
(c) a world swept by superficial and organised displays of emotion
(d) a community united by shared responsibilities.

Q.28 What does the speaker imply by expressing gladness at finding intellect on 'any sheet'?
(a) The speaker finds written expression particularly meaningful.
(b) The speaker prefers intellectual conversation over written communication.
(c) The speaker is critical of the lack of intellect in written works.
(d) The speaker values intellect only when it is explicitly expressed.

Q.29 Choose the option that lists the sequence of events in the correct order. **(Competency Based Que.)**
(i) He changes his mind when he notices something unusual about it.
(ii) The poet realises that the speck is a living mite with preferences of its own.
(iii) He intends to use the tip of his pen, dipped in ink, to erase the speck.
(iv) The poet notices a speck on the white paper he is writing on.
(a) (i), (ii), (iii), (iv)
(b) (iv), (ii), (iii), (i)
(c) (ii), (iii), (iv), (i)
(d) (iv), (iii), (i), (ii)

Q.30 Select the option that shows the correct relationship between statements (1) and (2). **(Competency Based Que.)**

Statement 1 The poet concludes that the mite proves to be an intelligent creature.

Statement 2 The mite seems to dislike the ink as it quickly whirls around to fly away.

(a) Statement 2 is the cause for Statement 1.
(b) Statement 2 is true, and Statement 1 is false.
(c) Statement 1 and Statement 2 are independent of each other.
(d) Statement 1 is true, and Statement 2 is false.

Q.31 What is the central idea in Frost's poem, 'A Considerable Speck'? **(Competency Based Que.)**
(a) The poet critiques society's disregard for smaller aspects of life.
(b) The idea is that every living being, no matter how small, has its own perspective and intelligence.
(c) The struggle between man-made creations and the natural world.
(d) The insignificance of individual thoughts in the grand scheme of the universe.

Q.32 'A Considerable Speck' captures **(ICSE Specimen 2025)**
(a) the journey of a mite across the sheet of paper.
(b) the poet's determination to kill the mite.
(c) the poet's encounter with the gigantic fly.
(d) the mite's attempt to escape from the fly.

Answers

1. (a)	2. (b)	3. (c)	4. (a)	5. (b)	6. (a)	7. (b)	8. (c)	9. (d)	10. (a)
11. (d)	12. (c)	13. (d)	14. (c)	15. (b)	16. (a)	17. (a)	18. (b)	19. (c)	20. (a)
21. (b)	22. (b)	23. (a)	24. (b)	25. (b)	26. (d)	27. (c)	28. (a)	29. (a)	30. (a)
31. (b)	32. (a)								

Explanations

6. An oxymoron is a figure of speech where two contradictory or opposing words are placed together to create a striking or thought-provoking effect.
The title combines two opposing ides—'considerable' meaning important and 'speck' meaning something small or insignificant.

10. In the poem, the poet's realisation progresses from curiosity to recognition and finally to admiration. Initially, Frost observes the tiny speck with interest, unsure of what it is. He soon realises it is a living mite, showing purposeful behaviour. This leads him to admire its determination and intelligence, despite its small size.

18. The phrase 'ran with terror and with cunning crept' contains contrasting ideas–running in fear versus creeping with calculated cunning. These opposing actions are placed side by side, creating a deliberate contrast.

TYPE - 2 Extract Based Questions

16 Marks

Extract 1

A speck that would have been beneath my sight
On any but a paper sheet so white
Set off across what I had written there.

(i) Discuss the use of colour imagery in the phrase 'paper sheet so white'.

How does it contribute to the visual and thematic aspects of the lines? **(3)**

Ans. The poet uses colour imagery to contrast the whiteness of the paper with the black tiny dot. The white paper symbolises purity, clarity, or a blank canvas of thought. The introduction of the speck disrupts this purity, making it visually impactful.

This imagery enhances the theme of contrast-between perfection and imperfection, order and disruption.

(ii) What might the 'speck' symbolise in a broader sense? Could it represent external forces, imperfections, or distractions? Justify your interpretation. **(3)**

Ans. The speck could symbolise distractions or imperfections that disrupt the poet's focus or peace. It may also represent external forces or challenges that intrude on personal or creative endeavours.

This interpretation is supported by its movement across the writing. This signifies the idea of interference in a deliberate act of creativity.

(iii) The title of the poem, 'A Considerable Speck' is oxymoronic. What does it imply? **(3)**

Ans. The title of the poem reflects its focus on how a tiny 'speck', though seemingly insignificant, draws the speaker's attention. It highlights how even the smallest details can disrupt or influence our thoughts. The title suggests that contrasts, like the speck on the white paper, make certain things more noticeable.

This indicates how minor imperfections or distractions can take on greater importance. Overall, the title captures the theme of finding meaning in the small and often overlooked aspects of life.

(iv) Critically assess how the presence of the speck shifts the tone of the speaker's engagement with their writing. Does it introduce tension, distraction, or another mood? **(3)**

Ans. The presence of the speck introduces a subtle tension and distraction. It shifts the tone from one of calm focus to one of mild irritation or introspection, as the speaker gets distracted with this minor intrusion. The mood reflects a broader human experience of being distracted by insignificant details.

(v) Comment on the structure of the poem. **(4)**

Ans. The structure of the poem is simple yet effective in conveying its themes. It follows a free verse form, meaning it does not adhere to a specific rhyme scheme or meter.

The poem's lines vary in length, reflecting the speaker's shifting focus and thoughts.

This irregularity adds to the sense of spontaneity and unpredictability, as the speaker is momentarily distracted by the speck.

The poem's lack of rhyme or formal structure could also suggest a certain informality, as if the speaker is reflecting casually on an experience, allowing the thoughts to flow organically.

Extract 2

And I had idly poised my pen in air
To stop it with a period of ink
When something strange about it made me think,
This was no dust speck by my breathing blown,
But unmistakably a living mite
With inclinations it could call its own.

(i) What was strange about the speck that attracted the speaker's attention?

What was it in reality?

Describe the speaker's attitude towards the speck. **(Competency Based Que., 3)**

Ans. The speaker realised that it was not a speck of dust blown over by his breath.

In reality, it was a living mite, having its own feelings and decision-making power.

His attitude was one of curiosity and wonder. This led to a broad reflection on life and existence.

(ii) What made the speaker realise that the mite had a mind of its own as well as intelligence?

Give three reasons to justify your answer. **(Competency Based Que., 3)**

Ans. It is evident that the mite had a mind and intelligence of its own. Three instances of the mite having its intelligence are

(a) The mite had stopped running as if frightened by the speaker's pen.

(b) Again, it started running wildly and came up to the place on the paper where the ink had not yet dried, and it stopped.

(c) The mite drank and smelt the ink but it got a feeling of intense dislike. It turned again to move.

(iii) **Analyse the speaker's decision to let the mite live. What does this reveal about his character?**

(Competency Based Que., 4)

Ans. The speaker's decision to let the mite live reveals a compassionate and thoughtful side to his character. Despite its tiny size and potential insignificance, the speaker chooses not to kill the mite, showing a respect for life, even in its smallest form and intelligence. This action suggests that the speaker values even the most seemingly trivial creatures and recognises their right to exist.

It also indicates a sense of empathy and a reluctance to cause harm unnecessarily.

(iv) **How would you evaluate the significance of the poem's ending? Why is the discovery of a 'display of mind' so important to the speaker?**

(Competency Based Que., 3)

Ans. The speaker feels delighted in finding intelligence and thought in unexpected places. He appreciates the display of mind in any written text highlighting life and reality.

It is important to the speaker as it affirms the presence of consciousness and life's value and intelligence beyond size and appearance.

(v) **What is the central theme of the poem?**

How does the speaker's action illustrate the theme of the poem?

If you have to give the poem a different title, what will it be? Give a reason for your answer.

(Competency Based Que., 4)

Ans. The central theme of the poem is importance of the human faculty of mind, its imagination and creativity. The poem also reflects on the value of small, often overlooked things and the speaker's reflection on imperfection and life. He gives importance to the intelligence displayed by the mite and refrains from killing it.

If I were to give an alternate title, it would be 'The Speck of Creation'. This title reflects how something small and seemingly insignificant, like the mite or the speck, can become a focal point of thought and creativity. It ties into the poem's theme of how even the tiniest details can inspire reflection and creativity in the human mind.

Extract 3

It paused as with suspicion of my pen,
And then came racing wildly on again
To where my manuscript was not yet dry;
Then paused again and either drank or smelt-
With loathing, for again it turned to fly.
Plainly with an intelligence I dealt.

(i) **What does the term 'intelligence' imply in the context of the poem?**

How does it apply to the mite's behaviour? (3)

Ans. The term 'intelligence' in the poem implies that the mite exhibits a certain awareness or instinctual decision-making ability, despite its small size.

The speaker suggests that the mite is not acting randomly but is instead reacting with a level of awareness, shown by its cautious behaviour and awareness of the manuscript. It indicates that even small creatures may possess some form of intelligence, albeit instinctive.

(ii) **Analyse the contrast between the mite's 'wild' movement and its cautious pauses.**

What does this reveal about its character or the poem's theme? (3)

Ans. The contrast between the mite's 'wild' movement and its cautious pauses illustrates the balance between impulsiveness and caution or intelligence.

The 'wild' movement shows a lack of control or direction, while the pauses show a moment of reflection or evaluation.

This duality may reflect the unpredictable nature of the human creativity-where ideas may rush forward impulsively but require moments of careful consideration. It also highlights how even the smallest creatures are capable of complex responses.

(iii) **What literary device is used in the poem when the poet gives human-like qualities of 'intelligence' to mite?**

How does this affect the reader's perception of the mite? (3)

Ans. The poet uses anthropomorphism, where the mite is attributed human-like intelligence.

This invites the reader to view the mite not just as an insect but as a creature with agency and purpose. This transforms the mite into more than a mere distraction, raising it to the status of a creature who is capable of conscious thought.

It also deepens the theme of creativity, suggesting that even the smallest, most insignificant things have a meaningful impact on the creative process.

(iv) **How does the description of the mite's movements help build the theme of unpredictability in the poem? Give reason for your answer. (3)**

Ans. The mite's movements like pausing, racing, drinking smelling, and flying away, perfectly capture the unpredictable nature of the creative process. Just as the mite does not follow a predictable path, creativity can also be spontaneous and fluctuating, moving between moments of uncertainty, inspiration, and hesitation.

This is because creativity and intelligence follow an unpredictable flow of ideas. Constant shifts occur during the process of writing or creating.

(v) **Do you think the poem has philosophical undertones? Why? Justify with reasons. (4)**

Ans. Yes, the poem has philosophical undertones as it explores themes of existence, perception, and the creative process.

The speaker's interaction with the tiny mite raises questions about the value of small things and how we assign meaning to them. The unpredictable behaviour of the mite mirrors the unpredictability of creativity and life itself, suggesting that both are influenced by forces beyond our control.

It invites reflection on how we perceive the world, the significance of even the smallest elements, and the uncertainty inherent in creation and existence.

Extract 4

It seemed too tiny to have room for feet,
Yet must have had a set of them complete
To express how much it didn't want to die.
It ran with terror and with cunning crept
It faltered: I could see it hesitate;
Then in the middle of the open sheet
Cower down in desperation to accept
Whatever I accorded it of fate.

(i) **How does the speaker describe the mite's behaviour? What does this suggest about the mite's state of mind? (3)**

Ans. The speaker describes the mite as hesitant, terrified, and desperate. It 'ran with terror' and 'crept with cunning' indicating fear and instinctive caution. The mite falters, hesitates, and 'cowers down' suggesting that it is in a state of distress, struggling to survive.

These actions show the mite's fear of its environment and possibly the impending danger (the speaker's pen).

(ii) **'It faltered: I could see it hesitate'. How does this line contribute to the tone of the poem? Justify. (3)**

Ans. The line 'It faltered: I could see it hesitate' contributes to the tone of uncertainty and tension in the poem. The mite's hesitation reflects its vulnerability and confusion about what to do next, which amplifies the sense of danger.

It adds to the theme of unpredictability in the creative process, where even the smallest, most insignificant elements can disrupt or alter the course of action.

(iii) **What can we infer about the relationship between the speaker and the mite? Explain in brief. (3)**

Ans. The relationship between the speaker and the mite seems to be one of dominance and control. The mite is described as being at the mercy of the speaker, having to 'accept whatever fate' is given.

This suggests that the speaker holds power over the mite, with the mite being unable to escape or influence its fate. This could symbolise the human tendency to control or impose meaning on smaller, powerless entities in life.

(iv) **Explain the meaning of 'Plainly with an intelligence I dealt'. What does it signify? (3)**

Ans. The phrase suggests that the speaker recognises the mite's behaviour as being more than just instinctive; it seems purposeful and calculated. The speaker is implying that the mite's actions are not random but show some form of awareness or intelligence.

This could signify that the mite is actively engaging with its environment and responding to the threat posed by the speaker's pen.

(v) **Analyse the attitude of the speaker towards the mite. What does it symbolise in a broader context? (4)**

Ans. The speaker's attitude toward the mite is one of detached observation. While he acknowledges the mite's fear and struggle, he doesn't intervene or show strong empathy. Instead, he seems more focused on the mite's behaviour, recognising its 'intelligence' and survival instinct. The speaker allows the mite to accept its fate, reflecting a passive attitude toward its struggle.

In a broader context, this attitude symbolises how humans often ignore the struggles of weaker or smaller beings. It may also represent how individuals must sometimes accept larger, uncontrollable forces in life.

Extract 5

I have none of the tenderer-than-thou
Collectivistic regimenting love
With which the modern world is being swept.
But this poor microscopic item now!
Since it was nothing I knew evil of
I let it lie there till I hope it slept.

(i) **'I have none of the tenderer-than-thou collectivistic regimenting love'.**
What does the speaker mean by this phrase? (3)

Ans. The speaker is rejecting the idea of the overly sentimental and controlling 'love' that is popular in modern society. The phrase 'tenderer-than-thou' suggests a pretentious or exaggerated form of love, while 'collectivistic regimenting love' refers to a love that forces conformity or order. The speaker contrasts this with a more individualistic, detached stance.

(ii) **Do you think the speaker's detachment from the mite is justified? Why or why not? (3)**

Ans. The speaker's detachment could be seen as justified in the context of his rejection of modern societal ideals of forced love and intervention. He seems to prefer a more passive approach to life, allowing things to unfold naturally.

However, one could argue that a little more empathy or action might have been justified, as the mite is a living creature, and a more compassionate response could have been better.

(iii) **How does the speaker's rejection of 'collectivistic regimenting love' reflect his broader worldview? (3)**

Ans. The rejection of 'collectivistic regimenting love' reflects the speaker's broader worldview of individualism and independence. He resists societal pressure to be overly sentimental and prefers a more detached and personal approach to life.

This worldview aligns with his passive treatment of the mite, where he doesn't impose any artificial emotions or actions on it.

(iv) **But this poor microscopic item now.**
Who does this line refer to? Why does the poet use this expression and what did he decide to do about it? (3)

Ans. The line 'But this poor microscopic item now' refers to the mite, a tiny creature.

The poet uses this expression to show that the mite is small and vulnerable. The word 'poor' suggests sympathy, but the speaker does not show deep emotion.

The poet decides to 'let it lie there till I hope it slept', meaning he chooses not to harm it but simply allows it to rest. This shows that the speaker is detached and doesn't interfere with the mite's fate.

(v) **What quality of the mite does the poet appreciate? Why? (4)**

Ans. The poet appreciates the mite's will to survive and determination. Despite its tiny size and vulnerability, the mite shows a strong desire to live. It is evident when it runs with terror, hesitates, and then cowers in desperation, accepting its fate. The poet acknowledges this instinctual drive for survival, even though the mite is powerless against the larger forces around it.

The poet seems to respect this quality because it reflects an inherent strength in the face of adversity, even in such a small, seemingly insignificant creature.

Extract 6

I have a mind myself and recognize
Mind when I meet with it in any guise
No one can know how glad I am to find
On any sheet the least display of mind.

(i) **What does the poet mean by 'I have a mind myself'? (3)**

Ans. The poet is asserting his own intellectual capacity and awareness. By saying 'I have a mind myself,' the poet is emphasising his ability to think, reason, and understand. It suggests that the poet is aware of his own intelligence and consciousness.

(ii) **Why does the poet express happiness upon finding 'the least display of mind' on any sheet? (3)**

Ans. The poet's joy at finding 'the least display of mind' reveals their appreciation for thought and intellect. The 'sheet' could refer to any surface where ideas are expressed.

This suggests that the poet values intellectual engagement. The speaker/poet is glad to find even small instances of creativity or reasoning, indicating that they are significant.

(iii) **Do you agree with the speaker's idea that any display of mind is worth appreciating? Justify your answer. (3)**

Ans. Yes, I agree with the speaker's idea that even smallest display of creativity and intelligence should be appreciated. This is because it encourages recognising and valuing all forms of intellectual expression, no matter how small. Appreciating even a small display of thought promotes a culture of creativity and learning.

(iv) **Describe the actions of mite throughout the poem. (3)**

Ans. The mite appears as a tiny speck on the poet's paper. As the poet raises his pen to stop it, he notices its movement. The mite pauses, then runs wildly, showing signs of fear and intelligence. It hesitates, then cowers down, as if accepting its fate. The poet, realizing it is a living creature, decides to let it be, respecting its tiny will to survive.

(v) **What does the poet say about the modern world? How does it add to the theme of the poem? (4)**

Ans. The poet criticises the modern world for its 'tenderer-than-thou collectivistic regimenting love' meaning that society today is obsessed with controlling and insincere forms of love. This contrasts with the speaker's more individual and natural view, focusing on intellect and survival.

This critique ties into the poem's theme by showing a difference between artificial, societal values and the natural survival instincts of the mite. The speaker rejects the controlling love of modern society and values authenticity which is symbolised by the mite's struggle to live.

05

THE POWER OF MUSIC

Sukumar Ray

Introduction

The Power of Music is a poem by Sukumar Ray, a famous Bengali poet known for his humorous and satirical writings. The poem talks about Bhisma Lochan Sharma, a man who sings passionately but without concern for how terrible his voice sounds. His loud and harsh singing creates chaos, disturbing people, animals and even nature. The poem belongs to the genre of nonsense verse, using exaggeration and humor to entertain the readers. Its unique charm lies in how it portrays the disastrous effects of lousy singing in a fun and imaginative manner.

About the Poem

The Power of Music by Sukumar Ray is a humorous poem that shows the often chaotic effects of music on both humans and animals. The poem tells the story of a musician whose unusual and different performance causes a range of surprising reactions, from funny to confusing.

People and animals are attracted to the music, and each responds in their own way, showing how music can affect everyone. Using fun language and imagery, the poem shows how music can capture attention, entertain and bring different beings together, even in chaos.

Exploring the Stanzas

When summer .... well-meant.

In this stanza, the poet introduces Bhisma Lochan Sharma, a passionate singer. His performances can be heard far and wide, from Delhi to Burma. He sings with intense dedication, as if he has given everything in his life to his singing. His efforts are sincere and well-meaning but his singing leaves people astonished and puzzled. They drive away in amazement.

The poem humorously exaggerates the contrast between Sharma's enthusiasm and the unexpected reactions of his audience.

They're .... out his broadside.

In this stanza, the readers see that Bhisma Lochan Sharma's singing causes chaos everywhere. People panic, fall sick, and beg him to stop, unable to bear his voice. They withdraw in confusion though they know that he is causing no harm. Even bullock-carts overturn, and horses are left stranded. Despite all this, Bhisma Lochan keeps singing loudly, completely unaware of the havoc he is causing. They hopelessly request him to stop singing but he continues.

The poem humorously exaggerates the chaos caused by his passionate singing.

The wretched .... quite confounded.

In this stanza, the poet describes that the animals are deeply disturbed by Bhisma Lochan Sharma's loud singing. They cry in desperation as they are totally confused not knowing what has hit them. Some are left bewildered by the sound. The lines humorously portray the dramatic reactions of animals to his overwhelming voice.

The fishes .... mansions tumble.

In this stanza, Bhisma Lochan Sharma's singing further causes chaos in the nature. Frightened fishes dive deep into the lake, desperate for peace. Trees collapse under the strain, their crashing heard from far away. Birds in the sky lose control and fall mid-flight. People, terrified by the noise, beg him to stop, fearing for their lives.

However, Bhisma remains unaffected, singing louder than ever. Even the skies seem to mourn his screech, and large buildings crumble under its impact. The lines humorously exaggerate the destructive power of his relentless singing.

But now there .... gift of silence.

In this stanza, a clever billy goat appears, ready to put an end to the chaos. He lowers his horns and charges directly at Bhisma Lochan Sharma, answering his loud singing with a mighty bellow of his own. The goat's powerful charge creates a blast of sound strong enough to disrupt Bhisma's singing. As a result, the music finally stops, and the world is gifted with the much-needed silence.

This moment brings relief after the overwhelming noise, and the poem humorously suggests that it took the courage and strength of a determined goat to silence Bhisma's relentless singing.

Theme of the Poem

The poem humorously shows the chaotic effects of music taken to extremes. Though sincere, Bhisma Lochan Sharma's loud and passionate singing creates panic and confusion everywhere. His enthusiasm represents how excessive passion can lead to unintended consequences. The poem contrasts human actions with nature's reactions, as animals and the environment respond dramatically to his voice. This highlights the difference between music and noise, showing how unchecked enthusiasm can turn music into a disturbance. The poem explores the fine balance between passion and its impact on the world through humour.

Message Conveyed by the Poem

The central message of the poem is that when passion and enthusiasm are taken to extremes, they can have unintended and chaotic consequences. While Bhisma Lochan Sharma's intense love for singing is sincere, it disrupts the world around him which causes panic and destruction among humans, animals and even buildings.

The poem highlights the importance of balance and moderation, suggesting that even something as powerful and beautiful as music can become harmful if not controlled. Through humour and exaggeration, Ray also implies that excessive enthusiasm–no matter how well-intentioned–can be overwhelming and disruptive to the natural order.

Style, Tone and Mood

- **Style** Sukumar Ray's style is humorous, exaggerated, and playful. The poem is written in a nonsensical way and comes under the category of nonsense poetry.
- **Tone** The tone of the poem is humorous and satirical.
- **Mood** The mood of the poem is light-hearted and comic, despite the chaos described in the poem.

Title

The title 'The Power of Music' is appropriate as the poem describes how Bhisma Lochan Sharma's music has a huge and disruptive effect on everything around him. His loud singing causes confusion, torture and chaos when animals panic, trees fall, and buildings collapse. The intended effect is comical.

This power of music highlights that while music can be powerful, too much of it can also cause harm. The title captures both the positive and negative sides of music's influence. However, in the end, the billy goat restores balance, showing that music's power must be controlled to prevent destruction.

Literary Devices

- **Alliteration** Welkin weeps ***[Stanza 4]***
  - Booming out his broadside ***[Stanza 3]***
  - Turn turtle ***[Stanza 4]***
  - Feathered fly ***[Stanza 4]***
  - Grants the world the golden gift of silence ***[Stanza 5]***

- Repetition Bellow answering bellow ***[Stanza 5]***
- Hyperbole Bullock carts overturned, horses line on roadside
  - People about to die
  - They whine and stare with feet in air mighty mansions tumble
  - Trees collapse
  - Birds turning turtle
  - The wretched brutes resent the blare the hour they hear it sounded.
  - A billy goat, most sagacious fellow
- Personification Welkin weeps ***[Stanza 4]***
  - Whine and stare
- Onomatopoeia Screech, Crash, Booming, Hums

Vocab Vault

Staked his mind Invested everything in life
Hell-bent Very determined
Dazed Disoriented
Retire Withdraw
Trampled Trodden under
Panic rout Chaos caused by anxiety
Languish Suffer
Plead Pray
Wretched Miserable
Brutes Animals
Resent Hate
Frantic Desperate
Collapse Fall
Feathered fly Birds
Turn turtle Turn upside down
Billy goat Male goat
Sagacious Wise
Bellow answering bellow Answering in the same manner
Tossed and whirled Thrown about

EXAM ORIENTED QUESTIONS

TYPE - 1 Multiple Choice Questions

01 Mark

Q.1 Which are the geographical locations mentioned in the poem 'The Power of Music'? **(Competency Based Que.)**

(i) Delhi (ii) Kolkata
(iii) Burma (iv) Bangalore

(a) (i) and (ii) (b) (i) and (iii)
(c) (ii) and (iv) (d) (iii) and (iv)

Q.2 In the context of the poem, the phrase 'staked his life' means

(a) he sings recklessly without caring about his safety.
(b) he sings with utmost passion and dedication.
(c) he is physically exhausted by his singing.
(d) he has faced life-threatening challenges to sing.

Q.3 What is the tone of the poem towards Bhisma Lochan Sharma?

(a) Sympathetic and encouraging
(b) Critical and disparaging
(c) Light-hearted and humorous
(d) Neutral and indifferent

Q.4 The repetition of 'he sings as though' emphasises

(a) The emotional intensity of Bhisma Lochan Sharma's performance.
(b) The uncertainty of his intentions.
(c) The monotony of his singing style.
(d) The audience's confusion about his motives.

Q.5 The poet's portrayal of Bhisma Lochan Sharma can be seen as a satire. Which of the following best supports this view?

(a) The poet exaggerates his passion to the point of absurdity.
(b) The poet focuses on his technical brilliance but mocks his audience.
(c) The poet contrasts his boldness with the timid reactions of others.
(d) The poet questions the relevance of art in modern society.

Q.6 Which of the following are not the reactions of the audience on Bhisma's singing?

(i) Fazed (ii) Dazed
(iii) Crazed (iv) Amazed

(a) (i) and (ii) (b) (ii) and (iii)
(c) (ii) and (iv) (d) (iii) and (i)

Q.7 'The people, dazed, retire amazed, although they know it's well meant'.
This line tells us that Bhisma Lochan's singing was ....

(a) melodious
(b) discordant
(c) soothing
(d) unbelievable

Q.8 What does the line "plead, 'My friend, we're near our end, oh stop your singing quickly'!" reveal about the audience?

(a) They find his singing melodious.
(b) They are deeply affected by the chaos his singing creates.
(c) They misunderstand his artistic intentions.
(d) They are trying to encourage him.

Q.9 From the poem, what do you gather about Bhisma's mindset?

(a) He is a master of entertainment
(b) He is generous
(c) He is not concerned about others
(d) He enjoys bullying

Q.10 What does the phrase 'panic rout' imply in the poem 'The Power of Music'? **(Competency Based Que.)**

(a) Solemn parade (b) Celebration
(c) Unhappy occasion (d) Chaotic situation

Q.11 Based on the imagery in the poem, what can be inferred about Bhisma Lochan Sharma's singing style?

(a) It is technically perfect but emotionally overwhelming.
(b) It is powerful but lacks harmony and appeal.
(c) It is both disruptive and mesmerising.
(d) It is misunderstood by the audience.

Q.12 'But Bhisma Lochan, unconcerned, goes/Booming out his broadside' Which of the following contains the figure of speech similar to what is used in the quoted line given above?

(a) Like glow worm golden in a dell of dew.
(b) She is as brave as a lion in the battlefield.
(c) His words were daggers that pierced my heart.
(d) The moon smiled down upon the lovers.

Q.13 What does the phrase 'resent the blare' suggest about the reaction of the animals?
(a) They are indifferent to the loud noise.
(b) They are overwhelmed and disturbed by the loud sound.
(c) They enjoy the blare and find it soothing.
(d) They react calmly and curiously to the noise.

Q.14 Which emotion is primarily conveyed by the animals in the poem?
(a) Joy (b) Awe
(c) Frustration (d) Indifference

Q.15 Pick the odd one out that does not tune with the context of the poem.
(a) Brutes whine and stare
(b) Trees collapse and shake
(c) Birds turn turtle
(d) People retaliate

Q.16 Which category does the poem fall in?
(a) Nonsense poetry (b) Comedy epic
(c) Narrative ballad (d) Pastoral elegy

Q.17 The use of visual imagery like 'feet in air' and 'whine and stare' achieves something in the poem. What is it?
(a) It conveys the animals' detailed physical distress.
(b) It makes the animals' reaction more relatable to humans.
(c) It emphasises the theatrical nature of the poem.
(d) It contrasts with the serenity of the natural setting.

Q.18 Which of the following is not the effect of Bhisma's singing as mentioned in the poem?
(ICSE Specimen 2025)
(a) The sky weeps tears
(b) The trees crash and shake
(c) The people retire amazed
(d) The turtles whine and stare

Q.19 And in the sky the feathered fly turn turtle while they're winging.
What does the phrase turn turtle mean?
(Competency Based Que.)
(a) Act like a turtle (b) Jump like a turtle
(c) Turn upside down (d) Become a turtle

Q.20 'The welkin weeps to hear his screech'. Identify the figure of speech used here.
(a) Alliteration (b) Onomatopoeia
(c) Personification (d) Oxymoron

Q.21 **Statement 1** Bhisma Lochan Sharma's singing causes mighty mansions to tumble.
Statement 2 This indicates that his singing is destructive beyond measure.
Select the option that correctly shows the relationship between statements (1) and (2).
(a) Both statements are true, and Statement 2 explains Statement 1.
(b) Both statements are true, but Statement 2 does not explain Statement 1.
(c) Statement 1 is true, but Statement 2 is false.
(d) Statement 1 is false, but Statement 2 is true.

Q.22 **Statement 1** The poet depicts Bhisma Lochan Sharma as a figure of reverence.
Statement 2 The poem portrays Bhisma Lochan Sharma humorously, focusing on the absurdity of his actions.
Select the option that correctly shows the relationship between statements (1) and (2).
(a) Both statements are true, and Statement 2 explains Statement 1.
(b) Both statements are true, but Statement 2 does not explain Statement 1.
(c) Statement 1 is true, but Statement 2 is false.
(d) Statement 1 is false, but Statement 2 is true.

Q.23 Complete the line.
'The fishes dived below the lake in ....'
(a) search for food (b) search for silence
(c) despair and fear (d) hopes of escape

Q.24 How does the poet use the reactions of nature to highlight the impact of Bhisma's singing?
(a) By portraying nature as resilient and unaffected.
(b) By exaggerating the destructive consequences.
(c) By focusing on harmony between art and the environment.
(d) By showing nature as a passive observer.

Q.25 What can be inferred about Bhisma Lochan Sharma's persistence despite the chaos he causes?
(a) He is unaware of the impact of his singing.
(b) He is determined to pursue his passion regardless of criticism.
(c) He believes the chaos is temporary and unimportant.
(d) He enjoys causing discomfort to his audience.

Q.26 The phrase 'a most sagacious fellow' suggest that ....
(a) the billy goat is physically strong
(b) the billy goat is wise and perceptive
(c) the billy goat is ferocious and violent
(d) the billy goat is indifferent to the singing

Q.27 Which figure of speech is used in the phrase 'bellow answ'ring bellow'?
(a) Alliteration (b) Onomatopoeia
(c) Personification (d) Hyperbole

Q.28 Identify the literary device present in 'strains of song are tossed and whirled by blast of brutal violence'. What does it imply?

(a) Metaphor, to depict the overwhelming force of the billy goat.
(b) Simile, comparing the song to a physical object.
(c) Hyperbole, exaggerating the impact of the billy goat's charge.
(d) Alliteration, emphasising the sound of the struggle.

Q.29 Complete the line.
'Bhisma Lochan grants the world the ....'.

(a) gift of joy (b) golden gift of silence
(c) sound of peace (d) precious melody

Q.30 Bhisma Lochan Sharma can be best described as ....

(a) Anti-hero (b) Caricature
(c) Cartoon (d) Hero

Q.31 What tone does the poet adopt in describing the billy goat's charge?

(a) Humorous and triumphant
(b) Serious and sombre
(c) Critical and analytical
(d) Sympathetic and emotional

Q.32 The conclusion of the poem could be interpreted differently if the billy goat were seen as a metaphor for natural justice. What does it imply?

(a) The billy goat represents the balance nature restores against disruption.
(b) The billy goat shows the futility of human creativity.
(c) The billy goat highlights the destructiveness of passion.
(d) The billy goat reveals the insignificance of individual actions.

Q.33 Arrange the following events in the correct sequence as they occur in the poem.

(i) The billy goat charges with his horns down.
(ii) Bhisma Lochan Sharma continues to sing despite the chaos.
(iii) The golden gift of silence is granted.
(iv) The creatures and trees react violently to the singing.

(a) (ii), (iv), (i), (iii) (b) (iv), (ii), (i), (iii)
(c) (ii), (i), (iv), (iii) (d) (i), (ii), (iii), (iv)

Answers

1. (b)	2. (d)	3. (c)	4. (a)	5. (a)	6. (d)	7. (b)	8. (b)	9. (c)	10. (d)
11. (b)	12. (a)	13. (b)	14. (c)	15. (d)	16. (a)	17. (a)	18. (d)	19. (c)	20. (c)
21. (a)	22. (d)	23. (b)	24. (b)	25. (b)	26. (b)	27. (b)	28. (a)	29. (b)	30. (b)
31. (a)	32. (a)	33. (a)							

Explanations

3. The tone of the poem is light – hearted and humorous. The poet uses humour to depict Bhisma Lochan Sharma's intense singing, highlighting its unintented and chaotic cons equences in a playful way.

15. In the context of the poem, option (a), (b) and (c) describe chaotic or unusual reactions to the intense music, such as animals and nature reacting in strange ways. Option (d) refers to human reaction. Thus, it is the odd one out.

16. The poem 'The Power of Music' falls under nonsense poetry as it uses exaggerated, whimsical and absurd imagery to create a humorous effect. In nonsense poetry, logic and reason are often set aside in favour of absurdity and fun.

28. The given phrase uses metaphor as it compares the song to something physical, tossed and whirled by the force of violence. The metaphor implies that the song is overwhelmed or destroyed by the sheer force of violence.

30. Bhisma Lochan Sharma can be best described as a caricature, as he is portrayed in exaggerated, humorous way.

31. The poet adopts a humorous and triumphant tone when describing billy goat's charge. The tone is light–hearted and the chaos created by the goat is presented humorously as if celebrating the goat's power and impact in a comic manner.

TYPE - 2 Extract Based Questions

16 Marks

Extract 1

When summer comes, we hear the hums
Bhisma Lochan Sharma.
You catch his strain on hill and plain from Delhi down to Burma
He sings as though he's staked his life, he sings as though he's hell-bent;
The people, dazed, retire amazed although they know it's well-meant.

(i) In which season would one hear Bhisma Lochan Sharma singing?
Where would one hear his voice? **(Competency Based Que., 3)**

Ans. One would hear Bhisma Lochan Sharma singing during summer.

They would hear his voice on the hill and on plains from Delhi to Burma.

(ii) How does the poet describe Bhisma Lochan Sharma's singing?
What effect does it have on the people? **(3)**

Ans. The poet describes Bhisma Lochan Sharma's singing as passionate and intense, comparing it to someone who has 'staked his life' and is 'hell-bent' on singing. This suggests that his singing is full of energy, urgency, and determination.

The people who hear his singing are dazed and amazed. The effect of the singing on the people is one of confusion, as they are left with mixed feelings.

(iii) The people retire 'amazed' after hearing Bhisma Lochan Sharma sing. How would you interpret the word 'amazed' in this context?
Do you think it conveys positive or negative feelings? Justify your answer. **(3)**

Ans. In this context, the word 'amazed' likely conveys a feeling of astonishment.

However, it is not purely positive. The people are amazed by the power and intensity of Bhisma Lochan Sharma's singing, but the use of the word in this setting suggests that the amazement might be accompanied by a sense of being overwhelmed. The amazement in this case could be viewed as a mixture of admiration and discomfort.

(iv) What do you think is the purpose of using such a wide geographical reference in the poem? **(3)**

Ans. Such a wide geographical reference is used to exaggerate the reach and impact of Bhisma Lochan Sharma's singing. It highlights the power of his voice-that it can be heard across vast distances, from the hills to the plains, and in places as far away as Burma.

This adds to the overall humorous tone of the poem.

(v) Which genre does the poem belong to? Justify your answer with appropriate reason. **(4)**

Ans. The poem belongs to the nonsensical genre, characterised by absurdity, exaggeration, and playful language.

It presents an exaggerated scene where Bhisma Lochan Sharma's singing causes trees to collapse, animals to panic, and people to be dazed. The billy goat, described as a 'sagacious fellow' ends the chaos with violence. This further adds to the absurdity and humour.

This nonsensical style allows the poem to entertain and engage readers through its imaginative and humorous exploration of the ridiculous, encouraging them to enjoy the fantastical without concern for logic or realism.

Extract 2

They're trampled in the panic rout or languish pale and sickly,
And plead,' My friend, we're near our end,oh stop your singing quickly! '
The bullock-carts are overturned, and horses line the roadside;
But Bhisma Lochan, unconcerned, goes booming out his broadside.
The wretched brutes resent the blare the hour they hear it sounded,
They whine and stare with feet in air or wonder quite confounded.

(i) What are the reactions of the animals and people to Bhisma Lochan Sharma's singing? **(3)**

Or How did animals react when they heard Bhisma Lochan Sharma? **(Competency Based Que.)**

Ans. The animals and people react with panic and distress to Bhisma Lochan Sharma's singing. The people are trodden under chaos while some feel pale and sickly. They plead for him to stop singing, fearing they are near their end.

The animals, including the bullocks and horses, are described as being in chaos, with the bullock-carts overturned and the horses lining the roadside. The animals resent the blaring sound and react in confusion, some with their feet in the air, staring in wonder at the noise.

(ii) **Do you think Bhisma Lochan Sharma is justified in continuing to sing despite the chaos he is causing? Why or why not?** **(3)**

Ans. From a logical perspective, Bhisma Lochan Sharma is not justified in continuing to sing despite the chaos. This is because his singing is causing panic, distress, and confusion among the people and animals around him.

However, from a poetic or artistic perspective, his unwavering commitment to singing could be seen as a metaphor for dedication and passion. This suggests that he is so absorbed in his own purpose that he ignores the consequences.

(iii) **What does the phrase 'they whine and stare with feet in air' reveal about the nature of the animals' distress?** **(3)**

Ans. The phrase 'they whine and stare with feet in air' conveys the animals extreme distress and confusion. The image of animals with their 'feet in air' suggests that they are disoriented, overwhelmed, and possibly even in a state of helplessness.

The use of 'whin' further indicates that the animals are not only physically affected but also emotionally distressed by the noise.

(iv) **What kind of people is Bhisma a caricature for?** **(3)**

Ans. Bhisma Lochan Sharma in the poem is a caricature of people who are overly focused on their own goals or passions and ignore the effects of their actions on others. His loud singing causes chaos, but he continues without caring about the discomfort he causes.

He represents people who, like stubborn idealists or self-absorbed artists, get so caught up in what they believe in that they don't realise when their actions are causing harm. The poem humorously points out how silly it is for someone to act without considering the impact on others.

(v) **The poet alludes to several aspects of music in the poem. Explain and Justify.** **(4)**

Ans. In the poem, the poet talks about different aspects of music, showing how powerful and intense it can be. Bhisma Lochan Sharma's singing is loud and overwhelming, showing how music can take over everything around it.

His singing is also full of passion and continues even though it causes chaos, showing how music can be unstoppable.

The poem shows how music affects everything in its path, with animals panicking and trees shaking. Overall, the poet shows that music can be both creative and disruptive.

Extract 3

The fishes dived below the lake in frantic search for silence,
The very trees collapse and shake - you hear the crash a mile hence -
And in the sky the feathered fly turn turtle while they're winging,
Again we cry,'We're goingto die, oh won't you stop your singing? '
But Bhisma's soared beyond our reach, howe'er we plead and grumble;
The welkin weeps to hear his screech, and mighty mansions tumble.

(i) **What do the fishes do in response to Bhisma Lochan Sharma's singing?** **(3)**

Ans. In response to Bhisma Lochan Sharma's singing, the fishes dive below the lake in a frantic search for silence. This suggests they are trying to escape the noise caused by his singing.

(ii) **Do you think the poet's portrayal of Bhisma Lochan Sharma's singing is exaggerated? Why or why not?** **(3)**

Ans. Yes, the poet's portrayal of Bhisma Lochan Sharma's singing is exaggerated. The description of fishes diving for silence, trees collapsing, and birds turning turtle in the sky is highly exaggerated, creating a comical effect.

The poet uses these exaggerated images to emphasise how overpowering and disruptive Bhisma's singing is, turning it into a humorous and absurd situation. The exaggeration serves to entertain the reader and highlight the absurdity of the scene.

(iii) **What is the significance of the phrase 'mighty mansions tumble' in the extract?** **(3)**

Ans. The phrase 'mighty mansions tumble' is significant as it emphasises the destructive and uncontrollable nature of Bhisma Lochan Sharma's singing. Even structures that are strong and grand, like mansions, are not immune to the chaos caused by his singing.

This image of 'tumbling' mansions highlights the overwhelming power of the noise, further exaggerating the impact Bhisma's singing has on everything around him. It underscores the absurdity of the situation and serves to enhance the comic and exaggerated tone of the poem.

(iv) **How does the poet describe the 'sky'? What does it do?** **(3)**

Ans. The poet describes the sky as the 'welkin', a term that refers to the heavens or the sky. In the poem, the sky is personified and is said to 'weep' upon hearing Bhisma Lochan Sharma's loud and disruptive singing. This personification suggests that the sky, like a human, is so affected by the singing that it expresses sorrow.

(v) **The poet uses a certain technique throughout the poem. What technique is it? How does he use it?** **(4)**

Ans. The poet uses hyperbole (exaggeration) throughout the poem. This technique makes things seem much bigger or more intense than they are. For example, the fishes are said to dive 'frantic[ally]' for silence, trees shake with a crash heard 'a mile hence', and birds 'turn turtle' while flying.

The sky is even described as 'weeping' from the noise. These exaggerations show how overwhelming and chaotic Bhisma Lochan Sharma's singing is, adding humour and emphasising its impact.

Extract 4

But now there comes a billy goat, a most
sagacious fellow,
He downs his horns and charges straight, with
bellow answ'ring bellow.
The strains of song are tossed and whirled by
blast of brutal violence,
And Bhisma Lochan grants the world the golden
gift of silence.

(i) **After reading the poem, give any three characteristic features that you can associate with Bhisma Lochan Sharma.** **(Competency Based Que., 3)**

Ans. Bhisma Lochan Sharma can be described as

Overzealous He sings with great passion and intensity, as if his life depends on it.

Oblivious He is unaware and unbothered about the chaos his singing causes around him.

Unstoppable His singing continues relentlessly, no matter the impact on others.

(ii) **How did the world get the golden gift of silence? Mention two ways in which music helps a person.** **(Competency Based Que., 3)**

Ans. The world got the golden gift of silence when Bhisma Lochan Sharma's singing was finally stopped by a billy goat, which charged at him, creating a blast of violence that silenced his singing.

Two ways in which music helps a person

(a) **Emotional Expression** Music allows a person to express their emotions, whether it's joy, sadness, or excitement.

(b) **Relaxation and Stress Relief** Music can calm the mind, reduce stress, and help a person relax.

(iii) **What is the significance of calling the billy goat 'sagacious'?** **(3)**

Ans. Calling the billy goat 'sagacious' is significant because it highlights the goat's wisdom and cleverness in knowing how to stop Bhisma Lochan Sharma's singing.

The term suggests that the goat is not only strong but also smart in stopping the chaos caused by the singing.

It adds a humorous and ironic touch, as the goat, often seen as a simple animal, is portrayed as the hero who saves the day.

(iv) **Why do you think the poet uses the phrase 'golden gift' to describe silence?** **(3)**

Ans. The poet uses the phrase 'golden gift' to describe silence because it emphasises how precious and valuable silence is after the overwhelming and disruptive noise of Bhisma Lochan Sharma's singing. The term 'golden' suggests that silence is a rare and cherished reward, highlighting its significance in contrast to the disruptive noise that preceded it.

(v) **The poet tries to furnish a message in the poem. What is the message? Does he do it successfully?** **(4)**

Ans. The poet conveys a message about the importance of balance and moderation in life. Bhisma Lochan Sharma's loud and constant singing, although done with passion and good intentions, causes chaos and discomfort to everyone around him. The billy goat's action, which silences the singing, represents the need for intervention when things get out of control.

The poet successfully conveys this message through humour and exaggeration. By using the exaggerated consequences of Bhisma's singing, the poet emphasises that too much of something, even if it's a comforting act like music, can be disruptive. The poem effectively shows that balance is needed to maintain peace and harmony.

QUESTION PAPER 2025

LITERATURE IN ENGLISH

(PAPER - 2)

General Instructions

Maximum Marks : 80

Time allowed : Two hours

Answers to this paper must be written on the paper provided separately.

You will **not** be allowed to write during the first **15** minutes.

This time is to be spent in reading the question paper.

The time given at the head of this paper is the time allowed for writing the answers.

The paper has **four** Sections.

Section A is compulsory—**All** questions in **Section A** must be answered.

You must attempt **one** question from each of the **Sections B, C** and **D** and **one** other question from **any Section** of your choice.

The intended marks for questions or parts of questions are given in brackets ().

Section (A)

*(Attempt **all** questions from this section.)*

Question 1

Choose the correct answers to the questions from the given options. **(16)**

(Do not copy the questions, write ONLY the correct answers.)

(i) What does Antony describe as, 'thou bleeding piece of earth,'?

(a) Caesar's robe that was stained with his blood
(b) The blood-soaked spot on which Caesar lies
(c) The bloodied pedestal on which Caesar fell
(d) Caesar's lifeless body covered in blood

(ii) When Brutus says, 'ambition's debt is paid', he means that ....

(a) Caesar's greed for power and possession had resulted in his death
(b) Caesar had left seventy-five drachmas for every citizen of Rome
(c) Mark Antony would be permitted to speak at Caesar's funeral
(d) The conspirators would be punished for assassinating Caesar

(iii) After Antony's speech following Caesar's assassination, the angry mob kills ....

(a) Cinna the conspirator (b) Cinna the poet (c) Decius Brutus (d) Cicero

(iv) When Antony says, 'He must be taught, and train'd, and bid go forth: A barren-spirited fellow,' he refers to ....

(a) Octavius (b) Lucilius (c) Lucius (d) Lepidus

(v) Who were the members of the Second Triumvirate, formed to rule over Rome after Caesar's assassination?

(a) Julius Caesar, Crassus, Pompey (b) Marcus Brutus, Caius Cassius, Casca
(c) Mark Antony, Octavius Caesar, Lepidus (d) Octavius Caesar, Julius Caesar, Mark Antony

(vi) Which of the following words best describes Cassius's mood when he says.

'Come, Antony, and young Octavius, come, Revenge yourselves alone on Cassius,'

(a) anxious (b) regretful (c) fearful (d) frustrated

(vii) In the poem, 'Haunted Houses', what does the speaker see at his fireside that the stranger cannot?

(a) The speaker only sees what is physically present
(b) The stranger can see the spirits while the speaker cannot
(c) The speaker sees both the present and the past
(d) The stranger sees both the present and the future

(viii) In the poem, 'The Glove and the Lions', who does Count de Lorge sigh for?

(a) The lions that ramped and roared (b) King Francis who loved a royal sport
(c) The nobles who filled the benches (d) The beauteous lively dame

(ix) Select the option that shows the correct relationship between Statements (1) and (2) from Maya Angelou's poem, 'When Great Trees Fall'.

Statement 1 When great trees fall, the world is left permanently unstable.

Statement 2 In the poem, the natural world is depicted as reacting with fear and uncertainty when great trees fall.

(a) (1) is false, but (2) is true. (b) Both (1) and (2) are false.
(c) (1) is true, but (2) is false. (d) Both (1) and (2) are true.

(x) The poem, 'A Considerable Speck', expresses Frost's

(a) love for the little organism (b) respect for intelligent life
(c) indifference to the tiny creature (d) anger at the mite's escape

(xi) Which of the given options contains the figure of speech that appears in the following line from the poem, 'The Power of Music'?

And in the sky the feathered fly turn turtle while

They're winging,

(a) You're one month on in the middle of May (b) Rainbow-tinted circles of light
(c) And life is too much like a pathless wood (d) The wind lies asleep in the arms of the dawn

(xii) In the short story, 'With the Photographer', the narrator asks the photographer, "Is it me?" because ....

(a) he is delighted with the photographer's skill (b) he looks very handsome in the photograph
(c) he is unable to recognise his own face (d) he is ashamed of how he looks in the picture

(xiii) In the short story, 'The Elevator', which of the following does Martin's father not do when Martin expresses his fear of the elevator?

(a) He dismisses Martin's concerns (b) He encourages Martin to use the stairs
(c) He tells Martin to grow up and be brave (d) He watches TV and ignores Martin's fear

(xiv) Choose the option that lists the sequence of events from Ray Bradbury's short story, 'The Pedestrian'.

1. One night, as he was nearing home, he was stopped by a police car.
2. Since his answers were considered odd and unacceptable, he was forced to enter the car and taken away.
3. Leonard Mead loved to walk through the empty streets at night.
4. A metallic voice from the car asked him a series of questions.

(a) 2, 1, 3, 4 (b) 1, 3, 4, 2 (c) 3, 1, 4, 2 (d) 4, 1, 2, 3

(xv) Where was Adjoa born?

(a) Nigeria (b) Ghana (c) Ethiopia (d) Kenya

(xvi) Why did M. Hamel have to leave the school after forty years of service?

(a) He was not allowed to teach French any longer (b) He had grown tired of his job as a school teacher
(c) He was thought to be too strict in his ways (d) He wanted to retire and take up farming

Section (B)

*(Answer **one or more** questions from this section.)*

DRAMA

(Julius Caesar by William Shakespeare)

Question 2

Read the extract from 'Julius Caesar' Act 3, Scene 2, given below and answer the questions that follow.

Antony

Friends, Romans, countrymen, lend me your ears;
I come to bury Caesar, not to praise him.
The evil that men do lives after them,
The good is oft interred with their bones;
So let it be with Caesar. The noble Brutus
Hath told you Caesar was ambitious;
If it were so, it was a grievous fault,
And grievously hath Caesar answer'd it.
Here, under leave of Brutus and the rest
For Brutus is an honourable man;
So are they all, all honourable men
Come I to speak in Caesar's funeral.

(i) What does Antony say he is there for?
What does he say he is not there for?
What do you think he is actually there for? **(3)**

(ii) What were the three conditions that Brutus had laid down before allowing Antony to speak to the citizens of Rome? **(3)**

(iii) List the three arguments that Antony uses immediately after he speaks these lines to prove conclusively that Julius Caesar was not ambitious. **(3)**

(iv) Antony repeatedly uses certain words in his speech to describe Brutus. What are they? Why does he do this? **(3)**

(v) Which one argument of Antony's do you think had the greatest impact on his listeners? Give a reason to support your answer.

What were the citizens' feelings towards Antony before he began his speech?

How do their feelings towards him change at the end of his speech? **(4)**

Question 3

Read the extract from 'Julius Caesar' Act 5, Scene 1, given below and answer the questions that follow.

Cassius Then, if we lose this battle,
You are contented to be led in triumph
Through the streets of Rome?
Brutus No, Cassius, no: think not, thou noble Roman,
That ever Brutus will go bound to Rome;
He bears too great a mind. But this same day
Must end that work the ides of March begun;
And whether we shall meet again I know not.
Therefore our everlasting farewell take:
Forever, and forever, farewell, Cassius.
If we do meet again, why, we shall smile;
If not, why then, this parting was well made.

(i) Why does Brutus say, 'No, Cassius, no'?

What conditions may force Brutus to go bound to Rome?

Brutus says, 'And whether we shall meet again I know not.' What do these words imply? **(3)**

(ii) To what does Brutus refer when he says, 'the work which the ides of March begun'?

How was 'that work' begun?

What political change would take place in Rome if Brutus and Cassius lose this battle? **(3)**

(iii) Earlier in this scene, Cassius had confided to Messala a strange occurrence that he had observed when his army was on its way from Sardis to Philippi.

Describe this strange occurrence. **(3)**

(iv) How does Brutus die?

How does his manner of dying contradict the philosophy by which he had lived his life? **(3)**

(v) At the end of the play, Antony calls Brutus, 'the noblest Roman of them all'. Why does he say this?

What does this reveal of Antony's character? **(4)**

Section (C)

*(Answer **one or more** questions from this section.)*

Prose - Short Stories

(Treasure Chest — A Collection of Poems and Short Stories)

Question 4

Read the following extract from William Sleater's short story, 'The Elevator' and answer the questions that follow.

Martin felt nervous when he got back to the building after school. But why should he be afraid of an old lady? He felt ashamed of himself. He pressed the button and stepped into the elevator, hoping that it would not stop, but it stopped on the third floor. Martin watched the door slide open ......

(i) Who entered the elevator when the door slid open? Describe this person. **(3)**

(ii) Why was Martin afraid of using this elevator? **(3)**

(iii) What led to Martin's fall down the stairs?

What did it result in? **(3)**

(iv) How does the story end? Bring out the element of horror in the ending. **(3)**

(v) What was Martin's father's opinion of him? What does this reveal to us about his father's character? **(4)**

Question 5

Read the following extract from Alphonse Daudet's short story, 'The Last Lesson' and answer the questions that follow.

"My children, this is the last lesson I shall give you. The order has come from Berlin to teach only German in the schools of Alsace and Lorraine. The new master comes tomorrow. This is your last French lesson. I want you to be very attentive.

What a thunder-clap these words were to me!

Oh the wretches; that was what they had put up at the town-hall!

(i) What does the word, 'that' in the extract refer to?

What other 'bad news' had the villagers received from the bulletin board outside the town-hall? **(3)**

(ii) How does the narrator describe the daily bustle at the start of a typical school day? **(3)**

(iii) What was different on that morning when he arrived late for school? **(3)**

(iv) What thoughts filled the narrator's head when he heard the above announcement? **(3)**

(v) What does M. Hamel urge his listeners never to forget?

M. Hamel writes a few words on the board at the end of the lesson. What were they?

What does he hope to inspire through his words and actions on that day? **(4)**

Section (D)

*(Answer **one or more** questions from this section.)*

Poetry

(Treasure Chest — A Collection of Poems and Short Stories)

Question 6

Read the following extract from Leigh Hunt's poem, 'The Glove and the Lions' and answer the questions that follow.

And truly 'twas a gallant thing to see that crowning show,
Valour and love, and a king above, and the royal beasts below.

(i) Describe the scene at the beginning of the poem. **(3)**

(ii) "Leigh Hunt uses vivid sound and visual images to describe the contest between the royal beasts in the pit." Justify with close reference to the text. **(3)**

(iii) Who was the 'beauteous lively dame' mentioned in the poem?
What did she do?
What prompted her to do this? **(3)**

(iv) Explain the following lines in your own words. **(3)**
(a) 'Smiling lips and sharp bright eyes which always seemed the same'
(b) 'The occasion is divine'
(c) 'Faith, gentlemen, we're better here than there'

(v) When King Francis exclaims, "rightly done!", what action of Count de Lorge does he applaud?
Why do you think the Count behaved the way he did? **(4)**

Question 7

Read the following extract from Robert Frost's poem, 'A Considerable Speck' and answer the questions that follow.

This was no dust speck by my breathing blown,
But unmistakably a living mite With inclinations it could call its own.

(i) What did the narrator first imagine the 'speck' to be?
What does his use of the words 'speck' and 'mite' tell us about it? **(3)**

(ii) What was the narrator doing when he spotted the speck?
Which two words from the poem helped you come to this conclusion? **(3)**

(iii) What made him realise that he was dealing with 'an intelligence'? **(3)**

(iv) Why did the narrator conclude that the mite had feet? **(3)**

(v) Describe the narrator's initial response to the speck.
What did he eventually decide to do about it?
Why does he make this decision?
What does this decision reveal of his character? **(4)**

Answers

1. (i) (b) The blood-soaked spot on which Caesar lies
   (ii) (a) Caesar's greed for power and possession had resulted in his death
   (iii) (b) Cinna the poet
   (iv) (d) Lepidus
   (v) (c) Mark Antony, Octavius Caesar, Lepidus
   (vi) (b) regretful
   (vii) (c) The speaker sees both the present and the past
   (viii) (d) The beauteous lively dame
   (ix) (a) (1) is false, but (2) is true.
   (x) (b) respect for intelligent life
   (xi) (a) You're one month on in the middle of May
   (xii) (c) He is unable to recognise his own face
   (xiii) (b) He encourages Martin to use the stairs
   (xiv) (c) 3, 1, 4, 2
   (xv) (b) Ghana
   (xvi) (a) He was not allowed to teach French any longer

2. (i) Antony says he is there to bury Caesar, not to praise him.

   He says he is not there to speak against Brutus and the conspirators.

   He is actually there to turn the people against the conspirators by making them realise that Caesar was not ambitious and was wrongfully killed.

   (ii) The three conditions that Brutus had laid down before allowing Antony to speak to the citizens of Rome were

   (a) Antony must not blame the conspirators in his speech.

   (b) He must speak only after Brutus has spoken.

   (c) He must say that he is speaking with the permission of the conspirators.

   (iii) The three arguments that Antony uses were

   (a) Caesar refused the crown three times. If he were ambitious, he would have accepted it.

   (b) He brought wealth to Rome. He filled Rome's treasury with money from his victories.

   (c) He cared for the poor. He wept for them and was not greedy for power.

   (iv) He calls Brutus and the other conspirators 'honourable man'. He repeats this phrase again and again, but in a sarcastic way, to make the people question whether Brutus and the others are truly honourable.

(v) The most powerful argument was reading Caesar's will, where he left money and land for the people. This made them realise that Caesar loved them and was not ambitious.

At first, the citizens supported Brutus and believed Caesar's killing was justified.

By the end, they were angry at the conspirators and ready to rebel. They wanted revenge for Caesar's murder.

3. (i) Brutus says this because he refuses to be captured and taken as a prisoner to Rome.

Brutus would be taken as a prisoner if they lost the battle and were captured by the enemy.

These words show that Brutus is unsure if he and Cassius will survive the battle. He knows that this might be their last meeting.

(ii) He is referring to the assassination of Julius Caesar.

It began when Brutus and the other conspirators killed Caesar on the Ides of March (March 15) to stop him from becoming a dictator.

If they lost, Antony and Octavius would take full control of Rome, making it an empire instead of a republic.

(iii) Cassius saw eagles flying with his army as they marched to Philippi. But later, the eagles left and instead, ravens, crows and kites (birds of death) flew above them. He took this as a bad omen, meaning they would lose the battle.

(iv) Brutus kills himself by running onto his own sword, which is held by his servant Strato.

Brutus believed in Stoicism, which teaches self-control and facing hardships without emotion. However, his suicide shows that he gave in to his emotions and fear of defeat.

(v) Antony says this because Brutus killed Caesar not out of personal hatred or jealousy but for what he thought was the good of Rome. Unlike the other conspirators, Brutus acted with honour.

It shows that Antony, despite being an enemy of Brutus, is fair and can recognise true nobility. He respects Brutus even after his death.

4. (i) A fat lady entered the elevator.

She was very large, wearing an old green coat. She had big, fleshy cheeks, no chin and a thick neck.

Her small blue eyes stared at Martin in a strange way.

(ii) Martin was scared of elevators in general. This one was small, dark and shaky, which made him more nervous.

His fear increased when the fat lady kept staring at him without saying anything.

(iii) Martin was terrified when he saw the fat lady waiting for him in the elevator. He panicked and ran down the stairs, which were dark. He tripped and fell.

He broke his leg and had to use crutches. This meant he could not take the stairs anymore and had to use the elevator.

(iv) The story ends with Martin trapped in the elevator with the fat lady. She presses the stop button, looks at him and laughs.

The ending is scary because Martin is stuck with the strange lady and no one is there to help him.

Her laugh and the stopped elevator create a sense of fear and mystery.

(v) Martin's father thought he was weak and a coward.

His father was strict and unsympathetic. He did not understand Martin's fears and often made fun of him instead of supporting him.

5. (i) The word 'that' refers to the order from Berlin that banned the teaching of French in Alsace and Lorraine.

The villagers had received other bad news from the bulletin board, such as lost battles, forced army recruitment (the draft) and orders from the Prussian officials.

(ii) The narrator describes the usual school morning as busy and noisy. There would be the sound of desks opening and closing, students repeating lessons loudly and M. Hamel's ruler tapping on the table.

(iii) That morning, everything was silent. There was no noise, no commotion and the classroom felt like a Sunday morning. The villagers were also sitting quietly in the back of the class.

(iv) When Franz heard the announcement, he felt shocked and regretful. He realised he had wasted time playing instead of studying. His books, which earlier felt like a burden, suddenly felt like dear friends.

(v) M. Hamel urges his listeners to never forget their language. He tells them that as long as people hold on to their language, they remain free.

At the end of the lesson, M. Hamel writes 'Vive La France!' on the board. Through his words and actions, he hopes to inspire love for their country and language.

6. (i) The poem begins with a grand royal event where King Francis and his court are watching a fierce fight between lions. Nobles and ladies are seated in the audience, enjoying the spectacle. Count de Lorge sits among them, admiring a beautiful lady. The scene is full of excitement, bravery and danger, with the king above and the wild beasts below.

(ii) The poet creates a lively picture of the violent lion fight using strong sound and visual imagery. The lions ramp and roar with horrid laughing jaws, making terrifying noises. Their blows are strong like beams and their paws create wind. They roll on one another, covering the pit with sand and flying manes. The bloody foam splashes into the air, making the scene even more wild and intense.

(iii) The beauteous lively dame was a young and beautiful lady whom Count de Lorge loved.

She dropped her glove into the lion's pit to test the Count's love and see if he would risk his life for her.

She wanted to show off in front of the king, nobles and other lovers. She believed that if Count de Lorge retrieved the glove, it would prove his bravery and love for her, making her feel proud.

(iv) (a) 'Smiling lips and sharp bright eyes which always seemed the same'

The lady always appeared cheerful and confident. Her sharp eyes showed she was clever and watchful and she always had the same charming expression, no matter the situation.

(b) 'The occasion is divine'

The lady thought this was the perfect moment to test Count de Lorge's love. She felt that with the king and nobles watching, it was a great opportunity to gain glory and admiration.

(c) 'Faith, gentlemen, we're better here than there'

King Francis says this after watching the violent fight between the lions. He means that it is safer to watch from a distance than to be in the dangerous pit. He acknowledges the risk and brutality of the scene.

(v) King Francis applauds Count de Lorge for throwing the glove back at the lady. He approves of the Count's decision not to be fooled by vanity.

The Count realised that the lady's test was foolish and vain. He felt insulted that she made him risk his life for her pride rather than true love. By throwing the glove back, he rejected her shallow demand and showed his self-respect and intelligence.

7. (i) The narrator first thought the speck was just a dust particle blown by his breath.

The words 'speck' and 'mite' show that it was very tiny but still a living creature.

(ii) The narrator was writing when he noticed the speck.

The words 'paper sheet' and 'manuscript' suggest this.

(iii) He realised the mite had intelligence because it moved with purpose, paused and reacted to his pen, showing it had its own will.

(iv) The narrator concluded that the mite had feet because it ran, crept and hesitated, showing controlled movement.

(v) At first, the narrator raised his pen to stop the speck with a dot of ink.

Later, he chose to let it live because he saw it was a thinking, living creature.

He made this decision because he respected its intelligence and saw no reason to harm it.

This shows that the narrator is thoughtful, observant and kind.

ICSE SPECIMEN PAPER
LITERATURE IN ENGLISH
(PAPER - 2)

General Instructions

Maximum Marks : 80

Time allowed : Two hours

Answers to this paper must be written on the paper provided separately.

You will **not** be allowed to write during the first **15** minutes.

This time is to be spent in reading the question paper.

The time given at the head of this paper is the time allowed for writing the answers.

The paper has **four** Sections.

Section A is compulsory—**All** questions in **Section A** must be answered.

You must attempt **one** question from each of the **Sections B, C** and **D** and **one** other question from **any Section** of your choice.

The intended marks for questions or parts of questions are given in brackets ().

Section (A)

*(Attempt **all** questions from this section.)*

Question 1

Choose the correct answer to the questions from the given options. **(16)**

(Do not copy the question, write the correct answers only.)

(i) Where was Caesar put to death?

(a) On a street in Rome (b) On the battleground of Philippi

(c) At the foot of Pompey's statue (d) In Brutus' orchard

(ii) Who asks permission to speak at Caesar's funeral?

(a) Brutus (b) Antony (c) Cassius (d) Octavius

(iii) "Woe to the hand that shed this costly blood! Over thy wounds now do I prophesy..." These lines tell us that Antony is......... .

(a) enraged (b) sorrowful (c) anxious (d) frustrated

(iv) When Antony says, 'This is a slight unmeritable man, / Meet to be sent on errands', he refers to

(a) Lepidus (b) Octavius (c) Pindarus (d) Lucilius

(i) To whom are these words addressed?

Why is Brutus angry with this person? **(3)**

(ii) How does this person feel when he hears these words?

What does he say to defend himself? **(3)**

(iii) Why did Brutus need 'certain sums of gold'?

Why was he unable to raise these sums of money? **(3)**

(iv) Earlier in this scene, Brutus refers to Lucius Pella.

What had he been accused of?

Who had supported him and how? **(3)**

(v) Mention any two aspects of Brutus' character that are revealed in the above extract.

What do you understand about the relationship between Brutus and the person he addresses? **(4)**

Section (C)

*(Answer **one or more** questions from this section.)*

Prose - Short Stories

(Treasure Chest — A Collection of Poems and Short Stories)

Question 4

Read the following extract from Stephen Leacock's short story 'With the Photographer' and answer the questions that follow.

"The photographer beckoned me in. I thought he seemed quieter and graver than before. I think, too, there was a certain pride in his manner.

He unfolded the proof of a large photograph, and we both looked at it in silence.

'Is it me'? I asked.

'Yes', 'he said quietly, 'it is you', and we went on looking at it.

(i) Where was the narrator?

Why had he gone there?

Why do you think that there was a certain pride in the photographer's manner? **(3)**

(ii) What does the word 'proof' mean in this context?

Why did the narrator ask, 'Is it me'? **(3)**

(iii) Which of the narrator's facial features had the photographer altered? **(3)**

(iv) What was the only part of the narrator's face that seemed original in the photograph?

How did the photographer plan to 'fix' this? **(3)**

(v) At the end of the story, the narrator flies into a rage.

What makes him angry?

How would you justify the narrator's angry outburst? **(4)**

Question 5

Read the following extract from Ray Bradbury's short story 'The Pedestrian' and answer the questions that follow.

"He would stand upon the corner of an intersection and peer down
long moonlit avenues of sidewalk in four directions, deciding which
way to go, but it really made no difference;"

(i) What was Leonard Mead's occupation?

What did he love to do?

When is the story set? **(3)**

(ii) To what does Mead compare his walk through the empty streets?

Mention two reasons he gives for making this comparison. **(3)**

(iii) Why had Mead decided to change his footwear from hard-heeled shoes to sneakers? **(3)**

(iv) What happened quite suddenly as he was making his way home?

What was Mead's immediate reaction? **(3)**

(v) Why was Mead taken away by the police car?

Would you call this a horror story or a piece of science fiction?

Give reasons for your answer. **(4)**

Section (D)

*(Answer **one or more** questions from this section.)*

Poetry

(Treasure Chest — A Collection of Poems and Short Stories)

Question 6

Read the following extract from H.W. Longfellow's poem 'Haunted Houses' and answer the questions that follow.

The stranger at my fireside cannot see
The forms I see, nor hear the sounds I hear;
He but perceives what is; while unto me
All that has been is visible and clear.

(i) What makes the poet-narrator different from the stranger at his fireside? **(3)**

(ii) According to the poet, what turns a house into a haunted house? **(3)**

(iii) Where is one likely to meet the 'phantoms' in a haunted house? **(3)**

(iv) What are the poet-narrator's views on owning property? **(3)**

(v) How do the poet's views of ghosts differ from the traditional perception of ghosts? How would you describe the mood that the poem evokes? Give one reason for your answer. **(4)**

Question 7

Read the following extract from Maya Angelou's poem 'When Great Trees Fall' and answer the questions that follow.

When great trees fall in forests,
small things recoil into silence,
their senses eroded beyond fear.

(i) What effect does the falling of a 'great tree' have on the creatures of the forest? **(3)**

(ii) How does the death of a great soul affect the lives of those left behind in the immediate aftermath of their passing? **(3)**

(iii) What long-term effect does the death of a 'great soul' have? **(3)**

(iv) What feeling is being expressed by the following lines/phrases? **(3)**

(a) Small things recoil into silence

(b) Kind words/ unsaid,

(c) be and be/ better. For they existed

(v) What is a 'Great tree' a metaphor for?

What is the central message of Angelou's poem, 'When Great Trees Fall'? **(4)**

Answers

1. (i) (c) At the foot of Pompey's statue

   (ii) (b) Antony

   (iii) (a) enraged

   (iv) (a) Lepidus

   (v) (b) Remain where they are

   (vi) (b) his life had come full circle

   (vii) (c) 'Rich gifts of raiment or grain or gold'?

   (viii) (d) The turtles whine and stare

   (ix) (b) Glide

   (x) (a) the impact of the death of a loved one on those left behind

   (xi) (a) the journey of a mite across a sheet of paper

   (xii) (d) reading magazines

   (xiii) (a) they were slender

   (xiv) (b) 2, 4, 1 and 3

   (xv) (c) (I) is the cause for (II).

   (xvi) (b) dystopian

2. (i) The speakers are at the Capitol in Rome, sitting at the Senate.

   The word 'puissant' means having great power or influence.

   The line 'Metellus Cimber throws before thy seat a humble heart' means that Metellus Cimber requests Caesar to listen to his plea with a humble heart.

   (ii) Previous to the given conversation, the Soothsayer had warned Caesar about the Ides of March as he predicted a threat around Caesar on that day. Caesar had dismissed his concerns.

   Caesar had said the above line to remind the Soothsayer that it was already ides of march and he was unharmed. The Soothsayer in response reminds him that the day is not over yet.

   (iii) Trebonius was given the task to lure Antony out of the Senate room so that Caesar is left alone with the conspirators. Casca was asked to be the first to attack and stab Caesar.

   Before entering the Senate room, Popillius Lena wishes Cassius good luck for his enterprise that day. Hearing his commendation, Cassius becomes nervous as he thinks Lena has discovered the conspirators' plans to assassinate Caesar.

   (iv) Artemidorus requests Caesar to address his letter as a matter of priority. He tries to entice Caesar into opening his letter first by informing Caesar that the contents of his letter pertain to Caesar directly.

Caesar refuses to open Artemidorus' letter. He decides to address any personal matters last as he wanted to address the matters of his people and subjects first. He establishes that the welfare of his people comes before his own.

(v) Based on the above short exchange, I sympathise with Caesar. He was not a perfect leader but he was a good and strong ruler.

He refused to read Artemidorus' letter as it addressed a personal issue. Instead, he insisted on reading matters of his people first. This shows his dedication and concern for his subjects over his own. He valued the welfare of his people over his own.

He was a just and stern ruler who upheld law and order above everything else. Even after several pleas from Metellus Cimber and other conspirators to allow Metellus's brother, Publius to return to Rome, Caesar refuses as Publius was banished by lawful means. This shows Caesar's honour and fair-mindedness.

Caesar was also known to share wealth with the poor. He redistributed land to the poor and soldiers. His will stated to share some part of his wealth among the poor after his death.

Being such a fair and powerful leader for Rome, he didn't deserve to be murdered by the hands of the conspirators, some that he considered friends.

3. (i) Brutus is addressing the above words to Cassius.

Brutus is expressing his anger and disappointment after learning that Cassius was accepting bribes in exchange of power. He also expresses his frustration when Cassius refused to send him money when he needed it.

(ii) Cassius felt angry and hurt after hearing Brutus's accusations.

He defends himself by clarifying that he didn't intend to refuse help. Instead, the messengers had made a mistake and caused a miscommunication between them.

(iii) Brutus needed the money to help pay the soldiers of his battalion.

He was unable to gather such a sum as he didn't have any funds of his own and refused to raise money using vile means. He argues that he would rather turn his own heart into gold and his blood drops into silver coins than rob poor and innocent villagers of their hard-earned money.

(iv) Lucius Pella was accused of siphoning off money from the Sardians. Brutus humiliated Pella by condemning his actions and disgraced him.

Cassius had written to Brutus defending Pella and requesting him to absolve Pella of these accusations. He says so because he knew the man well.

(v) The above extract showcases Brutus's high morals. He holds honesty and loyalty on the highest pedestal and expects others to do the same. In the extract, Brutus condemns Cassius for accepting bribes. He expresses his disappointment in Cassius for committing such a shameful act.

However, this scene also showcases the double standards. As he criticises Cassius's act of accepting bribes, he also argues with Cassius for not aiding him financially to pay his battalion using the bribe money. By doing this, he establishes that he can never extort money from the poor but doesn't mind using Cassius's 'loot' to pay his soldiers.

The relationship between Cassius and Brutus is shown to be strained in the above dialogue. They quarrel and find faults in each other without accepting their own mistakes. It showcases evident differences in their personalities and value system that leads to clashes between them.

4. (i) The narrator was at the Photographer's studio.

The narrator went to the studio to get a picture of him clicked. He wanted to get a good picture of him to serve as a memory for his friends and loved ones when he dies.

As the narrator's looks were not ideal or 'good' according to the photographer, he struggled with taking a good picture of the narrator. So, the photographer was proud of his work as, according to him, he was able to produce a 'good' picture of the narrator despite the narrator's bad features.

(ii) The 'proof' in the above extract means the sample or draft of a picture before it is finally printed.

The narrator enquired if the person in the picture was him as he could not recognise himself. The photographer had edited and distorted the image a lot and the narrator struggled to find any resemblance between him and the person in the picture.

(iii) The photographer had altered the narrator's eyes, eyebrows, forehead, facial hair and mouth.

(iv) The only part of the narrator that seemed original in the photograph was his ears.

The photographer planned to use a new technique called Sulphide to remove the ears entirely in the final edit to 'fix' them.

(v) The narrator was furious as the picture didn't look like him at all. The photographer had altered his appearance to match his own superficial standards.

The narrator is justified in his angry outburst. The photographer was unprofessional and insensitive to the narrator's feelings. The narrator simply wanted an image of his own. Instead, he got humiliated and body shamed by the photographer. Initially, the narrator was extremely amiable and patient to the photographer's criticism. He tried to amend himself as much as possible. However, the photographer's constant degrading remarks about his features had a negative impact on his self-worth and image, and eventually pushed him to fury.

5. (i) Leonard Mead was a writer by profession.

He loved to go out for long evening walks every day to get some fresh air after all his neighbours had retired inside their homes to watch television.

The story is set in 2053 A.D.

(ii) Mr. Mead compares his walk in the vacant streets to the shadow of a hawk in the Arizona desert.

He makes the comparison as the roads were empty and deserted in his neighbourhood in the evening. He only saw some dogs and had his own thoughts for company. The emptiness of the streets reminded him of his home. Being the only person out on the streets, he feels lonely and singled out. He feels like a hawk in the Arizona desert looking for civilisation.

(iii) Mr. Mead decided to change his footwear from heels to sneakers to avoid confrontations with the street dogs. His boots had hard heels which would make sound when he walked on concrete or pavement. This would gather the attention of the stray dogs who would chase after him. So, to avoid making loud noises to alert the attention of the stray dogs, he shifted to sneakers which would make a softer noise.

(iv) Mr. Mead saw a lone car turning around the corner. The car turned out to be the only police car out for patrolling.

Mr. Mead was surprised to see the car as he was not expecting anyone to be on the streets at that hour of the day. He knew that most people in the society were glued on their couch watching television shows at that time of the day.

(v) Mr. Mead was taken away by the police car for walking aimlessly around the town late in the evening.

I would call the story a piece of science fiction. The story sheds a light on the dangers of overdependence on technology in today's world.

In the world that Bradbury describes, the society is technologically-ruled. People are addicted to television and human interactions have become minimal. The crime rates have gone down so only one AI controlled cop car is used to patrol the whole city at night.

Through his story, Bradbury tries to display an admonishing tale which warns the world of the disadvantages of becoming technologically driven.

6. (i) The poet is different from the stranger at his fireside as the stranger can only feel the presence of people they could see around them. Whereas, the poet can see and hear the ghosts as well. He also suggests that the stranger can only see the present while the poet has the ability to also perceive the past.

(ii) The presence of the phantoms of people who used to live or died in the houses made the house 'haunted', according to the poet.

(iii) One can meet the 'phantoms' anywhere in the house. They can be found gliding around the house through the doors. We can meet them at the doorways, on the stairs or along the passages and halls of the house.

(iv) The poet believes that the living people in the houses don't own the houses or lands they inhabit. He states that the spirits who lived in these houses and lands are the original owners of those lands. They hold deeds to the houses in their hands, reaching their hands out of their graves.

(v) Traditionally, the presence of ghosts in a house or land is considered to be a frightful ordeal. Most people believe that ghosts are vengeful spirits that haunt the earth because of unfinished business or spite. However, the poet paints a harmless image of the ghosts in the poem. He believes that the ghosts are gentle and keep to themselves.

The poem tries to invoke the mood of security and comfort. Throughout the poem, the poet ensures the presence of phantoms in the house or around us is not malevolent. He constantly paints the image of the ghosts going about their day completing their own errands.

7. (i) When 'great trees' fall, the effect is felt in the whole forest. The loud noise frightens mighty animals like lions and elephants. Lions hunker down into tall grasses and elephants lumber to seek safety. Small animals also recoil into their places of safety till the vibrations die down.

(ii) After the loss of a great soul, the lives of the people they leave behind changes tremendously. In the initial days of grief, the air around them feels thin and rare. They find difficulty in breathing. They are overwhelmed by the hurtful reality of the absence of their loved one. They are flooded by their memories and guidance that helped them progress in life. They are consumed with remorse for kind words that were left unsaid or promises that were never fulfilled.

(iii) In the long term, our reality is forever plagued by the memory of the 'great soul'. Our souls that once flourished under the guidance of the 'great soul' start to shrink and shrivel from their absence. We struggle to cope with the emotional void we feel after they leave. The impact is so immense that sometimes we start to question our existence without them. We feel lonely and isolate ourselves from others to cope up with our grief.

(iv) The feeling being expressed in the given.

(a) Feelings of shock and panic

(b) Feeling of regret

(c) Feeling of optimism and bittersweet hope

(v) The 'great tree' is a metaphor for a great soul or significantly wise personality in our life. An old tree provides food and shelter to many small or big animals in a forest. When it falls, the entire forest is shocked and stunned by its loss. The animals who depended on it for food and shelter, don't have its protection now. It leaves a visibly large void where it stood, and the animals dependent on it have to eventually look for another way of survival.

Similarly, the poet uses the metaphor 'great tree' to emphasise on the loss of a loved one in our life and how their sudden absence impacts us. Our loved ones provide an environment of love and support. They guide us and help us learn the ways of life. But, their sudden demise is traumatic for us. The loss of their protection leaves us feeling clueless and helpless. Their absence leaves a void in our life which cannot be filled very easily. But eventually we heal and move on. Their memory and influence linger behind and help us shape our lives positively.

SAMPLE QUESTION PAPER
LITERATURE IN ENGLISH
(PAPER - 2)

General Instructions

Maximum Marks : 80

Time allowed : Two hours

Answers to this paper must be written on the paper provided separately.

You will **not** be allowed to write during the first **15** minutes.

This time is to be spent in reading the question paper.

The time given at the head of this paper is the time allowed for writing the answers.

The paper has **four** Sections.

Section A is compulsory—**All** questions in **Section A** must be answered.

You must attempt **one** question from each of the **Sections B, C** and **D** and **one** other question from **any Section** of your choice.

The intended marks for questions or parts of questions are given in brackets ().

Section (A)

*(Attempt **all** questions from this section.)*

Question 1

Choose the correct answer to the questions from the given options. **(16)**

(i) Cassius refers to himself as a 'coward' after Titinius is taken captive. Why?
- (a) He was hiding while his men were getting slaughtered in the battlefield.
- (b) He had lived long enough to see his friend be taken captive.
- (c) He allowed Brutus to run the battle strategy.
- (d) He asks Pindarus to kill him so no one else can.

(ii) 'Blood and destruction shall be so in use
And dreadful objects so familiar
That mothers shall but smile when they behold
Their infants quarter'd with the hands of war;
All pity choked with custom of fell deeds:'

What does the phrase 'All pity choked' mean here?
- (a) People will have no pity.
- (b) People will become sympathetic.
- (c) People will become choked.
- (d) People will have no anger.

(iii) Brutus condemns Cassius for siphoning off money. He asks Cassius to use the gold to ....
- (a) pay his soldiers
- (b) buy food and supplies for the army
- (c) buy gifts for his friends
- (d) return it back to the bribers

(iv) Caesar thought he was as constant as ....

(a) Rome (b) the Southern cross (c) Mount Olympus (d) the Northern star

(v) In Act IV Scene 3, what information does Messala deliver to Brutus and Cassius?

(a) Antony and Octavius are planning to attack Philippi.
(b) Antony is planning to execute Octavius.
(c) Antony is the new emperor.
(d) Octavius is planning to attack Philippi.

(vi) What does Antony claim lives on after men?

(a) Their ambitions (b) Their wealth (c) Their evil deeds (d) Their good deeds

(vii) In Robert Frost's poem 'A Considerable Speck', the mite paused because ....

(a) it was attracted to the ink on the paper
(b) it was suspicious of the writer
(c) it had an obstacle in his way
(d) it needed to think about its next steps

(viii) The Lady dropped her glove in the arena ....

(a) to distract the Count
(b) to test her lover
(c) to gain the King's love
(d) to be friend the lions

(ix) Who rescues everyone from Bhisma's bad singing in 'The Power of Music'?

(a) Cow (b) Horse (c) Goat (d) Turtle

(x) When great souls die, the air around us becomes light, rare, ...

Complete the given line from the poem 'When Great trees fall'.

(a) sterile (b) empty (c) soothing (d) electric

(xi) Select the option that shows the correct relationship between Statements (1) and (2) from H. W. Longfellow's poem 'Haunted Houses'.

Statement 1 The souls who depart from Earth still linger in their former living spaces.

Statement 2 The ghosts seek claim on their former living spaces by haunting them.

(a) (1) is true and (2) is false.
(b) (2) is true and (1) is false.
(c) (1) is the cause for (2).
(d) (1) and (2) are independent of each other.

(xii) In 'The Elevator', Martin felt like he was being chased on the stairs because ....

(a) the stairs were cold
(b) his footsteps echoed against the cement
(c) the stairs had dark shadows
(d) he kept hearing eerie voices behind him

(xiii) In Alphonse Daudet's short story 'The Last Lesson', M. Hamel complains that the parents preferred to send their kids to .... instead of school in the past.

(a) church (b) farms and mills (c) relative's house (d) work at the factory

(xiv) By the end of the short story 'The Girl Who Can', what does Nana realise?

(a) Her granddaughter was a great runner.
(b) Her daughter should get an education.
(c) Legs can have many uses.
(d) Her granddaughter is ready for marriage.

(xv) In the short story 'The Pedestrian', where is Mr. Mead taken to in the end?

(a) The police station (b) The psychiatric facility (c) The library (d) The homeless shelter

(xvi) Choose the option that lists the sequence of events from Stephen Leacock's short story 'With the photographer' in the correct order.

1. The photographer rolled the camera into the room.
2. The photographer put a black cloth over himself.
3. The photographer tore at the cotton sheet with a hooked stick.
4. The photographer went behind the camera again.

(a) 1, 3, 2 and 4 (b) 1, 3, 4 and 2 (c) 1, 2, 3 and 4 (d) 1, 4, 2 and 3

Section (B)

*(Answer **one or more** questions from this section.)*

DRAMA

(Julius Caesar by William Shakespeare)

Question 2

Read the extract given below and answer the questions that follow.

"Thou hast described
A hot friend cooling: ever note, Lucilius,
When love begins to sicken and decay,
It useth an enforced ceremony.
There are no tricks in plain and simple faith;
But hollow men, like horses hot at hand,
Make gallant show and promise of their mettle;
But when they should endure the bloody spur,
They fall their crests, and like deceitful jades,
Sink in the trial. Comes his army on" ?

(i) Are these lines spoken by Brutus?
Who is he speaking to (listener)?
Who are they talking about (subject of their conversation)? **(3)**

(ii) What is the meaning of the phrase 'A hot friend cooling'?
Why did the speaker say this? **(3)**

(iii) What is the meaning of "horse hot at hand"?
What are such 'horses' compared to? **(3)**

(iv) 'Comes his army on?' Who is 'his' in this sentence?
Where do they plan on approaching? **(3)**

(v) In Act IV Scene 2, what is the cause of the tense environment in Brutus' tent?
What does Brutus suggest to resolve it? **(4)**

Question 3

Read the extract given below and answer the questions that follow.

"Gentlemen all, - alas! What shall I say?
My credit now stands on such slippery ground,
That one of two bad ways you must conceit me,
Either a coward or a flatterer.
That I did love thee, Caesar, O'tis true:
If then thy spirit look upon us now,
Shall it not grieve thee dearer than thy death,"

(i) Who is the speaker of the above lines?
Who are the 'Gentlemen' he/she is addressing to? **(3)**

(ii) What sight does the speaker claim will make Caesar grieve dearer than death?
To whom does the speaker compare Caesar and the 'Gentlemen' to later in this scene? **(3)**

(iii) Later in this scene, the speaker requests Brutus for two things. What are they?
What are Brutus conditions for fulfilling the requests? **(3)**

(iv) Explain the meaning of the line 'My credit now stands on such slippery ground'.

What does the speaker think the 'Gentlemen' will perceive him as?

Which line expresses the speaker's love for Caesar? **(3)**

(v) Antony is a true friend and a skilled commander.

Do you agree with the above statement? Justify. **(4)**

Section (C)

*(Answer **one or more** questions from this section.)*

Prose - Short Stories

(Treasure Chest — A Collection of Poems and Short Stories)

Question 4

Read the following extract from William Sleator's short story 'The Elevator' and answer the questions that follow.

"Now she knows I live on the seventeen," he thought.

"Have you ever noticed a strange lady in the elevator?" he asked his father that evening.

"Can't say I have," he replied, not looking away from the television.

Martin knew he was probably making a mistake, but he had to tell somebody about the woman, "She was in the elevator with me twice today. She just kept staring at me. She never stopped looking at me for a minute".

(i) What floor did Martin live on?

Who is he referring to as 'she' in the first line?

Why does he not want her to know where he lived? **(3)**

(ii) What did Martin ask his father that evening?

What did his father reply? **(3)**

(iii) How did Martin feel about the fat lady? **(3)**

(iv) What mistake did Martin think he was making?

Was he correct? **(3)**

(v) Did Martin get any help from his father? Why or why not? **(4)**

Question 5

Read the following extract from Ray Bradbury's short story 'The Pedestrian' and answer the questions that follow.

The car hesitated, or rather gave a faint whirring click, as if information, somewhere, was dropping card by punch-slotted card under electric eyes. 'To the Psychiatric Center for Research on Regressive Tendencies.'

He got in. The door shut with a soft thud.

The police car rolled through the night avenues, flashing its dim lights ahead.

They passed one house on one street a moment later, one house in an entire city of houses that were dark, but this one particular house had all its electric lights brightly lit, every window a loud yellow illumination, square and warm in the cool darkness.

(i) What stops Mr. Mead on the streets?

What is he asked to do?

Describe how it looked from inside. **(3)**

(ii) Where is the car taking Mr. Mead?

Why? **(3)**

(iii) According to you, how is Mr. Mead feeling about his situation? **(3)**

(iv) What did they pass on their way to the facility?
Why does it stand out from its surroundings? **(3)**

(v) What is Mr. Mead's profession?
Does he have a family?
What could have saved Mr. Mead from his fate? **(4)**

Section (D)

*(Answer **one or more** questions from this section.)*

Poetry

(Treasure Chest — A Collection of Poems and Short Stories)

Question 6

Read the following extract from Leigh Hunt's poem 'The Glove and the Lions' and answer the questions that follow.

"De Lorge's love o'erheard the King, a beauteous lively dame
With smiling lips and sharp bright eyes, which always seemed the same;
She thought, the Count my lover is brave as brave can be;
He surely would do wondrous things to show his love of me;
King, ladies, lovers, all look on; the occasion is divine;
I'll drop my glove, to prove his love; great glory will be mine".

(i) Describe the Count's lady love. **(3)**

(ii) What did the lady think about the Count? **(3)**

(iii) What did the lady hear the King say? **(3)**

(iv) What does the lady plan to do in the above text? **(3)**

(v) List the reason behind the lady's plan. **(4)**

Question 7

Read the following extract from Robert Frost's poem 'A Considerable Speck' and answer the questions that follow.

"It faltered: I could see it hesitate;
Then in the middle of the open sheet
Cower down in desperation to accept
Whatever I accorded it of fate.
I have none of the tenderer-than-thou
Collectivistic regimenting love
With which the modern world is being swept".

(i) Why did the mite hesitate? **(3)**

(ii) Explain the line "Collectivistic regimenting love". **(3)**

(iii) What did the mite do after it reached the middle of the page? **(3)**

(iv) Do you think the mite made the correct decision?
Do you think it had a choice? Why? **(3)**

(v) What is the truth of the modern world according to the poet?
What flaws does he find in the mindset of people? **(4)**